Person, Personhood, and the Humanity of Christ

Princeton Theological Monograph Series

K. C. Hanson, Charles M. Collier, D. Christopher Spinks,
and Robin Parry, Series Editors

Recent volumes in the series:

Paul W. Chilcote
*Making Disciples in a World Parish:
Global Perspectives on Mission and Evangelism*

Nathan Montover
*Luther's Revolution:
The Political Dimensions of Martin Luther's Universal Priesthood*

Alan B. Wheatley
*Patronage in Early Christianity:
Its Use and Transformation from Jesus to Paul of Samosata*

Jon Paul Sydnor
*Ramanuja and Schleiermacher:
Toward a Constructive Comparative Theology*

Eric G. Flett
*Persons, Powers, and Pluralities:
Toward a Trinitarian Theology of Culture*

Vladimir Kharlamov
Theosis: Deification in Christian Theology, Volume Two

Mitzi J. Smith
*The Literary Construction of the Other in the Acts of the Apostles:
Charismatics, the Jews, and Women*

Person, Personhood, and the Humanity of Christ

Christocentric Anthropology and Ethics in Thomas F. Torrance

Hakbong Kim

Foreword by
David Fergusson

◆PICKWICK *Publications* · Eugene, Oregon

PERSON, PERSONHOOD, AND THE HUMANITY OF CHRIST
Christocentric Anthropology and Ethics in Thomas F. Torrance

Princeton Theological Monograph Series 245

Copyright © 2021 Hakbong Kim. All rights reserved. Except for brief quotations in critical publications or reviews, no part of this book may be reproduced in any manner without prior written permission from the publisher. Write: Permissions, Wipf and Stock Publishers, 199 W. 8th Ave., Suite 3, Eugene, OR 97401.

Pickwick Publications
An Imprint of Wipf and Stock Publishers
199 W. 8th Ave., Suite 3
Eugene, OR 97401

www.wipfandstock.com

PAPERBACK ISBN: 978-1-7252-8529-3
HARDCOVER ISBN: 978-1-7252-8530-9
EBOOK ISBN: 978-1-7252-8531-6

Cataloguing-in-Publication data:

Names: Kim, Hakbong, author. | Fergusson, David, foreword writer.

Title: Person, personhood, and the humanity of Christ : christocentric anthropology and ethics in Thomas F. Torrance / Hakbong Kim with a foreword by David A. S. Fergusson.

Description: Eugene, OR: Pickwick Publications, 2021 | Series: Princeton Theological Monograph Series 245 | Includes bibliographical references and index.

Identifiers: ISBN 978-1-7252-8529-3 (paperback) | ISBN 978-1-7252-8530-9 (hardcover) | ISBN 978-1-7252-8531-6 (ebook)

Subjects: LCSH: Torrance, Thomas F. (Thomas Forsyth), 1913–2007 | Theological anthropology | Jesus Christ—History of doctrines | Jesus Christ—Person and offices | Theology, Doctrinal—History—20th century

Classification: BX4827.T67 K56 2021 (print) | BX4827.T67 (ebook)

To my beloved children
Dohyun and Ruah

Contents

Foreword by David Fergusson ix

Acknowledgements xi

Introduction xiii

1 The Conception of the Human Being in Torrance: Persons in Relation 1

2 Trinitarian Personhood: The Ontological Ground of the Human Person and Personhood 45

3 The Humanity of Christ: The Onto-Relational Restoration of the Human Person and Personhood 85

4 The Sacramental and Diaconal Action of the Church: The Personal and Relational Outworking of Christ's New Humanity 141

Conclusion 180

Bibliography 189

General Index 201

Foreword

THE THEOLOGY OF T. F. Torrance continues to attract international attention, particularly amongst a younger generation of scholars who have explored his writings with skill and enthusiasm. The recent appearance of the *T. & T. Clark Handbook of Thomas F. Torrance* attests this diversity of geographical interest together with the broad scope of his theology. Yet, despite the significant attention devoted to Torrance's doctrine of God and his treatment of the person and work of Christ, his work on theological anthropology has received much less notice. Yet theological anthropology was an enduring concern from his early publication on *Calvin's Doctrine of Man* (1949), and it remained an embedded theme in his treatments of the Trinity, the incarnation, and the church.

Dr Hakbong Kim's study of Torrance's theological anthropology fulfils several important functions. He demonstrates its deep links with the constitutive elements of Torrance's thought, especially the intricate exposition of the doctrine of the Trinity in conversation with the early church. The extent to which this understanding of the human person is fundamentally relational and oriented towards God, the world, and our neighbours is thereby elucidated. And, within this setting, Kim points to ways in which the ethical and diaconal dimensions of our humanity are a constant feature of Torrance's work, notwithstanding criticisms that these was underdeveloped by contrast with the more vertical relation between the individual and God. In unfolding Torrance's anthropology, this study gestures towards ways in which the wider socio-political outcomes of his thought might be developed by scholars in the future. Both in its acute exposition and constructive reading of Torrance, Kim has produced a fine piece of work that provides a welcome addition to the growing secondary literature on his theology.

Professor David Fergusson
Regius Professor of Divinity
University of Cambridge

Acknowledgements

THIS STUDY IS THE outcome of a dissertation for the Doctor of Philosophy degree earned at the University of Edinburgh. I would like to express my heartfelt thanks to the many people who have helped and supported this study. Professor David Fergusson, my primary supervisor, encouraged my undeveloped theological thoughts and provided useful insights to improve the overall contents and directions of this study. He posed challenging questions from the beginning of this study so that I could consider how my research questions and arguments could be developed in a more critical and systematic way. This work, with its various critical and constructive discussions, is due to his gentle and careful guidance in my work and life. Dr Robert Walker, my secondary supervisor, supported and inspired me. He carefully went through my work and offered thoughtful feedback. As one of the leading Torrancian scholars, his supervision improved my knowledge and reading of Torrance's theology as a whole. Professor Tom Noble, my external examiner, offered the insightful comments and suggestions so that the original study could be made more solid.

I would like to convey my gratitude to Professor Eun Woo Lee of the Presbyterian University and Theological Seminary, Dr Tae In Kim of Hannam University, Dr Alexander Chow of New College, University of Edinburgh, Dr Sang Hoon Lee of Union School of Theology, Rev Yie Shik Kim of the Yeshim Church and Rev Hyung Cheon Rim of the Jamsil Church in Korea, Dr Jennifer Floether, Torrance Study Service and the Korean Students' Association at New College in Edinburgh, all of whom provided useful insights and unselfish help that benefitted this study, for which I am very grateful.

The prayers and encouragement of my family have sustained me in this work. I could not have finished this study without the prayers and support of my mother Myung Ok Lee, my parents-in-law Joong Hyun Cho and Hye Ok Kim, my sister Hyang Min Kim, my brothers-in-law Young Joo Cho and Ki Bum Kim, my nephew and nieces Joo Yong Kim, Yun Ji Kim and Sae Lim Kim. My loving wife Ara Cho and beloved children Do Hyun Kim and Ru Ah Kim have been the very impetus of this study and given strength each day to the process of completing this work.

Finally, and most importantly:

> I praise God who did not ignore my prayer
> or withdraw his unfailing love from me.
> (Psalm 66:22)

Introduction

THERE ARE NUMEROUS STUDIES on Thomas Forsyth Torrance (1913–2007), through which his works and contributions, particularly in the field of science and theology and trinitarian theology, have been introduced and articulated.[1] With the help of these studies providing interpretative lenses, we can see the key theological themes that Torrance has addressed in his various works and understand what matters in his theology.

Despite the revealing accounts of Torrance's theology in these studies, there is still room to further develop research on him. In particular, given that there has been a tendency to highlight the dogmatic significance of Torrance, research on the practical elements of his work has been relatively deficient; it is therefore necessary to discover and address the practicality of his theology. In this respect, we note that Torrance has been critiqued by theologians such as Colin Gunton, David Fergusson, and John Webster in virtue of the lack of practical significance, a fact

1. Commentators on Torrance, such as Alister McGrath, Elmer Colyer, and Paul Molnar, have regarded him as one of the leading Reformed theologians of the twentieth century, not only contributing to the field of theology and science but also to Reformation and patristic studies in which, for Torrance, the doctrine of the Trinity is located at the center, encompassing all other Christian doctrines (McGrath, *Thomas F. Torrance*, xi; Colyer, *How to Read T. F. Torrance*, 11, 45; Molnar, *Thomas F. Torrance*, 2, 31). Importantly, Torrance's engagement with the natural sciences and emphasis on scientific theology won him the Templeton Prize for Progress in Religion in 1978 and his deep theological exploration of patristic and Reformed theology enabled his ecumenical engagement with other theological traditions (Noble, "Thomas Forsyth Torrance," 823–24). It is evident that Torrance's theological accomplishments are not of practical but of doctrinal and epistemic importance, an understanding that explains why numerous studies on him have focused on the doctrinal significance, meaning, and implications of his theology. For example, see Habets, *Theosis in the Theology of Thomas Torrance*; Radcliff, *Thomas F. Torrance and the Church Fathers*; Morrison, *Knowledge of the Self-Revealing God*; Molnar, *Incarnation and Resurrection*; Chung, *Thomas Torrance's Mediations and Revelation*.

that questions the horizontally-focused theological considerations and requires further articulation of the practical facets in his theology.[2] Thus, exploring and unfolding the horizontal and practical implications in his theological system and logic, particularly the anthropological and ethical ones scattered in his theological *oeuvre*, can improve our comprehension of his entire theology. This book is dedicated to achieving this end.

A comprehensive study of the anthropology and ethics in the theology of Torrance is of course not new, albeit that works doing so are limited in number. For instance, in her doctoral thesis, "The Theological Anthropology of Thomas F. Torrance" (2013), Wei Jing explores how Torrance understands human beings in light of Christology, soteriology, and the doctrine of the Trinity.[3] In his book *Fully Human in Christ* (2016), Todd Speidell deals with Torrance's thought on Christ's vicarious humanity as the ontological foundation for human transformation and new moral life, arguing that his theology involves "an ethic of reconciliation."[4] In his book *Trinitarian Grace and Participation* (2017), Geordie Ziegler unpacks Torrance's logic of ethics, in which participation in Christ's ongoing humanity is not merely doxological, but also dynamic and practical, creating the Christian personal and ethical life.[5]

The above studies display anthropological and ethical themes and implications on Torrance, each with their own focus and direction; however, they do not fully reveal his inclusive and holistic understanding of

---

2. We will develop more detail on this as the book proceeds, but here it is necessary to briefly elucidate the key points of their critiques: (1) for Gunton, Torrance does not have a trinitarian model for anthropology because his emphasis, which is not on the relationality of the persons of the Trinity, but on the being of God, cannot unfold what the trinitarian personhood means for human personhood, (2) for Fergusson, Torrance's theology as a whole does not focus on horizontal (or practical), but on vertical (or doxological) movements and relations, a tendency that leads to insufficient attention to wider ethical, social, and political issues, such as social justice, human equality, and world peace, and (3) for Webster, Torrance's account of the vicariousness of Christ does not leave space for human ethical activity, so that the primacy of moral action is belittled (Gunton, "Being and Person," 129–31; Fergusson, "Ascension of Christ," 101; Webster, "Imitation of Christ," 95–96).

3. Jing, "Theological Anthropology of Thomas F. Torrance." For other PhD dissertation dealing with Torrance's anthropology, see Bevan, "Person of Christ."

4. Speidell, *Fully Human in Christ*, 1–37. In the first chapter of his book, "Soteriological Suspension of Ethics in the Theology of T. F. Torrance," Speidell explores the soteriological suspension of ethics and Christ's vicarious humanity in Torrance's theology and deals with some of the concrete moral issues that he occasionally addressed, thereby levelling against Torrance's critics: Webster and Fergusson.

5. Ziegler, *Trinitarian Grace and Participation*, 285–92.

human existence, transformation (or personalization), and new moral life and order. In effect he utilizes wide-ranging theological, philosophical, and scientific knowledge and epistemologies so as to expound and argue for the onto-relationality of the person and personhood. This in turn reveals the significance of Christ's humanity as the creative source of our new humanity in true relations with God and other persons and its resultant ethics affecting personal and relational reconstruction in the private and public dimensions.

In this context, the primary interest and aim of this book is to explore and articulate Torrance's anthropology and ethics in a more integrated and systematic way, thereby identifying and revealing the practicality of his theology. For this, we will consider in depth, shed light on, and develop: (1) his epistemological uses of person and personhood, (2) the ways in which he relates and moves them to christological discussions, particularly the pivotal role of Christ's humanity in personalization, and (3) the anthropological and ethical implications and effects that the humanity of Christ entails and engenders, not only in the individual and ecclesial, but also in the social realms. As this kind of research has not yet been attempted in relation to Torrance, this work will take the first step in this direction.

Importantly, Torrance's emphasis on the humanity of Christ in his anthropology and ethics displays a very different approach to Christian ethics from that of social trinitarianism, establishing the doctrine of the Trinity *per se* as "the best indicator of the proper relationship between individual and community."[6] For example, while for Torrance Christ's vicarious and new humanity and the *participatio Christi* are the key to understanding all ethical life and praxis, social trinitarians, such as Jürgen Moltmann, John Zizioulas, Catherine Mowry LaCugna, and Miroslav Volf, draw upon the personal and relational attributes of the persons of the Trinity as a trinitarian vision for ethical life and praxis in relative isolation from Christology.[7]

---

6. Tanner, *Christ the Key*, 207.

7. According to John O'Donnell, social trinitarians relate the Trinity to us or the world, i.e., to human lives in a practical sense on two related grounds. The first is the relationality of the three divine persons in which the three persons are united in *perichoresis* but they are distinctive, a perspective that sees human beings in relation to one another while continuing to regard them as real individuals, and therefore rules out an understanding of persons as exclusively individualistic. The second is the personal and social community of the Trinity in which this community provides human society with the ideal model in both structure and content (O'Donnell, *Mystery of the*

The difference between the Christocentric approach in Torrance and the trinitarian-centric approach in social trinitarianism draws our attention to whether Torrance could provide a more theologically appropriate understanding of and approach to Christian ethics and praxis in comparison to those of the social trinitarians. In this regard, the secondary interest and aim of this book (which is no less important than the primary ones in terms of its theological significance) is to assess and test the theological validity and effectiveness of his Christocentric anthropology and ethics in critical dialogue with social trinitarians.

With the above questions and purposes in mind, this book will set out to examine the Christocentric anthropology and ethics in the theology of Torrance and its theological validity and practicality within the four main chapters outlined below.

Chapter 1 will illustrate Torrance's understanding of human beings as persons in relation. The first point of focus will be on his critique of the dualist and individualistic Platonic-Aristotelian anthropology inherited and hardened by Boethius, Thomas Aquinas, and Descartes. Torrance's theological reflection on the human person, the relational *imago Dei* and uses of philosophical and scientific epistemology, i.e., the concepts of person in relation and personal knowledge will be then introduced in order to reveal and support the personal and relational dimensions of the human person and personhood in his anthropological thought.

Chapter 2 will deal with Torrance's understanding of trinitarian personhood as the ontological grounding for the human person and personhood. The onto-relationality of the three divine persons will first

---

Triune God, 106–9). On this basis, social trinitarians interpret and employ the practical relevance of the doctrine of the Trinity, that is, the social doctrine of the Trinity, for diverse anthropological, ethical, social, and political reforms.

However, the theological reasoning in social trinitarianism has been critiqued by theologians such as Karen Kilby, Kathryn Tanner, and Stephen Holmes. Put simply, three fundamental points dominate their criticism of social trinitarianism: (1) it is impossible to apply the ineffable nature and content of the Trinity to human societies directly without engendering "epistemological and ontological abstraction," (2) theological attempts to derive moral, social, and political ideas from the Trinity are not consonant with the trinitarian theology of the church fathers, and (3) hence social trinitarianism is just "the projection of human aspirations onto God" (Tanner, *Christ the Key*, 222; Kilby, "Perichoresis and Projection," 442; Holmes, *Quest for the Trinity*, 1–32). In this context, as we will see in more detail, Torrance's depiction of Christ as "the epistemological and ontological linchpin of trinitarian personhood and praxis" becomes a theological counterpart, with its own anthropological and ethical implications, to social trinitarianism.

be explored in a discussion about the *homoousion* and *perichoresis*. Then the practicality of the onto-relational concept of trinitarian personhood and the specifically Christocentric approach to trinitarian personhood and praxis in Torrance will be addressed and evaluated in a constructive dialogue with Moltmann, Zizioulas, and other social trinitarians.

Chapter 3 will articulate Torrance's understanding of the humanity of Christ as the epistemological and ontological linchpin in the onto-relational restoration of the human person and personhood. This will begin with the significance of Christ's humanity for revelation and reconciliation in a discussion of Torrance's critical realism, the *homoousion*, and the hypostatic union. The three themes will be considered in the following order: (1) the different aspects of Christ's humanity (fallen, vicarious, and new) that clarify his onto-relational connection to and the practical effect on our humanity, (2) personalization in the new humanity of Christ and its resulting new moral life, order, and social relations, and (3) a number of ethical issues, e.g., women in ministry, man-woman relations in marriage and divorce, abortion, and the priestly role of humanity in ecology addressed by Torrance's christological perspective.

Chapter 4 will address Torrance's understanding of the sacramental and diaconal action of the church as the personal and relational outworking of Christ's new humanity. This will first outline Torrance's view of the being, life, and mission of the church and the church's *participatio Christi* through the sacraments and its evangelical, ethical, and social implications and effects. The Christocentric ecclesiology and its practical significance in Torrance will then be compared to the ecclesiology of the social trinitarians and suggested as a corrective to this.

Through the above anthropological and ethical exploration, this book will first argue that Torrance does in fact involve and display horizontal concerns and practical implications in his theological system and reasoning. Despite his undue emphasis on Christology in ethical discussions and limited attention to ethical issues in the wider social realm, his articulation of human beings as persons in relation, and of the reconciling and personalizing humanity of Christ and its resultant ethics, reflects the outward considerations inherent in his trinitarian theology, providing the foundational and structural basis for Christian anthropology and ethics. This book will also assert that Torrance's approach to Christian ethics has a more appropriate theological validity and effectiveness than that of social trinitarianism. Inasmuch as the tendency in social trinitarianism, deriving practical implications and applications directly from the ineffable nature and content of the Trinity, brings about epistemological and ontological abstraction, Torrance's christological understanding of and approach to knowing and participating in the trinitarian personhood and communion and its resultant personalization and ethical transformation sheds important light on the christological deficiency of social trinitarianism and therefore should be considered as a complement or corrective to it.

I

The Conception of Human Being in Torrance

Persons in Relation

Introduction

THE QUEST FOR AN understanding of humanness has been significant. Since the ways in which we recognize and define our human being influence not only each of us individually, but also all humanity corporately, a wide range of discussions and questions about the human have taken place with significant theoretical and practical implications.

As Torrance elucidates it, it is Christian theology, particularly the doctrine of Christ in the early church, that gave rise to the conception of the human being as a person.[1] Theological elucidation of what had happened and been revealed about God in and through the incarnate Son produced an onto-relational understanding of trinitarian personhood, so that a personal and relational concept of person was created and applied to God.[2] This concept then came to be applied to human beings in virtue of their interpersonal relations to God and with one another which

---

1. Torrance, *Christian Frame of Mind*, 37–38.

2. Regarding the onto-relationality of the trinitarian personhood, Torrance states that "the divine Persons are who they are through their interrelations in being and act with one another" (Torrance, *Being and Nature of the Unborn Child*, 8). This means that the divine persons are to be understood as the distinct persons whose very being is to exist in interpersonal relations with other persons. For Torrance, it is this the "onto-relational" understanding of the trinitarian personhood that underlies our understanding of the human person and personhood.

clearly shows the fact that the constitution of human being should be understood as "persons in relation."

In this light, Torrance critiques ancient and modern dualistic patterns of thought which unfortunately have had such a damaging effect in individualistic, rationalistic, and psychological ways on the personal and relational concept of the human person. In particular, for Torrance, Plato, Aristotle, and Augustine are regarded as philosophical and theological foundations for the inward movement to self-identity so pervasive in the modern world. In opposition to Platonic-Aristotelian and Augustinian lines of thought, Torrance argues for an onto-relationality of the human person which takes place in all interpersonal relationships with God and our fellow humans, and which is demanded not only by theological and biblical reflections, but also by scientific and philosophical ones.[3]

However, it can be questioned whether, (1) the way in which Torrance advances and spells out a persons in relation approach over against the impersonal and non-relational concepts of person in the fields of scientific, anthropological, and theological knowledge is too simplistic, (2) his interpretation of the history of philosophy and theology as related to the concept of person is reasonable and defensible,[4] and (3) his epistemological utilization of theological, philosophical, and scientific knowledge can be regarded as a proper way to support his concept of person. Such questions invite us to think deeply about whether Torrance's critical reflections and responses to the history of philosophy and theology as related to the conception of the human being as a cognitive and self-sufficient being are acceptable and thus still significant for us.

---

3. In order to argue for personal and relational concepts of the human person and personhood, Torrance draws upon the following theological/biblical and philosophical/scientific understandings: (1) the Hebrew unitary view of humanity, (2) the concept of person in Richard of St. Victor, (3) a Christocentric understanding of "the image of God," (4) the concept of "personal knowledge" from Michael Polanyi, and (5) the concept of "person in relations" from John Macmurray. We will see more detail as the chapter proceeds.

4. In particular, as to Aristotle and Augustine, there are views different from Torrance's to which we need to draw our attention. For instance, there are discussions about whether (1) Aristotle is a monist/materialist or a dualist (Shields, "Soul and Body in Aristotle," 103–35; Everson, "Psychology," 168–94) and (2) it can be appropriate to regard Augustine as one of the main theologians for the rational and individual concept of the human person (Ayres, *Nicaea and Its Legacy*, 364–83; "Remember That You Are Catholic," 39–82; Barnes, "Regarding Augustine's Theology of the Trinity," 145–76; "Augustine in Contemporary Trinitarian Theology," 237–50).

With the questions above, this chapter will deal with first Torrance's historical understanding of humanness and the concept of the human person. It will then provide Torrance's theological and biblical reflections on human being in which his theological understanding of the human person will be addressed through discussions about the doctrine of the image of God. Lastly, it will offer Torrance's philosophical and scientific epistemology, i.e., the concepts of person in relation and personal knowledge to support the personal and relational dimensions of the human person.

In this theological exploration, it will be argued that despite the seemingly simplistic categorization of historical concepts of the human person (as a radical separation between personal/relational and impersonal/non-relational approaches), Torrance does carefully and properly utilize theological, scientific, and philosophical discourses on the concept of the human person. By drawing upon theological, scientific, and philosophical knowledge and epistemology, he does profoundly unfold the personal and relational characteristics of the human person and personhood, which would be an important anthropological and theological corrective to the rationalistic and impersonal concept of the human person pervading western thought.

Torrance's Understanding of Human Being as Persons in Relation: An Historical Overview

In Torrance's theological anthropology, human beings are to be regarded as persons in relation with God and other persons, a perspective which, though not hitherto dominant, is of great significance in the history of philosophy and theology related to the understanding of human being. Torrance critiques Platonic-Aristotelian anthropology in the ancient Greek and Roman traditions, for in its dualistic view of humanity it is difficult to find "any conception of human being as personal" and relational.[5] Despite the Hebrew unitary and personal view of humanity and the relational concept of the human person in the early church, the ancient classical impersonal and non-relational concept of humanity has unfortunately been inherited in the whole history of western thought with regard not only to anthropological but theological and scientific knowledge.

5. Torrance, *Christian Frame of Mind*, 37.

The Greek, the Roman, and the Hebrew Views of Humanity

In terms of the understanding of humanity, as Torrance expounds it, there are three great traditions pervading western thought, the Greek, the Roman and the Hebrew. While the Hebraic view of humanity was non-dualist, Greek and Roman views of humanity were governed by a radical dualism of body and soul (or mind), albeit in somewhat different ways.[6] For Torrance, it is the philosophies of Plato and Aristotle in particular which are regarded as the main philosophical grounds for the anthropological dualism effecting the impersonal and non-relational ways of thinking on humanity.[7]

---

6. Torrance, *Christian Frame of Mind*, 35–36. In order to engage properly in further discussion of dualism in the ancient and modern thought, it is important to spell out Torrance's definition of dualism: dualism is "the division of reality into two incompatible spheres of being. This may be cosmological, in the dualism between a sensible and an intelligible realm, neither of which can be reduced to the other. It may also be epistemological, in which the empirical and theoretical aspects of reality are separated from one another, thereby giving rise to the extremes of empiricism and rationalism. It may also be anthropological, in a dualism between the mind and the body, in which a physical and a mental substance are conceived as either interacting with one another or as running a parallel course without affecting one another" (Torrance, "Notes on Terms and Concepts," 136).

7. Here it is important to understand that Torrance deals with Platonic-Aristotelian (and Hebrew) anthropology not only in their notions of humanity, but in their ontology and epistemology with regard to God/ourselves/world relations. For Torrance, it is a fruitful way to address the notions of humanity in terms of such relations, for God/ourselves/world relations are not independent or isolated from one another but correlated together. Torrance's organic view of such relations is evident in his theology. As he argues, theology (and theological science) is not confined to just one relation, as it were, the God-human relation alone, for the world is a place where God not only created and was known to us through the incarnation in space and time, but we also *personally* know God and live together as an essential members and priests of creation. This implies of course that the relations between God, human beings and the world are not static and solitary or insular, which for Torrance is found in ancient and modern dualistic patterns of thought, but personal, relational and soteriological and so this is what we must operate with in a realist theology. See Torrance, *Reality and Evangelical Theology*, 21–30.

As we will see in more detail, this is Torrance's realist or interactionist view on theology which draws our attention to the ontological and epistemological role of the incarnation in which the impersonal/non-relational understanding of the God/ourselves/world relations in ancient and modern dualism is rejected and converted to an interpersonal understanding of such relations in a soteriological way. In this regard, Platonic-Aristotelian dualistic anthropology becomes an epistemological point of departure we must understand in relation and contrast to Torrance's own anthropology derived from his realist theology.

Plato's philosophical interest, as Torrance points out, lay in an "understanding and knowledge of the truth" in which the object of real knowledge is what is eternal, unchangeable and intelligible, that is, "ideas" or "forms," while the objects of sense-experience, i.e., natural events or actual facts, are regarded as not fully real, but, as it were, images or copies of forms.[8] In this regard, the visible world becomes a corollary of the noetic world.[9] In differentiating the two realms, Plato posits a good craftsman (Demiurge or God) as the ultimate being/reality *transcending* this mutable world. Plato's God accords mind (nous) and soul (psyche) with eternity and rationality to living beings in the visible (or finite) world so that a living being truly becomes endowed "with soul and mind by the providence of God."[10]

In Plato's cosmological and epistemological reflection, humanity is thought of in such a way that mind characterizes the human soul and the soul is temporally imprisoned within the human body in the visible world—that is, the body-soul separation.[11] In this sense, the soul is regarded as "the rational soul" having innate kinship with God, so that it is the nature of human beings with soul to contemplate "the eternal ideas or divine forms of truth, harmony, goodness and beauty."[12]

This is for Torrance the *a priori* structure or system of ideas that gives rise to the ontological/epistemological distortion and impossibility of any real knowing of what is known to us, which is fully in collision with the *a posteriori* experience and knowledge as we have it of the world and creaturely reality.[13] As Torrance claims, in this Plato's a priori structure of ideas, (1) this visible world or universe is not within the range of scientific knowledge, for the world we live and act in together is not regarded as fully real and thus empirical knowledge of the reality of this

---

8. Torrance, *Divine Interpretation*, 22–23.
9. Torrance, *Divine Interpretation*, 23.
10. Torrance, *Divine Interpretation*, 23.
11. Torrance, *Christian Frame of Mind*, 35.
12. Torrance, *Christian Frame of Mind*, 36.

13. Torrance, *Reality and Scientific Theology*, 104–5. As Torrance points out, the problem of Plato's cosmological/epistemological theory has been passed down through the ages with a great deal of speculation, "but in the early centuries of the Christian era, the theory took two basic forms, a Stoic form in which God came to be thought of in terms of a cosmic soul informing a cosmic body, and a Neo-Platonic form in which the distinction between the two realms was thrown into a sharp chasm between the world of sense perception and the world of thought" (Torrance, *Divine Interpretation*, 23).

world is therefore impossible,[14] and (2) we cannot have the actual experience and knowledge of the living God who is known to us in space and time by his personal and soteriological self-manifestation in and through the incarnation, for Plato's God is a God fully and wholly transcendent over this world.[15]

Anthropologically, this means that we human beings are isolated not only from our own ontological reality, but also from personal relations with objective realities, i.e., God and the world in our world of time and space. In this respect, Torrance argues that Plato's system of ideas in his dualism brings about a distorted conception of humanity in which human beings are not in personal interaction with the concrete realities we experience in space and time.

On the Aristotelian view, however, Plato's theory of transcendent and pre-existing ideas/forms is rejected. For Aristotle, as Torrance expounds him, the real or universal forms are not to be separated from the individual objects of the sensible world, i.e., matter, for they are essentially correlated together.[16] Accordingly, in Aristotle's view what it is (substance as it were), or form in Plato's thought, is not transcendent over an individual thing, but inherent in it, so that substance is understood as a whole individual entity or a composite of form and matter. Hence, substance (as an individual entity) is given ontological primacy.[17]

---

14. Torrance, *Divine Interpretation*, 22. This perspective of Plato, as Torrance argues, is particularly evident in the *Meno* "as the possibility of inquiry and learning." In order to critique and overcome this line of thought, Torrance draws upon Polanyi's solution to the problem, that is, his theory of "tacit knowing" in which to have knowledge is not to reminisce or recollect a priori knowledge/objective truth, but to commit to a posteriori to knowing in *personal* participation (Torrance, *Transformation and Convergence*, 113–14).

15. Torrance, *Trinitarian Faith*, 47–49.

16. Torrance, *Divine Interpretation*, 98. In this sense, the soul and the body are regarded as being related together in which "the soul informs the body and the body is the instrument for its expression and is appropriate to it" (Torrance, *Divine Interpretation*, 98).

17. As Torrance expounds it, Aristotle distinguishes between substance and accident and substance divides into primary and secondary substance, i.e., individual and the universal. As we will see in more detail as the chapter proceeds, in terms of Boethius's concept of person, Torrance maintains that, making use of Aristotelian distinction between primary and secondary substance, Boethius "distinguished between general and particular substance, and so reached the conclusion that person is the individual substance of rational nature" (Torrance, *Reality and Scientific Theology*, 174).

Despite Aristotle's materialist interpretation of reality, Torrance points out that Aristotle's emphasis remains on the conception of form "as the final determination of matter in the process of becoming."[18] This shows Aristotelian interest in the exposition of being, i.e., ontology, schematized in his teleological exposition of the given physical universe within a set of four causes starting from the what question (substance) to the how question (potentiality) and then the why and the whence question (actuality).[19] In teleological relations, natural processes such as the growth of the oak tree from an acorn is construed as purposeful behavior in a necessary process.[20]

However, for Torrance the Aristotelian line of thought, just like Plato but in different ways, excludes the human subject from cognitive and personal relations with the objective realities we experience, in that, as Bevan points out, "ontological primacy is given to concrete individual realities and to substance *over* relation."[21] In other words, for a living being is constituted as an individual substance, relations with objective realties does not become relevant to the constitution of an individual being.

Moreover, in the teleological movement, an individual substance is not construed as a personal being with personal intention, for this kind of teleological movement or development, from what it is (substance) to a description of "actuality" in causal and necessary terms, does not account for personal behavior, but only for purposeful behavior in a necessary process.[22] Further, there is no personal interaction between God and humanity, for the concept of God is defined as "the Unmoved Mover or Final Cause of motion in man and nature" and thought of as "acting in the world only indirectly, by way of inducing in its latent activity a change from a state of potentiality to a state of actuality."[23]

---

18. Torrance, *Ground and Grammar of Theology*, 63. In this respect, (1) in an anthropological sense the soul is inevitably thought as the substantial form of the body and (2) despite Aristotle's critique of Plato's "theory of division," it can be said that Plato's philosophical interest in the understanding and knowledge of the truth or the really real is nevertheless inherited in Aristotelian ontology and epistemology (Chiba, "Aristotle on Heuristic Inquiry," 174).

19. Torrance, *Christian Frame of Mind*, 43.

20. Torrance, *Christian Frame of Mind*, 43.

21. Bevan, "Person of Christ," 11 (italics added).

22. Torrance, *Christian Frame of Mind*, 43.

23. Torrance, *Ground and Grammar of Theology*, 63. This for Torrance is Aristotelian deism in which the possibility of a living interaction between God and the world and between God and us cannot but be restricted, which means in particular the

In this regard, Torrance argues that the order should be reversed in Aristotle's teleological movement as it focuses on an ontology that is not relevant to realities in relations, for all proper and actual knowledge of reality occurs in accordance with the question "what is the actual nature of this thing that we know?"[24] That is to say, for Torrance, as McGrath points out, our scientific and theological thinking takes place only "after the actuality of knowledge," following which every reality is investigated "*kata physin*—that is, according to its own distinct nature."[25]

This is what Torrance means by "a *posteriori*" in which as an individual knower the human subject can have the possibility not only to inquire into and have an actual knowledge of objective realities in the world by empirical science,[26] but also have the knowledge of God disclosed to us through his self-revelation in space and time.[27] Thus, in Torrance's argument about a posteriori knowledge of reality, we understand that epistemology has to follow ontology and ontology in the sense of actual knowledge of realities, for epistemology, as the study of how we know, can only begin from the actual knowledge of the objective realities with which we are already involved in epistemological and personal relations.

In sum, in Torrance's thought Platonic-Aristotelian dualism hinders a posteriori experience and knowledge of objective realities in different ways.[28] For in terms of anthropological implications, it is evident that

---

impossibility of the incarnation as the actual acting and real presence of the living God in space and time. See Torrance, *Ground and Grammar of Theology*, 63.

24. Torrance, *God and Rationality*, 33.

25. McGrath, *Thomas F. Torrance*, 234–35.

26. Torrance, *Transformation and Convergence*, 87–88.

27. Torrance, *Christian Doctrine of God*, 83; *Ground and Grammar of Theology*, 158. This is the central argument of Torrance in opposition to the ancient and modern dualistic patterns of thought. As the chapter proceeds, we will see the ways in which the Platonic-Aristotelian dualist and impersonal concepts of humanity have had a damaging effect not only on anthropological, but also on scientific and theological knowledge.

28. In this respect, although Aristotle sought to overcome Plato's theory of "division" (between eternal forms and material objects), Plato's dualistic way of thinking in his philosophical methodology is considered by Torrance as being taken over by Aristotle in quite different ways. Thus, Torrance insists that "the Platonic separation between the sensible world and the intelligible world, hardened by Aristotle, governed the disjunction between action and reflection, event and idea, becoming and being, the material and the spiritual, the visible and the invisible, the temporal and the eternal" (Torrance, *Trinitarian Faith*, 47). This dualistic epistemology and cosmology corrupted Ptolemaic cosmology, and led to a distorted concept of "intervening space

the dualistic structures negate the fact that human subjects are not only "unitary beings" who are composed of the body of their soul and the soul of their body (particularly in Platonic body-soul dualism), but also a "personal beings" in cognitive and interpersonal relations with the concrete realities of the creaturely world and particularly with God. In this regard, for Torrance the Platonic-Aristotelian dualism cannot denote any *personal* and *relational* conception of humanity.

By contrast as Torrance argues, the Hebrew view of humanity is not dualist but unitary, for (1) body and soul are considered as an integrated unity with human beings having the body of their soul and the soul of their body and (2) humanity is thought as beings in personal and relational intimacy with God and fellow humans.[29] This for Torrance is a conception of humanity derived not from philosophical grounds, but from the distinctive Hebrew conception of God.[30]

In the biblical account, God created humanity as unitary beings in personal relation to God and it is therefore the ontological and relational character of humanity that God has accorded human beings as their personal identity. As we will outline more in the following section, this is particularly evident in the doctrine of the image of God found in the Old Testament. Human beings are understood in the image of God, "not in virtue of our rational nature or of anything we are inherently in our own beings, but solely through a relation to God in grace into which he has brought us in the wholeness and integrity of our human being as body of our soul and soul of our body."[31]

For Torrance, the Hebrew view of humanity based on the conception of God offers significant anthropological and theological implications which are in sharp contrast to the dualist Platonic-Aristotelian anthropology. In the Hebrew framework, the spiritual and the physical are not separated but integrated under "the sustaining and holy presence

---

between God and man" which is far removed from the Nicene theology that spoke of "His actual presence in space and time and His personal interaction with our physical existence" (Torrance, *Space, Time and Incarnation*, 3).

29. Torrance, *Soul and Person of the Unborn Child*, 7; *Christian Frame of Mind*, 35. See also Torrance, *Trinitarian Faith*, 150.

30. Torrance, *Christian Frame of Mind*, 37. This is an important point telling us where Torrance's anthropology takes its starting point. Even though Torrance draws upon epistemological uses derived from philosophical and scientific knowledge (e.g., James Clerk Maxwell, Albert Einstein, Michael Polanyi, John Macmurray), Torrance begins with his anthropology from a trinitarian basis.

31. Torrance, *Christian Frame of Mind*, 39.

of God" which is also evident in "the teaching of the Old Testament about religious cleanness and uncleanness in physical life and behaviour."[32] This means that the physical invades the spiritual and *vice versa* within the intimate and reciprocal relation in which the soul is not regarded as being immortal but imprisoned in the body or as having ontological primacy over the body as its substantial form.[33]

Thus, the spiritual and the physical realms are not regarded as being in ontological disjunction but in intimate connection, which is particularly evident in the interrelation between God and his people. Not only does it create the personal and interactionist understanding of the God-human relation in the creaturely world we live in and experience, but it also affects our understanding of human relations and behavior to one another in every area of human life, thought, and activity. As Torrance puts it:

> God and his people were thought of as forming one covenanted society within the conditions of earthly existence; the people did not need to reach beyond those conditions or escape into some realm of timeless abstractions to enjoy spiritual communion with him. Integral to this Hebrew outlook was an essentially religious view of humankind, for human beings were regarded as related to one another and to the physical creation through the intimate presence of God and in reliance upon the constancy of his faithfulness and steadfast love. Hence . . . it became the inherent force affecting the way human beings regard and behave toward one another, and making for creative integration in everyday human life, thought and activity.[34]

In light of this, it is argued that only on such an understanding of humanity as personal beings can we have personal and interactionist God/ourselves/world relations in the conditions of creaturely existence, a view which is not understandable and acceptable in Greek and Roman dualist anthropology.

---

32. Torrance, *Christian Frame of Mind*, 36.

33. For Torrance, as Colyer points out, the Hebrew view of creation also so rejects Platonic anthropology that soul and body are created *ex nihilo* (out of nothing) and thus "corruptible like the rest of creation, with no inherent immortality, and subject to disintegration" (Colyer, *How to Read T. F. Torrance*, 174). For further understanding of the doctrine of creation *ex nihilo* and its relation to the contingent nature of the universe in discussion with natural theology, see Torrance, *Divine and Contingent Order*, 1–51.

34. Torrance, *Christian Frame of Mind*, 37.

Hence, as Torrance argues, even though it is difficult to find any specific concept of person in pre-Christian Jewish thought, the groundwork for the concept of human being as *personal* and *relational* is found in the Hebrew view of humanity. Moreover, the Hebrew unitary views of humanity were extended when we came to the Christian era, and here it was particularly the person of Jesus Christ (the incarnate God-human) and onto-relational thought about the persons of the Trinity that have had such a decisive impact on our understanding of the human being as a *person* and the *personal* in *relations*.

The Concept of Person: Tensions between the Personal/Relational and the Impersonal/Non-Relational

As Torrance argues, the conception of person arose as a result of christological and trinitarian debates in the early church. The Christian church came up with the concept of person applied to God through "intense theological elucidation of what had taken place in and through Jesus Christ and of what he had revealed of the triune nature of God."[35] Yet, the concept of person was not confined only to God, but applied to human beings, for their personal and relational nature as persons. As Torrance puts it:

> The Christian Church came up with the concept of *person*, applied in a unique way to God who is the source of all created personal being, and in another way to human beings who are personal in virtue of their relation to God and to one another within the interpersonal structure of humanity.[36]

In other words, theological discussion about the person of Christ in the early church discovered first "who God is" through Christ's mutual loving intimacy with the Father and the Spirit, and in that light human beings also were regarded as being in interpersonal relations with God

---

35. Torrance, *Christian Frame of Mind*, 38. In this respect, it is not surprising that there had been theological discussions, particularly on the meaning of and the relation between *hypostasis* (person) and *ousia* (being), for the Greek terms involved a wide range of theological implications and significance in relation to who God is and what God does in Christ. This will be addressed more in chapter 2 with regard to the persons and personhood of the Trinity as the creative source of human person and personhood.

36. Torrance, *Christian Frame of Mind*, 38. See also Torrance, "Soul and Person," 115.

and fellow humans which was their identification as person. This outlook reflects a personal and relational understanding of the human person in interpersonal relations with God and fellow humans, in other words, a person in relations.

In reference to the understanding of the term "person," Torrance elucidates that Greek theology adopted as an equivalent to "person" the term "*hypostasis*," using it to refer to "self-subsistent being in its external objective relations in distinction to *ousia* which was used to refer to being in its interior relations."[37] Although the Greek terms were conceptually impersonal, these were given "an intensely dynamic and personal significance" by the theological elucidation of the triune nature of God in the incarnation.[38] As Torrance puts it:

> Thus used in the doctrine of the Trinity *ousia* denotes being in its internal relations, while *hypostasis* denotes being in its interpersonal objective relations, for in himself God is One Being, Three Persons. In their Christian use *ousia* and *hypostasis* were now given a concrete dynamic and intensely personal sense governed by the Nature of the One living God revealed in his saving presence and activity as Father, Son and Holy Spirit.[39]

In this understanding, the concept of person in God is regarded as "an *onto-relational* concept," for what they are as persons is also predicated of the relations between the divine persons.[40] Therefore, in Torrance's trinitarian thought it is evident that personal relations are integral to what the persons themselves are, which is applied both to God and humanity.

As regards such a personal and relational understanding of person, Torrance finds a proper concept of person in the teaching of Richard of St. Victor that a "person is the incommunicable existence of intellectual nature."[41] This is ontologically derived from the Trinity in which person is defined not in accordance with "its own independence as self-subsistence," but "its ontic relations to other persons."[42]

---

37. Torrance, "Soul and Person," 114. In terms of the etymological development of the term "person" in the historical context, see Perlman, *Persona*, 4–5; Rudman, *Concepts of Person and Christian Ethics*, 125–26; Thiel, "Personal Identity," 869.

38. Torrance, *Trinitarian Perspectives*, 130.

39. Torrance, *Trinitarian Perspectives*, 131.

40. Torrance, *Christian Doctrine of God*, 157.

41. Richard of St. Victor, *De Trinitate* 4.22–24, quoted in Torrance, *Reality and Scientific Theology*, 175–76.

42. Torrance, *Reality and Scientific Theology*, 176.

Richard asserts that though a divine person is to be thought in terms of "what he is only through relations with other persons," a person retains the inalienable and ineffable mystery of who he is in "his own distinctive reality which may not be resolved away or be overwhelmed by other persons."[43] It is clear in the incarnation where God revealed "what he is in his self-manifestation toward us as Father, Son and Holy Spirit" in the personal and loving unity of his eternal being as the holy Trinity.[44] Thus, in trinitarian understanding, a person is at once distinct to the subject-being of the other and conditioned by personal relations with the other divine persons.

In this light, the term "the incommunicable existence" represents the fact that "a person is really objective to what is other than he and that this objectivity of one person to another is a constitutive ingredient in a personal being" and so is predicated of ontic relations with others.[45] When this onto-relational concept of person was applied to God and humanity, there were inherent theological and anthropological implications: (1) since God as the Trinity is a fullness of love and personal being who is "the creative, archetypal Source of all other personal beings and their interpersonal relations of love," all other personal being must be defined in terms of "its source and its end, that is, by reference to the fullness of Love and personal Being in the Trinity" and (2) human being is essentially personal being not in "its individuality, its self-subsistence or its self-belonging," but in personal relation to God as the objective source and end of all personal being.[46]

Thus, Torrance finds not just vertical but horizontal implications in Richard's concept of person. Inasmuch as "personal being is essentially *open* to others" in the onto-relational concept, human being must be defined as persons who are who they are through "person-evoking relation" to God and to their neighbors at the same time, which for Torrance means that personal and social belonging are essentially and inseparably together.[47]

It is on this basis that Torrance critiques Boethius's concept of person emphasizing individuality and rational substance, i.e., his "person

---

43. Torrance, *Reality and Scientific Theology*, 176.
44. Torrance, *Trinitarian Perspectives*, 50.
45. Torrance, *Reality and Scientific Theology*, 176.
46. Torrance, *Reality and Scientific Theology*, 176–77.
47. Torrance, *Reality and Scientific Theology*, 177.

is the individual substance of rational nature."[48] In such a concept, it is difficult to find any notion of human being as personal and relational, for Boethius's concept of person derives not ontologically from the Trinity, but *logically* from Aristotelian and Neoplatonic notions of universal substance.[49]

Boethius presupposes the distinction between person and nature and then distinguishes between two kinds of nature, substance and accident in the Aristotelian mode, arguing that only substances can be persons.[50] Boethius then distinguishes between substance and rational substance and between universal and particular substance using Aristotle's distinction between primary and secondary substances.[51] For Boethius here, substance can be either universals or particulars and universal substances are those that are predicated of individuals, while

---

48. Torrance, *Theological Science*, 305–6; Torrance, *Trinitarian Perspectives*, 50.

49. Torrance, *Reality and Evangelical Theology*, 43; *Reality and Scientific Theology*, 174–76. Put simply, Neoplatonism is a philosophical school of thought rooted in Plato's philosophy and in which Plotinus is a central scholar. According to Plotinus, there is an utterly ineffable and unknowable One as the supreme cause of all other realities, which is identified with the Good and the Beautiful. The One emanates *nous*, i.e., logos or reason, *psyche*, i.e., the world soul, and the material world. In this sense, human beings consist of material body and eternal soul with intellect, in which the human soul is regarded as being capable of returning to and even participating in the One or the Good. See Elsee, *Neoplatonism in Relation to Christianity*, 51–81. For Torrance, it is Augustine who brought ingredients of Neoplatonic dualism into Christian theology, and thereby a radical dichotomy between "God and the world, heaven and earth, the eternal and the temporal" has pervaded western thought (Torrance, *Ground and Grammar of Theology*, 22). Thus, for Torrance, Augustine is one of the theological foundations for a dualist understanding of God/ourselves/world relations in an impersonal and non-relational manner (Torrance, *Theology in Reconstruction*, 122).

However, it is evident that Torrance's critique of Augustine, specifically of his dualistic thought, remains not of the whole of his thought but only of certain areas, such as (1) Augustine's psychological and interiorizing concept of knowledge of God in which our knowledge of God is divided from God's actual act in the incarnation (Torrance, *Reality and Scientific Theology*, 169), (2) Augustine's theology of the sacraments separating outward and visible signs from inward and invisible grace (Torrance, *Theology in Reconciliation*, 95–99, 122–23), (3) the juridical understanding of the atonement that divides God from Christ (Torrance, "Karl Barth and the Latin Heresy," 470–79), and (4) the epistemological and cosmological dualism between the *mundus intelligibilis* and the *mundus sensibilis*, i.e., the intelligible world and the sensible world (Torrance, *Divine Meaning*, 193–95; *Theology in Reconciliation*, 46).

50. Torrance, *Reality and Scientific Theology*, 174.

51. Torrance, *Reality and Scientific Theology*, 174.

particulars are not.⁵² In this sense, since there is no general or universal person of a man or woman, but only the single persons of individuals, Plato, for example, or Cicero, for Boethius the word "person" cannot be applied to universals, but only to the concrete particulars or individuals of rational nature.⁵³

In his critique of Boethius's concept of person, Torrance argues firstly that this is an *impersonal* concept of person, for in Boethius's definition, "the person is defined in terms of itself in its cut-off particularity and private individuality."⁵⁴ This means that the becoming and the defining of a person has nothing to do with interpersonal relations with other personal beings. In this regard, Boethius's concept of person cannot be applied only to God regarded as simply one being and not to the three persons in *perichoretic* relations, nor equally and properly also to human subject-beings, for Boethius's concept "shuts the individual up in himself, so that his natural movement is one of self-determination over against other isolated individual subject-beings."⁵⁵

Secondly, Torrance insists that the concept of person derived from the notion of individuality and rational substance/nature is a *fateful* concept of person, for it has had a seriously damaging effect on the whole history of western thought, particularly on anthropological, scientific, and theological thought:⁵⁶ (1) in the anthropological perspective, the concept was adopted by Thomas Aquinas, then inherited in the philosophy of Descartes and assimilated to "the notion of the epistemological subject," i.e., self-certainty from self-consciousness (*cogito, ergo sum*),⁵⁷ (2) in scientific knowledge, when merged with Newtonian particle-theory, the concept of person brought about "the atomistic notion of the self-determining personality" which has distorted the infra-structure of

---

52. Boethius, *Theological Tractates*, 85.
53. Torrance, *Reality and Scientific Theology*, 174.
54. Torrance, *Reality and Scientific Theology*, 175.
55. Torrance, *Reality and Scientific Theology*, 175. The Geek term *perichoresis* refers to the interpenetration and mutual indwelling of the Trinity. For Torrance, *perichoresis*, "together with the conception of the *homoousion* . . . enables us to read back the interrelations between the Father, the Son and the Holy Spirit in the economy of salvation into the eternal relations immanent in the one Being of God" (Torrance, *Christian Doctrine of God*, 172). This will be addressed in more detail in chapter 2.
56. Torrance, *Theology in Reconciliation*, 285–86.
57. Torrance, *Theological Science*, 123.

all our social institutions and natural sciences,[58] and (3) in theological thinking, the concept denies that "God can be spoken of as personal" as is evident in the thought of G. W. F. Hegel and Paul Tillich, for "if it is applied to God it would seem to mean either that God is a restricted individual or that there are three finite Gods."[59]

---

58. Torrance, *Theology in Reconciliation*, 286.

59. Torrance, *Reality and Scientific Theology*, 175. Further explanation is required here. In anthropological and scientific thought, the Cartesian idea of self-consciousness locates "truth" in the subjective pole, so that the epistemological separation of subject from object occurs, which was accentuated through Newton's and Kant's philosophies in scientific knowledge. Newton's rigid and mathematical system of cause and effect gave rise to the dualistic division between absolute mathematical space and time and relative space and time and Kant's synthesis of rationalism and empiricism brought about the disjunction between the noumenal world and the phenomenal world. Here "the human mind itself is excluded from the field of scientific knowledge, in the mistaken belief that through elimination of the personal coefficient an absolutely dispassionate, impersonal, and exact scientific knowledge may be achieved," and God's salvific penetration into and interaction with the world and humanity is also excluded (Torrance, *Christian Frame of Mind*, 37). See also Morrison, *Knowledge of the Self-Revealing God*, 48–51.

In terms of theological thinking, God is defined in Hegel's thought as "Absolute Spirit," i.e., the universal self-subsistent and thinking existent and in Tillich's thought God is considered and mediated in our consciousness though "religious symbols." For Torrance, as Molnar points out, it is also Schleiermacher and Rudolf Bultmann who so refuse to think of God "as the object of our conceiving and knowing" that for them God is understood only so far as (1) God is "the co-determinant of our feeling of absolute dependence" (Schleiermacher) and (2) God can only be described in terms of "people's existential reactions to the gospel" (Bultmann). See Molnar, *Faith, Freedom and the Spirit*, 67–68; Torrance, *God and Rationality*, 106–7. For Torrance, it is apparent that in the thinking of Hegel, Tillich, Schleiermacher, and Bultmann, God was understood *not* as the triune God, i.e., as the divine three *persons*, Father, Son and Holy Spirit in the *loving* and *personal relations* of the eternal being disclosed to us and experienced in his self-manifestation, *but by* allowing their thoughts to be diverted to their own psychological, rationalistic, and existential thinking of God.

However, as elucidated, for Torrance our scientific and theological thinking takes place only after the actuality of knowledge, that is, *kata physin*. According to McGrath, in Torrance's thought there have been three fundamental transitions in scientific and cosmological thinking: (1) "from primitive Hellenistic cosmology, characterized by a thorough and pervasive dualism, to a Ptolemaic cosmology," (2) "from a Ptolemaic to Copernican and Newtonian cosmology" in a modified form of dualism, and (3) "the Maxwellian-Einsteinian revolution, which abandoned the dualist assumptions of earlier understandings of the world in favour of a unitary approach based on the notion of continuous fields" (McGrath, *Thomas F. Torrance*, 213–14). In theological thinking, the transition for Torrance was "Barth's reconstruction of the doctrine of the Trinity" in which our knowledge of God is so interlocked with the dynamic interaction of God with humanity through his self-revelation in Christ to us, that "to know God from

For Torrance what is notable is the fact that the individualistic and rationalistic concept of person derived from the dualisms of Plato and Aristotle has led to the epistemological and ontological separation not only of the human subject (or human knower) from the object (or objective realities), but also of God from both the universe and humanity in proper scientific and theological ways of thinking. This also means that through this concept of person becoming such a universally accepted category of thought, the ancient impersonal/non-relational frame of mind has been deeply entrenched in our understanding not only of anthropology, but also of theology and the natural sciences.

Such is the epistemic center of the reason why Torrance critiques the impersonal and non-relational concept of person and its infection of human thinking and life. In that case, we may be concerned about the extent to which he proposes an alternative or corrective without just remaining critical of the concept. In response, Torrance argues that "the introduction into human thought of the category of the personal has far-reaching consequences, of a general and a particular kind."[60] To put it another way, it is when and as *the personal and onto-relational concept of person* in the trinitarian and christological tradition penetrates into our thought, that real epistemological and ontological inversion of and corrective to the *impersonal* and *fateful* concept of person can take place. As Torrance puts it:

> The effect of Christianity is to replace the impersonal *Id* with the intensely personal *Ego Sum* of the living God, but that brings the Christian faith into a wide-ranging struggle with the ancient impersonalism that still exercises considerable if inertial force in sensitive areas of our culture and way of life. Our immediate concern here is with the reforming of our basic conception of God by using *the concept of the person* or rational agent as a disclosure model through which to allow God's own ultimate

---

the very start is to know him as Triune" through Christ (Torrance, *Theology in Reconciliation*, 286). Thus, in both scientific and theological transitions, Torrance finds an "epistemological inversion" in which the objective reality is disclosed to the subjective reality, i.e., the human knower in an a posteriori experience of the reality (Torrance, *Theological Science*, 131). This is Torrance's scientific and theological response to reality in the manner appropriate to it where it is investigated according to its own distinct nature. As we will see further in more detail in chapter 3, it is a realist epistemology based on Torrance's critical realism in which it is the humanity of Christ which has a pivotal role in his critical realism in relation to theological epistemology and ontology.

60. Torrance, *Reality and Scientific Theology*, 173.

personal and personalising nature to control and shape our understanding of his dynamic interaction with the world he has made.[61]

By using the onto-relational concept of person, where personal relations are integral to what persons are, the impersonal/non-relational concept of person in human mind and thought is reformed. This means that the schizoid God/ourselves/world relations and the gulf between subject and object in theological and scientific ways of thinking are overcome through being understood in the personal and relational framework where subject and object are properly related in interpersonal and interactive relations. In this light, Torrance argues that the fact that the concept of person derived from the doctrines of the incarnation and the trinitarian personhood means that "personal relations belong to the structure of reality itself" and this becomes a theological corrective to "the impersonal model of the detached observer over against the object."[62] As Torrance puts it:

> Hence a recovery of the concept of the human being as personal agent, actively related to the world of things and personas around him, erases the radical dualism upon which the old model of thought depended (i.e., the model built up from the concept of man as a detached observer over against inert, determinate being), and produces a new orientation of mind to the universe in which the idea of a God who interacts with us and our world is not automatically excluded.[63]

This draws our attention to two significant implications: (1) the importance of the concept of person in Torrance's theology in terms of his critique of the ancient and modern dualisms and (2) the decisive role or factor of the incarnation, God's personal self-communication through Christ which leads us to fully understand the onto-relational concept of person.

First, given that a wide range of studies on Torrance have generally suggested the concepts of "critical realism" and "the incarnation" as

---

61. Torrance, *Reality and Scientific Theology*, 173.

62. Torrance, *Reality and Scientific Theology*, 173.

63. Torrance, *Reality and Scientific Theology*, 57. Here Torrance mentions that "the model of active agency" and "the place of action" are recurring themes in the philosophy of Macmurray. Torrance also asserts that a bridgeable relation between subject and object in scientific and philosophical knowledge is evident in the various writings of Polanyi and Macmurray (Torrance, *Reality and Scientific Theology*, 173).

his central responses to the dualistic patterns of thought in scientific and theological thinking, we must consider the concept of person in Torrance as one of the most significant epistemological methods he used.[64] Second, for Torrance the concept of person is properly understood only in and through the mediation of Christ, for here we are allowed to know not only the personal relations in the Trinity as the source of all personal relations/beings, but also his personal relations with us in and through Christ. This for Torrance is one of the main consequences of what Christ achieved for us which will be addressed more in the next section and in chapter 3.

In summary, as we have seen for Torrance the concept of person has to be regarded as onto-relational which enables us to have a proper understanding of humanity as persons in relations with God and others. In the following sections, the onto-relational concept of human person in Torrance's thought will be illustrated further by the theological, scientific, and philosophical epistemology on which he drew.

Torrance's Theological Concept of Human Being: The Relational Imago Dei

For Torrance, as elucidated, the fact that we human beings are persons in relation with God and with others is grounded in the being-constituting relation of the divine persons in which the onto-relational concept of person first arises. This draws our attention to the biblical and Christian understanding of the nature of human identity, that is, the nature of the *imago Dei*, for humanity created in the image of God clearly shows human beings, as ontologically contingent on God, to be persons in relation vertically, to God and horizontally with others. In this regard, for Torrance it is the humanity of Christ which enables us to fully recognize "the true image and the reality" of both humanity and God, the truth of

---

64. There has been a wide range of studies on Torrance's theology. In particular, with regard to Torrance's critique of ancient and modern forms of dualisms, we find a stereotypical understanding of it which has been endorsed by numerous theologians. In this understanding, there are at least three related topics and points where Torrance's rejection of dualism becomes clear: (1) his understanding of the God-world relation revealed in the incarnation and critical realist epistemology (Colyer, *How to Read T. F. Torrance*, 57), (2) a realist epistemology in theology and natural sciences and Christ as the epistemological center and focus of his realism (McGrath, *Thomas F. Torrance*, 212, 219), and (3) his realist theological and scientific view, the Nicene *homoousion*, and the incarnation (Molnar, *Thomas F. Torrance*, 41, 46, 303).

humanity as image and of God as the reality, and to which we are restored as personal and relational beings created in the image of God.

Imago Dei in the Biblical Tradition

In the Old Testament, humanity is created by God as unitary in being with body and soul (or mind) *ex nihilo*, out of nothing.[65] This shows that as created beings humanity is contingent on God, for their "sustaining ground and sufficient reason" is ontologically rooted in him alone.[66] Despite the contingent nature of all created beings, however, for Torrance it is human beings who have the distinctively contingent nature grounded in "the direct address of God to man which has the effect of sealing and destining him for communion with God."[67] This means that only in vertical contingency on God and interaction with him in personal/relational ways, is human being an image of God, which therefore rejects not only the Platonic notion of any pre-existing soul, but also the Aristotelian static relation between God in his deity and humanity. As Torrance puts it:

> Man is a creature in total dependence of being, and motion, and life, upon the gracious will of God. He is created out of nothing, and has neither origin nor being in himself, but is given being, and maintained in being, by the grace of God. *In relation to God, therefore, man is only an image.* That is to say, his life is absolutely reflexive of the action of God, and can be lived only in a motion of continued reflection. This is a very important point in the Reformed doctrine of man, for it is just here that a decisive break is made with the Aristotelian man of scholastic theology, in which the living, dynamic relation of man to God is translated into a substantival and logical relation.[68]

65. For Torrance, God's nature as persons in relation and love is the reason why humanity was created by God in his image. As Torrance notes, in the biblical tradition "God does not wish to exist alone, and has freely brought into being alongside of himself and yet in utter distinction from himself another upon whom he may pour out his love, with whom he may share his divine Life in covenant-partnership." This for Torrance underlies our understanding of anthropology entailing the very nature of man in relation and the essential goodness and dignity of humanity (Torrance, "Goodness and Dignity of Man," 314). See also Torrance, *School of Faith*, 1xxiii.

66. Torrance, "Goodness and Dignity of Man," 310.

67. Torrance, "Goodness and Dignity of Man," 310.

68. Torrance, *Theology in Reconstruction*, 99. See also Torrance, "Goodness and Dignity of Man," 310–12; "Soul and Person," 110–12.

In this respect, we human beings must be regarded as the image of God "not in virtue of our rational nature or of anything we are inherently in our own beings, but solely through a relation to God in grace into which he has brought us in the wholeness and integrity of our human being."[69] This relational *imago Dei* is evident already in the "spirit-Spirit relation" and the "male-female relation" found in the creation of human beings.

In terms of the spirit/Spirit relation, as Torrance notes, the Bible speaks of God's personal relation to human beings in creation as realized through his Spirit not only upholding human contingent existence, but also sustaining the human creature in "his/her contingent openness to God and the address of his Word."[70] It is this relation constituted *through* God's Creator Spirit that the Bible called "*spirit*."[71] Through "the power and presence of the Spirit" the human spirit is related to the triune God and given "the capacity to think and act in accordance with the nature (*kata physin*) of what is other than himself": that is the essence of *human rationality*.[72]

In this regard, the human spirit—not a third thing in human beings, with soul and body—is to be understood only in essential and dynamic correlation with the divine "Spirit." It is thereby apparent that the human spirit is a "transcendental determination" of his/her existence, not something human beings have, or as "a spark of the divine, but the *ontological qualification* of his/her soul" given and sustained by the Spirit.[73] Thus, in the light of this spirit/Spirit relation the human creature as *imago Dei* is thought of only as "an essentially relational being" who is what he/she is only through the "being-constituting relation of the Creator."[74]

However, the relational *imago Dei* is found not only in the spirit/Spirit relation, the vertical relation, but also in the male-female relation, the horizontal relation. In the biblical tradition, as Torrance notes, human beings are created in God's image, not as solitary individuals, but as men and women in love and marriage to become "one flesh" by act of

---

69. Torrance, "Goodness and Dignity of Man," 317.

70. Torrance, "Goodness and Dignity of Man," 310.

71. Torrance, "Goodness and Dignity of Man," 310. In this sense, for Torrance, the term "spirit" is to be thought only in a personal and relational sense, particularly the spirit-Spirit relation.

72. Torrance, "Soul and Person," 110.

73. Torrance, "Soul and Person," 110 (italics added).

74. Torrance, "Goodness and Dignity of Man," 311.

God.[75] This means that they need each other to be fully human and in "their union the basic unit of humanity," so that "co-humanity belongs to the essential fabric of human existence."[76] Thus, it is evident that the human creature as the image of God is a relational being not simply through a vertical relation to God, but also through a horizontal relation within human created existence as man and woman. Then through procreation this intra-human relation within the family flows in "the intrinsic social structure of humanity."[77]

For Torrance this is "the *personal* or *inter-personal* structure of humanity in which there is imaged the ineffable personal relations of the Holy Trinity."[78] In the creation of man and woman as God's image and in their love and marriage, the *otherness* and *togetherness* of man and woman are embedded in each of them and each is "an independent and distinctive human being *in* partnership with the other."[79] This is what Torrance means by "the being-constituting relation"[80] in which there is "an inherent relatedness in human being which is a creaturely reflection of a transcendent relatedness in divine Being."[81] In this regard for Torrance, it is clear that in the biblical tradition the human being created

---

75. Torrance, "Goodness and Dignity of Man," 311. See also Torrance, *Christian Doctrine of Marriage*, 4.

76. Torrance, "Goodness and Dignity of Man," 311.

77. Torrance, "Goodness and Dignity of Man," 311.

78. Torrance, "Soul and Person," 109.

79. Torrance, "Soul and Person," 109.

80. Torrance, "Goodness and Dignity of Man," 311.

81. Torrance, "Soul and Person," 109. According to Habets, in Torrance the fact that the inherent relatedness in human being, particularly in marriage and family is in turn a creaturely reflection of a transcendent relatedness in divine Being, is clearly influenced by Barth (Habets, *Theosis in the Theology of Thomas Torrance*, 40; cf. Barth, *CD* 3/4:117). Here Habets seems to find Barth as the central theological ground for Torrance's understanding of the image of God in this point. But for Torrance it is evident that in the Old Testament the relation between Adam and Eve as man and wife points to the mutuality of the society between them and in the New Testament through Christ the imago-relation between the Son and the Father is seen in the relation between man and woman. Torrance found a similar thought in Calvin in his commentary on Paul's statement that "the woman is the glory of man as he is the image and glory of God" (Torrance, *Calvin's Doctrine of Man*, 44). Hence, it can be argued that on this point Torrance's understanding of the creaturely reflection of a transcendent relatedness in divine being is essentially based on the biblical tradition that both Calvin and Barth have used in Reformed theology.

in the *imago Dei* is constituted as a personal/relational being only in the being-constituting, onto-relations with God and others.

Imago Dei in the Christian Tradition

As Torrance asserts, the Old Testament view of humanity created in the *imago Dei* is considerably deepened and reinforced through "the acute personalisation of human relations with God in Jesus Christ."[82] Put another way, in union with the incarnate Son through the Spirit, the being-constituting relations with God and others are fully restored, for in him we are personalized as persons created in the image of God. This has significant implications for the nature of sin and the ontological significance and necessity of Christ's personalizing ministry for the restoration of the relational *imago Dei*.

In reference to the nature of sin, sin for Torrance is to be regarded not primarily in legal terms, but as the breach of vertical and horizontal relations with God and others, for sinful or fallen human beings are no longer "the beings they ought to be either in relation to God or in relation to one another."[83] This is because sin is the ontological contradiction in humanity in which human beings are trapped within their inverted and distorted nature and being through their onto-relations with God and others becoming displaced and twisted into alienation and estrangement.[84] Thus, for Torrance sinful human beings are considered as beings in need of ontological restoration and transformation from the existential contradiction obstructing their interpersonal vertical and horizontal relations, which means that sinful nature and being in humanity have to be restored and renewed to being fully personal and human, created in God's image.

For Torrance here, it is Jesus Christ who is "the decisive factor and controlling centre of the Christian tradition" as it relates to our understanding of humanity as the *imago Dei*, for it is in and through him alone that we penetrate through "all the distortion, depravity and degradation

---

82. Torrance, *Christian Frame of Mind*, 39.

83. Torrance, "Goodness and Dignity of Man," 312.

84. For Torrance in this regard, God's forgiveness of human sin through the atoning incarnation and cross of Jesus Christ must be said to resolve not our forensic or legal problem, but the ontological one in which we are trapped in estranged and alienated relations from God and others in the very ontological depths of our sinful humanity (Torrance, *Mediation of Christ*, 39).

of humanity to the true nature of man hidden beneath it all."[85] As we will see more detail in chapter 3, Christ is not only "the one true Man who is properly and completely in the image of God," but also "the only One who is both the *Image* and the *Reality* of God, for in his incarnate Person God and Man, divine and human nature, are inseparably united."[86] As such and since our actual human being and nature are taken up and perfectly united to his divine being and nature in his person, in Christ the dehumanizing breach between God and humanity was and is healed and restored.

In other words, this means that our relations with God are personalized in and through Christ who is "the one *personalising Person,* while we are *personalised persons* who draw from him the true substance of our personal being both in relation to God and in relation to one another."[87] In and through Christ, sinful and fallen human beings are transmuted into persons as the relational *imago Dei* and alienated and estranged relations into personal and interpersonal onto-relations with God and our follow humans.

In the light of Torrance's Christocentric approach to the *imago Dei* and its restoration, we may crystallize its anthropological and christological implications in terms of a set of affirmations:

1. Human beings as we are, we can be the very image of God in being-constituting relations with God and others only in and through union with Christ by the Spirit.[88]

85. Torrance, "Goodness and Dignity of Man," 315.

86. Torrance, "Goodness and Dignity of Man," 317.

87. Torrance, *Christian Frame of Mind*, 39. For Torrance it is the humanity of Christ which provides us with the ways in which the restoration of the *imago Dei* and of onto-relations with God and others occurs and which therefore engenders important anthropological and ethical implications. This will be addressed further in chapter 3 through a wide range of christological discussions entailing a Christian anthropology and ethic.

88. For Torrance, "union with Christ" was *objectively* or *ontologically* accomplished for all of humankind in the incarnation, where the actual conditions of our estranged humanity were taken up and brought into perfect atoning, sanctifying, justifying, and reconciling union with divine nature in the person of Christ (Torrance, *Mediation of Christ*, 64–66). It is the role of the Spirit to *subjectively* actualize what has already been *objectively* accomplished in the incarnational reconciliation of Christ and through his entire vicarious life. Through "the communion of the Spirit," we are given to participate or share in the *ontological* transformation of our humanity in Jesus Christ so that new and true human being, life, and relations are set up (Torrance, *School of Faith*, cvi–cxviii). In this regard, for Torrance the theme of union with Christ through the

2. The epistemological and ontological problem and distortion of humanity found in the Platonic-Aristotelian dualistic anthropology and the nature of sin, i.e., the epistemic and ontological estrangement from God and our neighbors is broken up and corrected by the mediation of Christ.

3. As Christ is both the image and reality of God and humanity and the one who restores the relational *imago Dei* in his person, we may truly reach the knowledge of God, not one inherently possessed in our human existence, but ontologically contingent upon onto-relation with God restored in Christ.

Inasmuch as it is the christological personalization and reconstruction of the relational *imago Dei* which is all important, for Torrance it is Christ who must be regarded as the absolute epistemic and ontological hinge of the biblical/Christian anthropology, which is the line of thought that was not taken seriously in Augustine's psychological and interiorizing movement of thought to God.[89] Moreover, for Torrance the fact that Christ became incarnate in "the creaturely world of time and space we experience," taking our fallen humanity and uniting it to his divinity in his own incarnate person in actual historical event, dictates that all knowledge must begin with the a posteriori encounter with Christ which is so germane to his epistemology and leads to the stratified model of the knowledge of God.[90] Hence, for Torrance it is Christ who underlies our understanding of the relational *imago Dei* and the knowledge of God.

Spirit has a central place in his anthropology and ethics. We will see how our union with Christ has anthropological and ethical implications and effects more in greater depth as this thesis proceeds.

89. Torrance, *Reality and Scientific Theology*, 174. We will examine this in more detail as the chapter proceeds.

90. Torrance expounds "the stratification of the knowledge of God" in accordance with the three levels which come to light and through an a posteriori reconstruction of our actual knowledge of God as it has arisen. The three levels are: the evangelical and doxological level (the personal and communal experience of God), the theological level (or the economic level), and a higher theological and scientific level (or the ontological/immanent level). In this stratified structure, we move from the first level to the level of the economic Trinity (*ad extra*) and lastly to the level of the ontological or immanent Trinity (*ad intra*). In other words, in and through the incarnation in our history, "we are compelled, under pressure from God's self-communication, to acknowledge [that] what God is toward us" as Father, Son and Spirit in Christ, he is in himself in his own eternal being (Torrance, *Ground and Grammar of Theology*, 156–58).

Interestingly, Torrance finds a similar procedure in Einstein's stratified structure

Torrance's Scientific and Philosophical Concept of Human Being: The Personal Agent and Person in Relation

As we have seen, Torrance finds the concept of human being as persons in relation in biblical/theological traditions, in which our vertical and horizontal relations with God and others, i.e., the being-constituting relations clearly show that human beings are persons as personal/relational beings created in the *image Dei*. Torrance, then, draws upon philosophical and scientific epistemology so as to support and deepen his theological concept of humanity. Torrance undergirds his own epistemic thought of subject-object, knowing-being, and human-God/human-human relations particularly in the scientific and philosophical concepts of Polanyi and Macmurray, "personal knowledge" and "persons in relation." Here we will see the ways in which Torrance employs their scientific and philosophical epistemology in his own interpretation and reconstruction of their thought for his trinitarian and Christocentric anthropology.

Personal Knowledge: Michael Polanyi

As a Hungarian chemist Michael Polanyi (1891–1976) is one of the most influential writers in the field of the philosophy of science. In particular, Polanyi's book *Personal Knowledge: Towards a Post-Critical Philosophy* (1958) is widely accepted as his most significant work where he unfolds the "fiduciary" (faith or belief) element of human knowledge in his critical response to dualisms in the field of scientific knowledge.[91] Torrance makes use of Polanyi's philosophy of science in selective and

---

of scientific knowledge in which, as Myers expounds it, "our conceptual knowledge arises from the ground level of our intuitive apprehension of reality; and, even as this knowledge becomes increasingly formalised, it remains closely coordinated with our basic intuitive experience of reality. Thus, we advance towards ever more refined conceptuality not by moving away from concrete reality, but by penetrating more deeply into it" (Myers, "Stratification of Knowledge," 5–6). In this regard, Loder states that we find an intriguing point in Torrance's analogy between our theological understanding of God and of the intelligible universe as Einstein expounds it, an analogy which may be used as "an instrument of grace" to disclose the actual knowledge of God in both a scientific and a theological context (Loder and Neidhardt, *Knight's Move*, 199). This a posteriori logic is also found in Polanyi's theory of "tactic knowing" and Macmurray's notion of "person in relation" which will be addressed more in the following section.

91. Polanyi, *Personal Knowledge*, 266–67.

sometimes critical ways to demonstrate the fundamental correspondence between scientific inquiry and theological inquiry essentially based on belief or faith.[92]

In terms of Polanyi's understanding of belief as the source of all knowledge, it is necessary to begin first with Torrance's exposition of what Polanyi calls the "absurd mechanisation of knowledge" deeply entrenched in modern dualistic sciences, particularly in Newton's system of the universe.[93] This offers a good understanding of the tension between mechanistic-rationalistic and personal knowledge in Polanyi's thought.

In Newton's concept of the universe inherited from the ancient epistemological dualism, there is dichotomy between "absolute mathematical time and space" ("noumenal" in Kant's term) with the infinite presence of God and "relative apparent time and space" ("phenomena") of this world.[94] God conceived of as beyond and independent of the universe plays a role in conferring natural laws and regulating efficient causes and mechanical connections within the universe and the universe is thereby defined as a closed system of cause and effect governed by natural laws, i.e., "a mechanically conceived universe."[95]

In the mechanistically conceived structure of the universe, we find a dualism between the theoretical and the empirical aspects of reality,[96] in which "every one begins with a mind that is devoid of any innate or intuitive ideas and gains knowledge *only through* sense impressions received under the impact of material substances or through reflection on those impressions."[97] This is the empiricist theory of knowledge by

---

92. Colin Weightman states that Polanyi's influence on Torrance is clearly presented in Torrance's writings from 1963 onwards. For instance, Torrance's numerous references to Polanyi are found in his book *Theological Science*, which is based on the 1959 Hewett Lectures on "The Nature of Theology and Scientific Method" and published in 1969. Torrance's first-published systematic treatment of theology, *The School of Faith* (1959), also refers in the introduction to "references to the personal and communal dimensions of knowledge, two typical Polanyian themes" (Weightman, *Theology in a Polanyian Universe*, 203). For further understanding of Weightman's work on how Polanyi offers "the capstone of Torrance's assessment of the nature of science and how it is to be related to theology," see Weightman, *Theology in a Polanyian Universe*, 129–274.

93. Torrance, *Christian Frame of Mind*, 39.

94. Torrance, *Divine and Contingent Order*, 8–9.

95. Torrance, *Divine and Contingent Order*, 9; *Christian Theology and Scientific Culture*, 25.

96. Torrance, *Christian Frame of Mind*, 46; *Ground and Grammar of Theology*, 32.

97. Torrance, *Christian Theology and Scientific Culture*, 45 (italics added).

Locke, corresponding to that of Galileo and Newton, which is taken over by Hume and Kant "in shift in the centre of gravity from a theocentric to an anthropocentric point of view," identifying the law of the autonomous reason with an identification of natural law.[98] Thus, a consistent impersonalization of science and human culture was introduced, erecting "a completely mechanistic conception of the universe and of human existence" in the enterprise of science.[99]

In the mechanistic-causal interpretation, Polanyi argues, the absurd mechanization of knowledge or the "massive modern absurdity" occurs.[100] In this, the human conscious mind and personal convictions and actions are themselves excluded from the field of scientific knowledge in the mistaken belief that "through elimination of the personal coefficient an absolutely dispassionate, impersonal, and exact scientific knowledge may be achieved."[101]

This has a damaging effect not only on the relation between the mind of the knowing agent and the objective reality, but also on the relation between faith and reason or belief and rational knowledge in such an extent that "belief is no more than an ungrounded persuasion or private opinion of the mind which falls short of knowledge, for it is not based on the evidence of the senses and is only extraneously related to what is believed."[102] That is to say, belief or faith is not regarded as a source of knowledge and demonstrative reasoning in scientific observations.

However, for Polanyi as Torrance expounds him, belief or intuitive apprehension must be recognized as the source of knowledge integral to "an intuitive grasp of a reality" in which there takes place, in the mind of human knower, direct intuitive contact with the objective reality.[103] This rejects the idea that "scientific discovery is a logical process" to knowledge through deductive reasoning from observations, for there is no logical bridge between experience and scientific ideas/concepts as Einstein already demonstrated in his principle of relativity.[104] In this sense, the

---

98. Torrance, *Christian Theology and Scientific Culture*, 47.

99. Torrance, *Christian Theology and Scientific Culture*, 47.

100. Polanyi, *Personal Knowledge*, 9.

101. Torrance, *Christian Frame of Mind*, 47.

102. Torrance, *Christian Theology and Scientific Culture*, 45.

103. Torrance, *Transformation and Convergence*, 114.

104. Torrance, *Transformation and Convergence*, 114; "Framework of Belief," 12. In terms of the way in which Einstein opposes and crushes the mechanistic concept of the universe and its impact on scientific knowledge in his theory of relativity, see Polanyi, *Science, Faith, and Society*, 87–90.

intelligibility of the objective reality is to be thought of as being inherent in nature, invisible and independent of ourselves, but through belief or intuitive apprehension the mind of the knowing agent is able to penetrate into the intelligible features of the objective reality. As Torrance puts it:

> [Polanyi] insisted that we must recognise belief or intuitive apprehension once more as the source of knowledge from which our acts of discovery take their rise, for it is in belief that we are in direct touch with reality, in belief that our minds are open to the invisible realm of intelligibility independent of ourselves, and through belief that we entrust our minds to the orderly and reliable nature of the universe.[105]

By the fiduciary component of knowledge, the mechanistic knowledge claimed by Newtonians is transmuted into personal knowledge in which "no scientific discovery or verification is possible without the responsible participation of the person as an active rational centre of consciousness in all acts of human understanding and knowing."[106] In this light, for Polanyi as Torrance elucidates him, beliefs are certainly personal acts, for only persons are capable of engaging in objective operations and knowing what is known through responsible commitment to and personal participation in the claims of reality, therefore knowledge can only be personal and is what Polanyi calls "personal knowledge."[107]

Torrance regards Polanyi's priority of belief as not only the proper reorientation of scientific knowledge, but also as the transition from abstract and impersonal knowledge to a personal coefficient of knowledge. In an anthropological sense, it is an affirmation that humanity is *personal*

---

105. Torrance, "Framework of Belief," 9.

106. Torrance, *Christian Frame of Mind*, 45.

107. Torrance, *Transformation and Convergence*, 134–35; "Notes on Terms and Concepts," 141–42. This does not mean, however, that the human knower is capable of determining the knowledge of the objective reality purely in his/her subjective pole. Personal knowledge, of course, entails personal judgement, that is, responsible self-criticism in relation to the objective reality in which a person distinguishes what is known from his/her subjective notions (Torrance, "Framework of Belief," 19). But for Polanyi personal knowledge and judgment take place tacitly or implicitly "in relating evidence to an aspect of external reality" that he/she acknowledges and which is objectively imposed on the mind of the knowing agent by reality itself in the fiduciary framework (Torrance, *Transformation and Convergence*, 123). Thus, personal knowledge or belief is far from being merely "a subjective or private concern," but is rather "the obedience of the mind to objective reality in recognition of its universal and normative authority," and that is truth as "the external pole of belief" (Torrance, "Framework of Belief," 13–14).

and therefore as rational and personal agents equipped for the personal knowledge necessary in knowing and engaging in what is known. It is also the exclusion of the false ideal of objectivism, the detaching of subjectivity (or the human knower) from objectivity (or the objective reality) in order to achieve pure exteriority in knowledge. Thus, following Polanyi, Torrance argues that in scientific knowledge humanity must be considered as persons in relation with the objective reality through the fiduciary framework—that is, belief or faith.[108]

Interestingly and importantly, Torrance relates the nature and status of belief in scientific knowledge to the nature and status of belief in our knowledge of God. Despite significant differences between them, in both theology and science we believe the nature of beliefs derived from the intelligibility inherent in what we believe, which clearly shows that theological activity and scientific activity share the fiduciary component of knowledge.[109] They also have a shared rational procedure, that is, rationality or objectivity in which "the mind of the knower acts in strict conformity to the nature of what is given, and refuses to take up a standing in regard to it prior to actual knowledge or in abstraction from actual knowledge."[110]

In this regard then, for Torrance it is evident that both scientific and theological knowledge are based on the same fiduciary and rational framework of knowledge, whether to the objective reality or to God. In this framework, first, the fact that the human knower is a personal, rational agent, unfolds the further fact that both the mode of assent, and the nature of the personal convictions aroused in the heuristic process and relation with the objective reality or God, are and must be personal and not impersonal.[111] In addition, the damaging split between subject and object, or thought and experience, is recovered in the natural unity of knowing and being.[112] As beliefs arise in the mind of the knowing agent by the experience of the reality known to us, the human knower personally commits to and participates in the reality and so is able to inquire more deeply into it. In this heuristic process of knowing and being, persons reach not only the knowledge of reality in a scientific sense, but also

---

108. Torrance, "Framework of Belief," 12.
109. Torrance, "Framework of Belief," 12.
110. Torrance, *Karl Barth*, 67–68.
111. Torrance, "Framework of Belief," 12.
112. Torrance, *Christian Theology and Scientific Culture*, 63.

the knowledge of God in a theological sense. Thus, for Torrance it has to be argued that it is persons who are *the bearer of objectivity* in personal relation with the objective reality or with God.

Persons in Relation: John Macmurray

In a way similar to his use of Polanyi's philosophy of science, Torrance also draws upon the personalist philosophy of John Macmurray (1891–1976) who was one of the greater Scottish philosophers in the humanist tradition. Even with the significant input from Polanyi, Macmurray has had a decisive influence on Torrance's understanding of the unitary relation between knowing and being in action, even though as Fergusson asserts, he has often not been stressed as an important influence on Torrance.[113] Yet Torrance in his numerous books utilizes Macmurray's concepts of the self as agent, reason and reality, and persons in relation.[114] In this respect, Macmurray is undoubtedly to be regarded as one of the influential thinkers on the thought of Torrance.

Torrance's epistemological uses of Macmurray are closely linked to his critique and rejection of dualistic patterns of thought in the fields of scientific, anthropological, and theological knowledge where such a split has been engendered a split between subject and object. The emergence of Macmurray's personalist philosophy is particularly evident here with regard to the Cartesian impersonal approach to knowledge.

Descartes's approach to knowledge, as Torrance elucidates it, rests upon "doubt" as a form of self-certainty (*cogito, ergo sum*) in which a theoretical and egocentric process is developed with the complete

---

113. According to Fergusson, in terms of the influences on Torrance's thought commentators on Torrance have often focused on patristic writers (particularly Athanasius), John Calvin and other Reformers, Barth, and modern scientific thinkers, e.g., Clerk Maxwell, Einstein, and Polanyi. But as Fergusson rightly points out, Torrance's realist theology is reinforced by Macmurray's epistemology and Torrance's anthropological understanding of embodiedness and sociality of human life is strongly Hebraic and also supported by Macmurray's writings (Fergusson, "Influence of Macmurray on Scottish Theology," 146–47).

114. See Torrance, *God and Rationality*, 81; *Reality and Scientific Theology*, 57–58; *Space, Time and Resurrection*, 41–42; *Theological Science*, 3–4, 11–12, 75–76, 123, 208; *Theology in Reconstruction*, 15, 232–33; *Christian Frame of Mind*, 43; *Theology in Reconciliation*, 28; *Transformation and Convergence*, 194, 213. For further understanding of Macmurray's contributions to Torrance's thought on overcoming dualism, creating an integrated realist philosophy, and elucidating the form of the personal, see Folsom, "John Macmurray's Influence," 339–58.

bifurcation of subject and object.[115] To put it another way, if a human person is regarded only as the thinking self and then by the process of doubting or observing phenomena *within the self* infers and so gets to knowledge of the objective reality, it is inevitable that (1) the self is an isolated individual and (2) the knowledge of reality is reduced to rational representations which arise within the states of self-consciousness or thought. In this sense, the objective reality such as the world or God is not something with which humanity interacts as "a personal agent" and this engenders the impersonal and non-interactive conception of God/ourselves/world relations.[116] Such is the subject-object split in space and time we experience.

Making use of the language of Macmurray, Torrance critiques the Cartesian theoretical and egocentric approach to reality, arguing for a realist relation between reason and reality where reason is not itself determinative but follows reality as it is disclosed to us. As Torrance puts it:

> In the language of Professor John Macmurray, reason is our capacity to behave consciously in terms of the nature of what is not ourselves, that is to say, the capacity to act in accordance with the nature of the object. Hence true thoughts are thoughts which refer properly to reality and which are thought in accordance with the nature of the object to which they refer.[117]

This, as we have seen, is the a posteriori or heuristic category of thought which must be followed in the fields of scientific, anthropological, and theological knowledge. Torrance relates this personalistic metaphysic found in Macmurray to its anthropological and social implications.[118] Inasmuch as to be rational is to behave in terms of actual knowledge of the world, of things and persons in accordance with their natures, reason or objectivity is not to be confined to the intellect alone, but characterizes

---

115. Torrance, *Theological Science*, 122; *Reality and Scientific Theology*, 57.

116. Torrance, *Reality and Scientific Theology*, 57.

117. Torrance, *Theology in Reconstruction*, 232; cf. Macmurray, *Reason and Emotion*, 7–9.

118. This seems to follow a transition from Macmurray's metaphysic of the personal to its moral implications. As Fergusson points out, in his book *The Self as Agent*, Macmurray shows the way in which the self is identified as a personal agent, which is objectively actualized when the agent interacts with other agents in action. In his book *Persons in Relation*, Macmurray develops the concept of what it means to be an agent in dynamic relations with others, i.e., a "persons in relation approach" with its moral implications (Fergusson, "Contours of Macmurray's Philosophy," 44–45).

"every aspect of our human life and activity as rational personas."[119] That is to say, an essential characteristic of rational reason must be its personal element embodied in action in which it is the nature of persons to be rational through relating themselves objectively not only to the world, but to other persons around them.[120]

It is in *action*, as we behave personally in accordance with the natures of the world and other persons, that we are to be thought of as personal agents in relation with the world and other persons in their own rational and personal activity. This rejects the distorted Cartesian notion of humanity as isolated individuals or detached observers, establishing instead a personal reorientation of mind in human life and activity.

In this regard, Torrance asserts that "in the sphere of the ethical and social life we develop a capacity to act objectively in relation to other persons, by behaving towards them in accordance with their natures, not in terms of the nature of things and not in terms of our own subjective determinations."[121] His assertion is fundamentally aligned with Macmurray's affirmation that "against the assumption that the Self is an isolated individual, I have set the view that the Self is a *person*, and that personal existence is *constituted* by the relation of persons."[122]

Torrance insists that *love* then becomes the critical point where persons interact with one another in inter-personal relations. Since "the capacity to love objectively is the capacity in which we live as persons," love has a quintessential place in personal relations.[123] Inasmuch as the fact that it is irrational to treat to things as persons and *vice versa*, loving persons as persons and not as things is to behave objectively and personally in accordance with their very natures as persons. Thus, following Macmurray, for Torrance love is "the ultimate source of our capacity to behave in terms of the nature of the object," which is "the core of objectivity."[124]

---

119. Torrance, *Theology in Reconstruction*, 232.

120. Torrance, *Theology in Reconstruction*, 232; *Reality and Scientific Theology*, 57.

121. Torrance, *Theology in Reconstruction*, 232; cf. Macmurray, *Persons in Relation*, 40–43

122. Macmurray, *Self as Agent*, 12.

123. Torrance, *Theology in Reconstruction*, 232; cf. Macmurray, *Reason and Emotion*, 15.

124. Torrance, *Theology in Reconstruction*, 232; Macmurray, *Reason and Emotion*, 15.

It is important to take note of the way in which Torrance's anthropological and social concerns are related to his theological concerns, particularly those of christological significance. As Torrance argues, through God's self-communication and the objectivity of his love to us in Jesus Christ, we learn what true rationality and objectivity are and in this, we learn to act toward God in accordance with his nature as Lord, developing the capacity to relate ourselves objectively to him, to other persons and even to the world around us. This takes place when we allow God in his being and act to impress himself on us, to "press us within the structured objectivities of things and other persons in which we have our human existence in space and time, and open us up for truly objective relation toward himself, in which we are reconciled to him and healed of our mental alienation and estrangement."[125] This for Torrance means the reconstitution of our relations to God and with other persons in the objectivity of God's love revealed in Jesus Christ who is the ontological ground for all such anthropological and social implications.

Here is the locus at which Torrance diverges from Macmurray with regard to the role of Christianity in the recovery of the personal. In Macmurray's religious thought the proper task of Christianity is to shape and itself become a universal and practical community for "the creation of a total human fellowship" in which not doctrine, but ritual is the appropriate means of promoting human fellowship and community in a true and actual sense.[126] Even though Macmurray draws our attention to the practicability of Christianity, Torrance takes his "from/to relation" (from the self to the other and *vice versa*) first into account but with Christ as the key to the recovery and transformation of personal relations to God and with other persons. In this regard for Torrance, Macmurray's thought is one that excludes the significance of Christology from our understanding of anthropology, and that reduces the ritual of communion in the church simply to the social unity necessary for establishing a universal community of persons.

Critical Appreciation of Torrance's Concept of Person

As we have seen, Torrance advances the onto-relational concept of person found in the relations of the divine persons and then applied to all of

---

125. Torrance, *Theology in Reconstruction*, 233.
126. Macmurray, *Religion, Art, and Science*, 74.

humanity. For Torrance this is fundamentally rooted in Christology, for it is God's self-revelation in Jesus Christ which enables us to know the personal relations of the divine persons as Father, Son, and Holy Spirit in the economy of salvation. But Torrance does not limit his understanding of humanity as persons in relation to simply expressing the biblical and theological concepts and meaning. However, while retaining the significance of Christology in the understanding of the human person and restoration of human personhood, Torrance draws upon scientific and philosophical epistemology. In this integration of theological, scientific, and philosophical knowledge, Torrance's persons in relation approach to humanity offers a profound epistemic understanding which undergirds his anthropology. This ultimately challenges the impersonal and non-relational concept of person derived from the ancient and modern dualistic patterns of thought.[127]

However, Torrance's critical interpretation of the history of philosophy and theology as it relates to the concept of person, particularly his critique of Aristotle and Augustine needs to fully respond to arguments different from the ones he uses. This will judge whether or not Torrance's persons in relation approach is rooted in a proper interpretation of the history of philosophy and theology. It will also determine whether Torrance's onto-relational concept of person is acceptable and can be a corrective to the impersonal/non-relational concepts of person pervasive in western thought.

First, as to the derivation of the concept of person, Vogel critiques the theologically inclined understanding that it was impossible for the

---

127. Here Torrance indicates a divergence from Barth with regard to the concept of person. For Barth, the terminology of "persons" is problematic, because it, through analogy with human persons, can imply a form of tritheism, especially given the modern emphasis on self-consciousness and persons as substantive and isolated individuals (Deddo, *Karl Barth's Theology of Relations*, 23). However, by revealing and developing an onto-relational concept of person, as found in biblical and theological traditions and underpinned by wide-ranging theological, philosophical, and scientific epistemologies, Torrance employs the concept of person in his rejection of dualistic ways of thinking that are so pervasive in western thought. Although at this point Torrance is differentiated from Barth, who understands persons as "modes of being," the fact that Jesus Christ has a pivotal role in revealing the triune God as Father, Son and Holy Spirit in Torrance's theology seems to be the Barthian starting point of Torrance. For further understanding of Barth's preference for "modes of being" over "persons" and some theological critiques/defences of this, see Torrance, *Persons in Communion*, 121, 214–301; Hart, *Regarding Karl Barth*, 100–116; Molnar, *Divine Freedom and the Doctrine*, 242–45.

ancient world to have a concept of person without the help of Christian theology. Vogel asserts that there was a wide range of Greek reflections on human beings in discussion about their rational and individual character, which was prior to Boethius's definition of a person in terms of individuality and rational nature.[128] Hence Torrance might be subjected to Vogel's criticism, for he states that the concept of person is "a direct product of Christian theology," particularly of christological and the trinitarian discussions in the early church.[129]

However, Torrance's understanding of the concept of person is related to its personal and relational nature. Trinitarian personhood as revealed in Christ enables us to properly understand the interpersonal and relational meanings of person as applied to both God and humanity, a relational characteristic of the human person (in relation to both God and other persons) which is not found in Greek thought of humanity. Thus, for Torrance it is not the individual/rational but the personal/relational characteristics of the concept of person which are rooted in Christian theology and it is this which rejects and contrasts sharply with Boethius's definition of person that Vogel mentions.

Second, Torrance's interpretation of Aristotle as a dualist (just like Plato but in different ways) needs to be assessed, for Aristotle has been characterized as a materialist, dualist, attribute (or property) theorist in large and very diverse reflections on his account of soul/body relations.[130] Therefore, it is necessary to examine whether Torrance's critique of Aristotle can be considered defensible and acceptable.

Before going further here, it is important to note the reason why such a wide range of interpretations of Aristotle's account of body/soul relations has occurred. Put simply, Aristotle's exposition of the soul and its capacities in relation to the body is so cryptic and subtle that it has caused diverse interpretations. On the one hand, Aristotle in his *de Anima* (*On the Soul*) II.1 in Greek argues that soul and body are one (412b 5–9)[131] and the soul cannot be separated from the body (413a 1–4).[132] This rejects Platonic body-soul dualism and offers a monist or materialist

---

128. Vogel, "Concept of Personality," 40–60.
129. Torrance, *Reality and Evangelical Theology*, 43.
130. Shields, "Soul and Body in Aristotle," 103.
131. Aristotle, *De Anima*, 51.
132. Aristotle, *De Anima*, 53.

interpretation of Aristotle's body/soul relations.[133] On the other hand, Aristotle refers to the soul as the form or actuality of the body having in it the capacity of life (412a 20–28)[134] and the final cause of the body (415b 10–14),[135] which leads him to commit himself to a form of dualism.[136]

The diverse reflections above draw our attention to some possible criticisms of Torrance. One of the possible criticisms is that Torrance offers *insufficient reasoning* to reach the conclusion that although Aristotle sought the unity of the body/soul relation, he argued for the ontological primacy of the soul as the form of the body and the final determination of matter in the process of becoming. Even though Torrance compares Plato

---

133. According to Hartman, Aristotle is regarded as "a materialist in the most important sense of the world," for the soul as an internal part of the body is located in the heart (Hartman, *Substance, Body and Soul*, 6, 137). Charles thinks of Aristotle as "an ontological materialist," for psychological states, the natural properties of the soul such as human thought, sense, desire, and perception necessitate the occurrence of their accompanying states *in* bodily movement such that the action of the body is ontologically able to have both "physical and psychological efficient causes" (Charles, *Aristotle's Philosophy of Action*, 213–17).

134. Aristotle, *De Anima*, 48–51.

135. Aristotle, *De Anima*, 65.

136. In terms of the dualistic view, it is fashionable to regard Aristotle as "a property/attribute dualist," for unlike Plato and Descartes he does not conceive of a total division between body and soul. Even though the body/soul relation is inseparable and the human agent or person is a compound of soul and body, it is nevertheless true, as Heinaman points out, that the soul is "an immaterial entity" of a living being that supervenes on bodily parts (Heinaman, "Aristotle and the Mind-Body Problem," 84, 90). Robinson, too, asserts that the soul for Aristotle is "the *efficient* as well as the final and formal cause of the body (*de An*. 415b8ff)." This is a distinct property of the soul which determines a creature's behavior and so rejects any materialistic explanation of the form of the body by mechanistic means (Robinson, "Aristotelian Dualism," 138–39).

It is important to understand that the immateriality or incorporeality of the soul in Aristotle's thought is related to his rejections of previous atomist and mechanist philosophers such as Thales, Heraclitus, Empedocles, Democritus, and the Pythagoreans who regarded the soul as a material, the mere cause of its movement and its self-moving. But Aristotle rejects the materialism and motility of the soul. If the soul moves or is moved, this means that the soul has a magnitude which is a property of material (Aristotle, *De Anima*, 11–29). Then does this mean that Aristotle asserts the substantial immateriality or eternity of the soul like Descartes and Plato? The answer to this is found, as elucidated, in his theory of form and matter. Thus, it is argued that Aristotle rejected both materialism and dualism in his hylomorphism, for he carries over into his analysis of body/soul relations a unifying concept that body and soul are one but not identical with regard to their properties. See Shields, "Soul and Body in Aristotle," 104–5.

with Aristotle in terms of body/soul relations and then takes the teleological development as an example to support his argument, it appears an insufficient exploration inasmuch as he could/should have participated in wider, more extensive philosophical reflections on this subject, i.e., the materialist and dualist characteristics of Aristotle's body/soul relations, in order to unfold and undergird his position.[137]

In addition, the inadequacy of Torrance's philosophical work on Aristotle makes it seem that Aristotle was a *mechanical dualist*. In Torrance's argument, despite the unity of the body/soul relation, for Aristotle the soul is the form and the final determination of matter. This for Torrance means the priority of "being" over "becoming." In this sense, the soul is regarded as not being affected by the natural body but on the contrary as itself affecting or moving the body and matter in the process of becoming, and this depicts the soul as a mechanical principle in non-interactive events with the body. But Aristotle asserts that the soul is affected by the body, for the attributes of the soul, such as anger, mildness, fear, pity, courage, joy, love, and hate, are attended by the corresponding particular affections of the body and *vice versa* (403a 16–24).[138] This clearly shows the interplay between the body and the soul which appears to be a factor that Torrance did not fully take into account in his work on Aristotle.[139]

In reference to the critiques above, therefore, it can be argued that for Aristotle the soul functions as the effective, formal, and final cause in the interplay with the body, which can lead to a charge of an over-domination of the soul over the body, form over matter, being over becoming, substance over relation in Torrance's interpretation of Aristotle. This also poses the question whether it is indeed Aristotle, as Torrance states, who has had a damaging effect on the concept of person by providing a

---

137. This kind of critique can be supported by pointing to Torrance's profound works on trinitarian and christological theology in which he did profoundly and sufficiently participate in a wide range of discussions to show his deep understanding and reflection.

138. Aristotle, *De Anima*, 7–9.

139. It cannot be denied, of course, that Aristotle consistently regards the soul as the real cause of the body which commits him to a form of dualism. But the interplay between body and soul is widely accepted in both materialist and dualist views on Aristotle even in different interpretations of him. In this sense, if Torrance had known this and even so wanted to argue for the non-interactionist view of Aristotle, he should have given further exposition of it.

dualistic and individualistic category of thought which has been inherited and hardened by Boethius, Thomas Aquinas, and Descartes.[140]

However, it cannot be denied that regardless of his intention Aristotle's cryptic and subtle exposition of body/soul relations and teleological development did pass down through the ages, engendering dualist and individualist ways of thinking pervasive in western thought. This is one of the main criticisms that Torrance raises. Further, although Torrance has a firm basis for arguing that Aristotle's anthropology does not sufficiently stress the importance of relationality for human identity and flourishing, without sufficient philosophical research with regard to the diverse interpretations of Aristotle, especially considering Heinaman and Robinson's views, it is difficult to affirm that Torrance's interpretation of Aristotle as a dualist (similar to Plato) is wrong. It is nevertheless clear that Torrance's work on Aristotle requires greater nuancing.

Third, Torrance's interpretation of Augustine as one of the main theological foundations for the individualistic and rationalistic concept of person can be critiqued by such theologians as Ayres and Barnes who have led to the recent revision of Augustinian interpretation.[141] The key point in this line of thought is that it is a mistake to read Augustine's trinitarian theology as (1) an overemphasis on the unity of God, i.e., substance ontology, (2) impersonal Neoplatonic metaphysics, and (3) an anthropocentric and psychological approach to the knowledge of God.[142] The re-interpretation raises the question whether it is valid to view Augustine in the light of Neoplatonism and in contrast with Greek patristic theology.[143]

---

140. According to Shields, despite Aristotle's "concurrent commitments to immateriality and inseparability" of the soul in body/soul relations, Aristotle is not a sort of Cartesian, because unlike Descartes he regards the soul as ontologically dependent on the body which is denied by Descartes (Shields, "Soul and Body in Aristotle," 131–32).

141. This criticism is also expressed by Tanner who argues that for Augustine human consciousness can be an image of God in isolation from any relations with anything else (Tanner, *Christ the Key*, 3).

142. See Ayres, *Nicaea and Its Legacy*, 364–65; Barnes, "Exegesis and Polemic," 58; Cavadini, "Structure and Intention," 103–23; Muller, "Rhetorical and Theological Issues," 356–63.

143. In order to have a proper understanding of this discussion, it is necessary to first spell out that it is a western theological presupposition that Augustinian psychological analogy of God was derived from a Neoplatonic understanding of God in which knowing God means an inward turn to contemplate the *imago Dei* in the soul. In this charge against Augustine, (1) the *imago Dei* is found in the human soul or mind reflecting the divine mind, and (2) the result of the inward turn engenders a severe

In a critical response, Ayres argues that despite some Neoplatonic impact on Augustine, particularly the concept of God as immaterial, unchangeable, and the Truth *per se*, Augustine's understanding of God is based not on Neoplatonic metaphysics but on a conception of God's simplicity in order to articulate "a concept of Father, Son, and Spirit as each God, and as the one God."[144] In this sense, it is the grammar of simplicity which unfolds both the substantiality and relations of the triune God that enables Augustine to follow Nicene trinitarian theology so that "Augustine's God is not one thing or substance with secondary internal divisions."[145]

As regards Augustine's approach to the knowledge of God, Barnes asserts that for Augustine the knowledge of God is actualized by Christ in such a way that the Son brings us to the fulfilment of beatific vision.[146] For Augustine it is Christ who purifies the human mind first in his sacrifice,

bifurcation of *theologia* (God's transcendence) and *oikonomia* (God's self-revelation as the Trinity in redemptive history). It is then an inevitable corollary, so far as the influence of Neoplatonic concept of God on Augustine is concerned, to emphasize the essence/substance (*ousia*) of God (and the primacy of soul) rather than the threefold manifestation (*hypostasis*) of the Trinity as the Father, Son and Spirit in the actual event of self-revelation. As regards this presupposition, see Allen and Springsted, *Philosophy for Understanding Theology*, 74; Grenz, *Rediscovering the Triune God*, 9; LaCugna, *God for Us*, 10, 102.

144. Ayres, *Nicaea and Its Legacy*, 379. Put simply, the conception of the divine simplicity is related to what it means to be divine or what may be said about God. For Augustine God is *simple*, which means that God "is" what God is said to "have," i.e., God *is* Wisdom, Beauty, Justice and Goodness *per se*. Yet the language of divine simplicity does not enable us to progress to God's existence but does help to identify what may and may not be said about God (Ayres, "Augustine on the Trinity," 126–27). In discussion with the Homoians, who argue that the Son is like (*homoi*) but not identical to the Father, and therefore reject the Nicene *ousia* language that the Son is of the same substance (*homoousios*) as the Father, Augustine, in the context of divine simplicity, states three things about the divine relation between the Father and the Son in one substance without division: (1) on the one hand, we *cannot* comprehend the ineffable God in *corporeal* analogies which cannot lead us to the divine nature of the God who *is*, (2) on the other hand, we *can* comprehend God in such a way that "the Father does all things through the Word who is the Power and Wisdom of God (1 Cor 1:24)" and thus the relationship between the Father and the Son enables us to understand not only the fact of "the Son being from the Father's substance," but also that here is "a true revelation of the Father through the Son." This shows that the Father and the Son in the irreducible relation of persons are of one substance, a concept which is then applied to the Spirit without any subordination or division (Ayres, *Nicaea and Its Legacy*, 138–39, 370–72).

145. Ayres, *Nicaea and Its Legacy*, 377.

146. Barnes, "Exegesis and Polemic," 58.

thereby making sinful humans capable of obtaining the eternal.[147] Thus, Augustine's approach to the knowledge of God is not anthropocentric or psychological but *Christocentric*, a perspective which therefore rejects Torrance's interpretation of Augustine's approach to the knowledge of God as non-christological.

In terms of Augustine's trinitarian theology, Torrance recognizes that Augustine's real interest was not to detect "traces of the Trinity" in the human mind or soul, but to find the proper concepts and terms with regard to the ways in which God can be intelligibly and properly referred to.[148] Torrance also understands that Augustine did outline his doctrine of the Trinity in relation to the Nicene principle of *homoousion* in which "there is a relation of indivisible oneness in being between what God is toward us as Father, Son and Holy Spirit and what he is eternally in himself."[149]

But for Torrance, the problem is Augustine's *insufficient* theological understanding of "the rational structure of faith" that only "becomes embodied in our understanding in the *actual event* of our knowledge of God."[150] Torrance states that Augustine worked rather with "a rational structure" that is already embedded in "the constitution of human nature" and must be considered as "a necessary precondition for the realisation of knowledge of God in the human mind or soul."[151] Even though Augustine did not apparently identify human rational nature, i.e., the human mind or soul with the image of God, God's image for him is present in the mind or soul that can participate in God. It is when the human soul is engaged in remembering, understanding, and loving the Creator that this activity enables human subjects to attain the knowledge of God.[152]

This is one fundamental difference between Augustine's a priori and Torrance's a posteriori approaches to the image of God and its relation to Christ. Although as Barnes argued, the knowledge of God begins for Augustine with the purifying work of Christ, what actually occupies the center of knowing God is *not* Christ *but* the mind or soul, for the soteriological work of Christ functions as something evoking the image of

---

147. Muller, "Rhetorical and Theological Issues," 359.

148. Torrance, *Reality and Scientific Theology*, 171.

149. Torrance, *Reality and Scientific Theology*, 168. See also Torrance, *Trinitarian Perspectives*, 22.

150. Torrance, *Reality and Scientific Theology*, 169 (italics added).

151. Torrance, *Reality and Scientific Theology*, 169–70.

152. Torrance, *Reality and Scientific Theology*, 171.

God present in the soul. In the light of this, it is evident that Augustine's thought is *psychologically* (not *christologically*) slanted and that human subjectivity plays a determinative role in attaining knowledge of God with the emphasis upon self-consciousness in acts of the self-remembering, understanding, and loving.

Moreover, in internal cognitive activity toward God, the persons of the Trinity are understood through "various triadic patterns in human subjectivity, in the soul" when the knowledge of God strikes into and affects our consciousness.[153] In this respect, Augustine's exploration of knowledge of God is derived not from the *onto-relations in God's self-revelation* to us, but from an *interiorizing* movement of thought in which we "let the patterns of our understanding take shape under the impact of his reality" in our soul.[154]

Hence, in Augustine's thought (1) we find an understanding of humanity centered on the in-turned movement of the soul or as a *self-transcendent being* participating in God or his reality by means of self-contemplation where the soul transcends itself in God and (2) in Augustine's psychological slant, the onto-relational concept of person is not relevant to the knowledge of God or the persons of the Trinity.

This had an influence upon the theological anthropology and understanding of person which as elucidated was taken and developed by Boethius and Thomas Aquinas with an Aristotelian line of thought. This is the reason why Torrance regards Augustine as a theological foundation for the rational, individual, and autonomous concept of person. Further, Torrance rejects the Augustinian-Thomist thought where triune knowledge of God is the result of a turning inward which locates "the doctrine of the one God and the doctrine of the Trinity" in different conceptual systems.[155] This separates God's being and work and thus Torrance supports the Athanasius-Cyril axis in Greek patristic theology, particularly that of Gregory Nazianzen as will be addressed more in chapter 2.

Conclusion

This chapter set out to examine Torrance's onto-relational concept of person in terms of a wide range of theological/biblical, philosophical,

---

153. Torrance, *Reality and Scientific Theology*, 166.
154. Torrance, *Reality and Scientific Theology*, 166.
155. Torrance, *Reality and Scientific Theology*, 171.

and scientific discussions. What we have found is that humanity must be regarded as persons in relation to God and to fellow humans, a concept which specifies the distinctive identity of a human being to be that of a person and personal agent in interpersonal relations with other objective realities in space and time. The onto-relational characteristic of the concept of person in Torrance is unpacked and supported by his use of theological/philosophical/scientific epistemology in rejection of the impersonal and non-relational patterns of thought found in the ancient and modern dualisms so pervasive in the fields of anthropology, theology, philosophy, and science.

This chapter also dealt with some critiques of Torrance, particularly his interpretation of Aristotle and Augustine in the context of the history of philosophy and theology as related to the concept of person. We found insufficient philosophical research behind Torrance's interpretation of Aristotle on the one hand, but on the other hand his reflection on Augustine, that by offering a psychological/interiorizing and not a Christocentric approach to God he committed himself to the individual and rational concept of person, was defensible.

In reference to the findings of this chapter, we find some significant points. First, Jesus Christ is presented as the ontological and epistemological fulcrum of the concept of person. It unfolds Torrance's trinitarian and Christocentric understanding of anthropology.[156] Yet in making use of philosophical and scientific epistemology, Torrance not only offers a profounder understanding and argument, but also opens the possibilities of dialogue with philosophical and scientific discourse.[157] This is one of the theological merits of Torrance which can be thought of as surpassing Barth.

Second, the onto-relational concept of person, particularly as found in the biblical and theological tradition shows that the concept of trinitarian personhood underlies that of human person and personhood. In other words, we must begin with trinitarian theology and Christology when and as we think of Christian anthropology and ethics. Further, since the onto-relational concept of person has not only dogmatic but practical significance and implications, it can become a distinct theological response

---

156. We will see in the following chapters the ways in which Torrance address anthropology and ethics in his trinitarian theology and Christology.

157. According to McGrath, Torrance's study of the intellectual foundations of dialogue between theology and science is to be regarded as his most original contribution (McGrath, *Thomas F. Torrance*, xii).

or corrective to any kind of impersonal and non-relational anthropology, and this is what Torrance has. Thus, although commentators on Torrance have not focused on the onto-relational concept of person as one of his critical responses to dualistic ways of thinking, Torrance's concept of person should be examined and developed in more depth with this in mind.

In conclusion, the onto-relational concept of person in Torrance clearly locates and unfolds the personal and relational nature of the human person and personhood in the being-constituting relation with God and other persons. But in order to fully understand the onto-relationality of the human person it is necessary to spell out God's onto-relationality in deeper and more adequate discussion. Therefore, in the following chapter we will address Torrance's understanding of trinitarian personhood as the ontological foundation of human person and personhood.

2

Trinitarian Personhood

The Ontological Ground of the Human Person and Personhood

Introduction

WE HAVE SEEN THAT for Torrance humanity is to be regarded as consisting of "persons in relation" to God and one another, a perspective which is rooted in the onto-relational concept of trinitarian personhood. This means that the human person and personhood is ontologically contingent upon the divine persons and personhood. Thus, it is necessary to spell out the onto-relational characteristics of trinitarian personhood in order to have a proper understanding of the ontological ground of human personhood in Torrance's thought.

Following Athanasius and Gregory Nazianzen, Torrance sees God's *onto-relationality* as encapsulated in the patristic terms *homoousion* and *perichoresis*. The terms unfold not only the oneness of the Father, Son, and Holy Spirit in being and act (the *homoousion*),[1] but also the ontic relations of the divine persons as distinctive *hypostases* in dynamic and personal communion with one another within the eternal Godhead (*perichoresis*).[2] Homoousial and perichoretic relations shed light on the dynamic, personal, and relational concept of person as applied to God who is thought of not as isolated in himself but as a *"Being for others."*[3]

---

1. Torrance, *Christian Doctrine of God*, 95.
2. Torrance, *Christian Doctrine of God*, 102.
3. Torrance, *Christian Doctrine of God*, 131.

And since the onto-relational structure and life of the triune God is known to us only in space and time through the incarnate Son, for Torrance it is Jesus Christ who is the epistemological and ontological center of all understanding of trinitarian personhood.

However, Torrance's understanding of the ontic relations of the divine persons and his Christocentric approach to trinitarian personhood bring to the fore questions about the ways in which (1) the ontic relations of the divine persons can be truly outlined in their dynamic, personal, and relational structure without the theological risks of modalism, subordinationism, and one-sided theological emphasis on either the oneness or the threeness and (2) whether Torrance's Christocentric understanding of trinitarian personhood can avoid remaining merely dogmatic and doxological and whether it can unfold implications of practical significance.

The two questions above are related to theological reflections opposed to Torrance. For instance, in terms of the former, Gunton critiques Torrance's Augustinian or western view of the *homoousion* and *perichoresis* whereby (1) the divine persons in the economy are undermined and flattened out through the emphasis on the complete equality of being and act and (2) persons are not understood as "persons" who are constituted by their relations but more as "relations" belonging to what they are.[4] This for Gunton obscures the particularity of the divine persons and opens the door to modalism.[5] The latter point is related to the "social trinitarian vision" of establishing the doctrine of the Trinity *per se* as "the best indicator of the proper relationship between individual and community."[6] Inasmuch as social trinitarianism draws upon the Trinity alone in *relative isolation from Christology*, it is important to unfold how the christological approach in Torrance's thought could provide anthropological, ethical, and social implications in comparison to those of the social trinitarian.[7] Thus, there is a need to test and assess not only

4. Gunton, "Being and Person," 121, 126.

5. Gunton's critique is not restricted to the dogmatic area but expanded to the anthropological. In this respect, Torrance is criticized for not engaging in discussion with Zizioulas with regard to "what the concept of person means for the human personhood." In other words, it is a critique that Torrance did not pay attention to the particular characteristics of the persons of the Trinity in virtue of his *Augustinian* tendency, a perspective which cannot offer a "trinitarian and *ethical* insight" to the understanding of human society (Gunton, "Being and Person," 131).

6. Tanner, *Christ the Key*, 207.

7. In their criticism of traditional monotheism and the Augustinian-Thomist

whether the onto-relational concept of the divine persons and a Christocentric approach to trinitarian personhood in Torrance's thought are rooted in a proper dogmatic basis, but whether also they can present and fully display the practicality of trinitarian personhood.

With the above questions in mind, this chapter will deal first with Torrance's understanding of the onto-relationality of the divine persons in discussion about the *homoousion* and *perichoresis*. It will then address how Torrance's onto-relational concept of trinitarian personhood in general unpacks its practicality in constructive dialogue with Jürgen Moltmann and John Zizioulas, social trinitarians standing respectively on Reformed theology and Orthodox theology. Lastly, Torrance's specifically Christocentric understanding of trinitarian personhood and its practical significance will be evaluated in relation to social trinitarianism.

Through this theological exploration, it will be argued that for Torrance homoousial and perichoretic relations of the divine persons clearly show "the oneness" of the Father, Son, and Spirit in their divinity and activity and "the ontic relations" of the persons as belonging to what they essentially are as distinctive *hypostases* within the eternal Godhead. This not only reveals the dynamic, personal, and relational characteristics of trinitarian personhood as the creative source for all personal being and community, but also rejects both subordinationism and modalism, for there is no degree of deity in relations where the Father, Son, and Spirit exist as one being, three distinctive persons. Further, the fact that the ineffability of such relations of the persons can be known only in and through the incarnate Son means that it is Christ who is the key to trinitarian personhood and Christian anthropology, a perspective which becomes a theological supplement or corrective to social trinitarianism.

Onto-Relational Understanding of the Divine Persons

Torrance finds the ontic relations of trinitarian personhood in the patristic terms *homoousion* and *perichoresis* in which the dynamic, personal,

---

approach that arguably separates the doctrine of the One God (*theologia*) from God's redemptive self-revelation in time and space (*oikonomia*), social trinitarians such as Jürgen Moltmann, John Zizioulas, Catherine Mowry LaCugna, Miroslav Volf, and Leonardo Boff have proposed the social doctrine of the Trinity as a theological answer to human conflicts, interlaced as they are with political, socio-economic, and ethical issues. However, as we will see in more detail, social trinitarianism shows theological deficiencies, particularly in its insufficient christological reasoning with regard to knowing trinitarian personhood and participating in trinitarian communion.

and relational being and life of the triune God is unfolded. Through the homoousial and perichoretic relations, the triune God is known to us as one God, three persons, the Father, Son, and Holy Spirit in personal and onto-relational communion. The eternal and ineffable ontic relations of trinitarian personhood were revealed in the incarnate Son who has equal divinity with the Father and Spirit but became one of us for our sake in the economic salvation. Thus, in and through Jesus Christ we know the ontic relations of trinitarian personhood in which God is thought of not as an *isolated being* but as a *being for others, a being who loves.*

Homoousion

The term *homoousion*, from the Greek, *homo-ousios* meaning *same-being* or of one being with, was used by Nicene theologians, particularly Athanasius, in opposition to Arianism which argued that "Jesus was not of the same being as God and therefore not God but the highest of creatures, created by God for a mediatory and creative role."[8] Therefore, the *homoousion* was a theological affirmation that the Son is of one being with the Father, such that "the Son and the Father are equally God within the one being of God."[9] This was adopted at the council of Nicaea in AD 325, and in AD 381 the council of Constantinople described and declared the full divinity of the Spirit not in the Nicene language of *homoousios* but directly in terms of biblical language to depict the Spirit as "Lord" who is to be worshiped and glorified together with the Father and the Son.[10]

For Torrance, the doctrine of the *homoousion* is regarded as "the ontological and epistemological linchpin of Christian theology," for in and through the incarnation the *homoousion* reveals the life and being of God both *ad extra* and *ad intra*.[11] The *homoousion* enables us to deepen and refine our grasp of the being and life of God disclosed in his self-revelation

---

8. Walker, "Glossary," 348.

9. Torrance, *Trinitarian Faith*, 122.

10. Following Athanasius, Torrance states that the *homoousion* expresses not only the oneness between the Son and the Father, but also the distinction between them in such a way that "the Father is unchangeably the Father and not the Son and the Son is unchangeably the Son and not the Father," which is applied likewise to the Spirit. Thus, the *homoousion* was "a bulwark against Sabellianism and Arianism, against Unitarianism and polytheism, alike" in the Nicene era (Torrance, *Trinitarian Faith*, 125). See also Torrance, *Divine Meaning*, 199.

11. Torrance, *Christian Doctrine of God*, 95.

to us as the Father, Son, and Spirit, whereby our thought moves "from the secondary level in which we have to do with the economic Trinity to the tertiary or higher theological level where we have to do with the ontological Trinity, that is, in patristic language, the move from *oikonomia* to *theologia*."[12] Although the eternal relations of God and his relations with us are ineffable, in and through Christ, who is homoousial with the Father and Spirit, the life and being of God is freely known to us in the economic salvation and we are then united with the personal and relational communion of the eternal God.[13] But what exactly does the life and being of God disclosed to us in the *homoousion* refer to?

Torrance understands that it is the *homoousion* that unfolds the personal and relational characteristics of the life and being of God. As Torrance asserts, the *homoousion* states that God's self-revelation and self-communication to us as the Father, Son, and Holy Spirit in the economy of salvation are rooted in and derived from God as he is in own eternal being, life, and nature.[14] This unpacks not only the evangelical and ontological relation between the economic Trinity and immanent Trinity, but also the personal and relational life and being of the triune God in such a way that

> what God is toward us and has freely done for us in love and grace, and continues to do in the midst of us through his Word and Spirit, he really is *in himself* and that he really is *in the internal relations and personal properties* of his transcendent Being as the Holy Trinity the very same Father Son, and Holy Spirit, that he is in his revealing and saving activity in time and space toward mankind, and ever will be.[15]

---

12. Torrance, *Christian Doctrine of God*, 95. In terms of Torrance's concept of "the stratification of the knowledge of God," see further chapter 1, footnote 90 [x-ref].

13. When it comes to knowing God in and through revelation, we must understand that there is limitation in our knowledge of God, for we do not know God as God knows himself. In this sense, following Athanasius, Torrance states that "to know God in this way [through his self-revelation] does not mean that we can know *what* the being of God is, but it does mean that we are given knowledge of God that is directly and objectively grounded in eternal being" (Torrance, *Trinitarian Faith*, 67). This clearly shows that Torrance's Christocentric approach to trinitarian personhood is rooted in Athanasius as well as in Barth who speaks of "God's Being as his Being in his Act, and his Act as his Act in his Being" (Torrance, *Christian Doctrine of God*, 120).

14. Torrance, *Christian Doctrine of God*, 80.

15. Torrance, *Christian Doctrine of God*, 130.

Just as in the *homoousion* the economic Trinity and the immanent Trinity belong to one another and the act and being of God cannot be separated, so the personal being and life of God who is known to us in the economic salvation derives from and reflects the very personal being and life of the eternal God.[16] In this regard and following Athanasius, Torrance insists that the *homoousion* unpacks not only the homoousial relation of each person, but also the inner relations of the Trinity, that is, "the coinherent relations" of the divine persons in the one being of God.[17]

Moreover, the *homoousion* sheds light on the personal being and life of God through the new meaning of *ousia*. As Torrance elucidates it, the Greek fathers used the term *ousia* to speak of the being of God, not in the metaphysical and static sense of "being" originally found in Greek philosophy, particularly in Aristotle, but in a living and personal sense governed by God's redemptive revelation and communication to us in

---

16. Torrance states that the economic Trinity and the ontological Trinity are identical, for there is only one God in himself and in his redemptive and revealing act toward us in space and time (Torrance, *Ground and Grammar of Theology*, 158). If the economic Trinity is divided from the ontological Trinity and there is no real bond between the economic and the ontological Trinity, it would bring into question whether God himself was the actual content of his self-revelation, and then the redemptive act of God in the salvation history would become an event "without any divine validity and lacking any ultimate divine truth" (Torrance, *Christian Doctrine of God*, 7–8). However, Torrance argues that despite their essential oneness, the economic Trinity and the ontological Trinity have their *own distinction* in the sense that the ontological Trinity is *not* constituted by or dependent on the economic Trinity. Following Athanasius, Torrance states that we must think of the economic Trinity as "the freely predetermined manifestation in the history of salvation of the eternal Trinity," which means that the economy, i.e., creation and the incarnation, is *not necessary for the existence of the eternal God* so that we cannot apply some economic elements, e.g., the time pattern of human life in the incarnate Son, to the eternal life and being of God. For this reason, Torrance rejects Rahner's statement that "the immanent Trinity is the necessary condition of the possibility of God's free self-communication." This is a rejection of "a logical necessity" between the economic and the immanent Trinity found in Rahner (Torrance, *Trinitarian Perspectives*, 79). For further discussion, see Molnar, "Function of the Immanent Trinity," 267–70.

17. Torrance, *Christian Doctrine of God*, 126. Torrance states that even though the actual term "coinherence" or *perichoresis* was not used by Athanasius, the conception of a relation of coinhering in God was developed in his stress on "a complete mutual indwelling in which each Person, while remaining what he is by himself as Father, Son, or Holy Spirit, is wholly in the others as the others are wholly in him" (Torrance, *Trinitarian Perspectives*, 10). Thus, for Athanasius the coinherent relation of the divine persons was not merely "a linking or intercommunication" of the distinct divine persons, but rather an actual *personal* communion (Torrance, *Trinitarian Perspectives*, 10).

history.[18] The transformed term *ousia* was accepted by the Council of Nicaea in light of the truth that "the fullness of the Father's Being is the Being of the Son and of the Spirit."[19] And when associated with God's self-revelation in "three distinct objective Persons or *hypostaseis* as Father, Son and Holy Spirit," *ousia* or being signified "the one eternal Being of God in the indivisible reality and fulness of his intrinsic *personal* relations as the Holy Trinity."[20] In this sense, *ousia* is being considered in "its internal relations" and *hypostasis* is being considered in "its otherness, i.e., in the objective relations between the persons."[21] The *homoousion*, thus, refers to "immanent personal relations in the Godhead" in which the persons of the Trinity are all consubstantial *yet* in relation to one another as three *hypostaseis*, which is the trinitarian formula "one Being, three Persons (*mia ousia treis hypostaseis*)."[22]

In this regard, Torrance asserts that the *homoousion* discloses "the nature of God's Being as a Communion of divine Persons, who in and through their distinctive properties and their indivisible relations with and for one another are the triune Being of God."[23] Further, the *homousion* unfolds the fact that the being of God is "personal, living and active Being, fellowship-seeking and communion-constituting Being" *for others* which is evident in his self-revelation and communication to us in the gospel.[24] As Torrance puts it:

> We learn that the one Being of God *is* the Being of the Father who did not spare his only Son but freely gave him up in atoning sacrifice for us, and *is* the Being of the Son who loved us and gave himself for us, and *is* the Being of the Holy Spirit who for our sakes brings us through himself into communion with the Father and the Son. God's whole Being as three divine Persons is

---

18. Torrance, *Christian Doctrine of God*, 116. Torrance, as Colyer points out, finds a dynamic and intensely personal understanding of the being (*ousia*) of God in God's self-naming as *Yahweh*, i.e., "I am who I am / I will be who I will be," who revealed himself, established a covenant communion with Israel and delivered them. God's self-naming in relation to Israel was related to the "I am" of Jesus Christ in the New Testament so that the early church was able to think out "the nature of God's *ousia* with greater faithfulness and precision" (Colyer, *How to Read T. F. Torrance*, 304–5).

19. Torrance, *Christian Doctrine of God*, 116.
20. Torrance, *Trinitarian Perspectives*, 16.
21. Torrance, *Christian Doctrine of God*, 131.
22. Torrance, *Trinitarian Faith*, 131.
23. Torrance, *Christian Doctrine of God*, 128.
24. Torrance, *Christian Doctrine of God*, 132.

> his Being for others, but to his Being for others beyond himself, his Being with us in our human existence in time and space, there corresponds his Being for within himself, for that is the eternal ground in God for what he is and promises in the Gospel to be for others beyond himself.[25]

God's *being for others* in his economy of salvation reflects God's *being for others* in homoousial and hypostatic relations. The Father is not properly Father apart from his relationship with the Son and Spirit and *vice versa*, which clearly shows that the divine persons exist in, belong to and live for one another "by virtue of their one Being for one Another and by virtue of the dynamic Communion which they constitute in their belonging to one Another."[26] As such, for Torrance the *homoousion* delineates God as "*Being for others, Being who loves*" which is indeed the onto-relational being and life of the triune God as the creative source of all created personal being and communion.[27]

However, Gunton argues that when Torrance over emphasizes the unity of God's being and work or life in the *homoousion*, the elements of subordination in the economy, i.e., commanding and obeying and superordination and subordination are downplayed.[28] Further for Gunton, Torrance's understanding of the relation of *ousia* and *hypostasis* undermines and flattens out the distinctiveness of the persons of the Trinity.[29] The key point in Gunton's criticisms is that Torrance tends to understand the doctrine of the Trinity through "western or Augustinian eyes" where the unity or being of God is stressed at the expense of his triunity.[30]

---

25. Torrance, *Christian Doctrine of God*, 132.

26. Torrance, *Christian Doctrine of God*, 133.

27. Torrance, *Christian Doctrine of God*, 131, 133. Inasmuch as social trinitarianism regards the equal, personal, and relational communion of the Trinity as a theological response to individualism and communism, Torrance's understanding that the personal being of God is the creative source of personal communion and that he wants to establish a personal communion between himself and us in his consistent love for others, might be seen very compatible. However, for Torrance such communion is not theoretical or merely a social model of the Trinity, but actual and a personal communion embodied in having communion with God only in and through Christ. This will be further addressed as this chapter proceeds.

28. Gunton, "Being and Person," 120–21.

29. Gunton, "Being and Person," 129.

30. Gunton, "Being and Person," 129–34. Interestingly, in his book *The One, the Three and the Many*, Gunton critiques the concept of God in western thought for its influence on modern disengagement and displacement by stressing the one at the expense of the many in the sense that "the real *substance* of God, what he substantially

TRINITARIAN PERSONHOOD   53

In term of subordination, Gunton takes the fourth gospel's Christology and 1 Corinthians 15:24–28 as examples to prove that "the Son obeys the Father, does the Father's work and will hand over the kingdom of the Father."[31] This for him is concrete evidence that the Son is subordinate in himself to the Father, not simply in the economy, a perspective which is supported by Barth who states that subordination does belong not only to the economic Trinity, but also to the immanent Trinity.[32] In this sense, Gunton reads Torrance's theology as a theology that is based on patristic grounds not biblical.[33]

But when Torrance states that the biblical statement "My Father is greater than I" is to be construed not ontologically but soteriologically or economically, it is clear that he fully recognizes the subordination of the Son to the Farther as belonging to the economy.[34] This means that the subordination of Christ as the suffering and obedient servant in his economy "cannot be read back into the eternal hypostatic interrelations and distinctions subsisting in the Trinity," for here the Father, Son, and Spirit eternally coexist as "three fully co-equal Persons in a perichoretic togetherness and in-each-otherness."[35] Thus, for Torrance subordination itself must be understood only in the economy and the homoousial and perichoretic relations of God have the function of rejecting any degrees of deity among the divine persons with the result that the monarchy of

---

is, is the being that underlies the particular persons" (Gunton, *One, the Three and the Many*, 191). When the unity of God was over emphasized by western theologians, this undermined the particularity of a divine person with a resultant emphasis on "the unity of God and a corresponding one on the unity of society" or the world, an understanding which for him is evident in the one Christendom and regimes labelled fascist. Hence, many modern social and political ways of thinking here are to be regarded as "the revolt of the many against the one, and at the same time that of humanity against divinity" so that modernity is outlined as "disengagement" and "displacement" (11–40). In this regard, he argues that the western concept of God did pay little attention to the true particularity and relationality of the divine persons and thus Gunton is an advocate for the Cappadocians and John Zizioulas who state that "the being of God is not a blank unity, but a being in communion" (214). This offers a trinitarian model for anthropology with social, political, and ethical implications.

31. Gunton, "Being and Person," 120.
32. Gunton, "Being and Person," 121.
33. Gunton, "Being and Person," 130.
34. Torrance, *Christian Doctrine of God*, 180.
35. Torrance, *Christian Doctrine of God*, 180.

God or "the one ultimate Principle of Godhead" is located in the whole Trinity.[36]

In relation to the second critique that Torrance's understanding of the relation of *ousia* and *hypostasis* undercuts the particularity of the divine persons, Gunton states that in Torrance's thought the divine persons are absorbed into the being or unity of God. When Torrance cites Prestige's remark that *ousia* refers to being in its internal reality, while *hypostasis* denotes being in its outward reference, *ousia* is being used to refer to God's unity or *oneness*, while *hypostasis* is being used to describe God's *threeness*.[37] In the light of this, the terms *ousia* and *hypostasis* together denote that the divine persons are the being of God and thus for Gunton they merely unpack "different aspects of the one divine being."[38] This in turn leads to the further criticism of modalism, for Torrance's

---

36. Torrance, *Trinitarian Perspectives*, 112. In this regard, Torrance's view on subordination is different from that of Barth who understands that subordination belongs to both the economic and the ontological Trinity. Of course, for Barth subordination does not mean the ontological inferiority of the Son, but his free "self-emptying and self-humbling" as an act of obedience which happens in both the economy and God himself (Barth, *CD* 4/1:209). Yet following Athanasius, Torrance insists that all the human affections, human prayer and worship, receiving of divine blessings, and obedience of the Son "in the form of a servant and the whole of his becoming flesh" are to be construed in terms of the mediatorial work belonging to his economic condescension (Torrance, *Theology in Reconciliation*, 151). This means that the economic properties of the Son must be understood only in the economy of salvation for our sake, for the historical events, i.e., suffering, death, and resurrection in the whole life of Jesus Christ, cannot project historical happening into the eternal being of God (Torrance, *Divine Meaning*, 343–44).

However, it is important to note that when Torrance states that on the cross Christ's "spiritual and physical pain interpenetrated each other," then the economic suffering becomes the immanent suffering and the inconsistency in his argument seems to occur. But following Barth, Torrance asserts that "the suffering is not his own, but the alien suffering of the creature, of man, which he takes to himself in the Son" (Torrance, *Christian Doctrine of God*, 249). This means that the suffering in the economic salvation must be understood not permanently but *temporally* in the sense that the Son never did and never would suffer simply as the eternal Son. In this sense, it can be argued that for Torrance although it is true that the economic property cannot be read back into the immanent one, God *freely* chose to suffer in Christ for our salvation. This for him is based on a seemingly paradoxical relation between the passibility and impassibility of God which is to be understood in terms of its soteriological significance (249–54).

37. Gunton, "Being and Person," 127.
38. Gunton, "Being and Person," 127.

understanding at this point shows that God exists inwardly on the one hand and outwardly on the other hand.[39]

But for Torrance, *ousia* does not refer simply to an internal reality and *hypostasis* does not mean an independent substance but an objective otherness.[40] As elucidated, both *ousia* and *hypostasis* refer to "being" in the sense that *ousia* is being considered in its internal relations and *hypostasis* is being considered in its otherness, that is, in its objective relations. In the case of the Father, for example, Father is considered absolutely as he is in himself and at the same time Father is considered relatively in regard to the Son. Although it is one and the same Fatherly being, we can think of the "Father considered absolutely *in se* as *ousia* and relatively *ad alium* as *hypostasis*."[41]

In this sense, it can be argued that in Torrance's understanding of the *homoousion* the particularity of the divine persons is not undermined by being absorbed into or separated from the being of God, but rather underlined in their homoousial and coinherent relations, for the ontic relations between the persons "belong to what they essentially are in themselves in their distinctive *hypostasis*."[42] Hence, the suspicion of modalism is to be removed, for in Torrance's trinitarian thought the persons are not understood as just different aspects of the one divine being, or relations that merely reflect the eternal being of God, but rather as distinctive and objective realities in distinction with one another as the Father, Son, and Spirit in the communion of the eternal Godhead.

Perichoresis

As Torrance elucidates it, the word *perichoresis* derives from *chora*, the Greek term for "space" or "room," or from *chorein* meaning both "to make room" and "to contain," which indicates "mutual containing or mutual involution of realities," i.e., a *coinherence*.[43] Gregory Nazianzen first used "*perichoresis*" in this manner to express "the way in which the divine

---

39. Gunton, "Being and Person," 125–26.
40. Torrance, "Thomas Torrance Responds," 316.
41. Torrance, *Christian Doctrine of God*, 131.
42. Torrance, *Christian Doctrine of God*, 102.
43. Torrance, *Ground and Grammar of Theology*, 17; *Trinitarian Perspectives*, 141.

and human natures in the one Person of Christ interpenetrate each other without the integrity of either being damaged by the other."[44]

It was then applied to the Trinity to speak of "the way in which the three divine persons mutually dwell in one another and coinhere or inexist in one another while nevertheless remaining other than one another and distinct from one another."[45] The Father, Son, and Spirit are distinctive persons, but they dwell in and with one another in such an intimate way that "their individual characteristics instead of dividing them from one another unite them indivisibly together, the Father in the Son and the Spirit, the Son in the Father and the Spirit, and the Spirit in the Father and the Son."[46] This is the trinitarian content of Athanasius's formulation "Unity in Trinity and Trinity in Unity."[47]

For Torrance, perichoresis is not a static and speculative but a dynamic concept, for it unfolds an eternal movement in the love of Father, Son, and Spirit for one another which flows outward unceasingly toward us.[48] Together with the *homoousion* the perichoretic relations enable us to read back the interrelations between the Father, Son, and Spirit in the economic salvation into the eternal relations in the one being of God. Thus, the concept of *perichoresis* reveals the personal and intimate relations in the divine being and life, which, as with the *homoousion*, is known to us only in and through Jesus Christ.

Moreover, Torrance argues that *perichoresis*, in connection with the *homoousion*, spells out the *ontic relations* of the divine persons. By interpreting the biblical teaching about the mutual indwelling or coinherent relations of Father, Son, and Spirit in the consubstantial communion, the concept of *perichoresis* unpacks "the identity of the divine Being and the intrinsic unity of the three divine persons."[49] That is to say, the perichoretic relation clearly reveals the onto-relational characteristic of the

---

44. Torrance, *Ground and Grammar of Theology*, 172.

45. Torrance, *Christian Doctrine of God*, 102.

46. Torrance, *Christian Doctrine of God*, 172.

47. Torrance, *Trinitarian Faith*, 10. Torrance points out that the formulation of Athanasius was derived from the Nicene *homoousion* and developed by Epiphanius who offered "a powerful development of that Athanasian doctrine of the Trinity in Unity and the Unity in Trinity, or the consubstantial unity of three perfect co-equal enhypostatic Persons in the one indivisible being of the Godhead" (Torrance, *Trinitarian Faith*, 10–11). See also, Torrance, *Trinitarian Perspectives*, 138–39.

48. Torrance, *Trinitarian Perspectives*, 141; *Christian Doctrine of God*, 102.

49. Torrance, *Christian Doctrine of God*, 102.

trinitarian personhood in such a way that the divine persons are seen to be distinct *persons* whose very *being* is to exist in and belong to the *coinherent relations* with one another.

This is what Torrance calls "the onto-relational concept of the divine person" which the early church developed on the basis of the concepts of the *homoousion* and *perichoresis* and which was a *new concept of person* unknown in human thought until then.[50] As elucidated in chapter 1, this onto-relational concept of person, originally derived from the doctrines of Jesus Christ and the Trinity, was then applied to humanity so that human beings are regarded as persons in relation reflecting the trinitarian relations in God in a created way. Thus in Torrance's thought, as Molnar rightly points out, "the *homoousion, perichoresis* and the *onto-relational concept of persons* function together with the result that God is understood as three fully distinct persons in communion with one another within the eternal Godhead," and that human persons are understood "in ways appropriate to their created nature and reflective of the uncreated way in which God exists as three Persons, one Being."[51]

However, Gunton critiques that, as with the *homoousion*, Torrance's understanding of *perichoresis* downplays the distinctiveness of the persons. Gunton insists that it has to be *perichoresis* in order to indicate how the distinct three divine persons constitute one God, but Torrance uses it to show how the one God has a relationality in the relations of the divine persons whereby *perichoresis* begins from "one God" and moves to "persons" instead of from "persons" to "one God."[52] This for Gunton

---

50. Torrance, *Christian Doctrine of God*, 102.

51. Molnar, *Thomas F. Torrance*, 63.

52. Gunton, "Being and Person," 124–25. In order to properly understand Gunton's critique, we need to grasp how Gunton sees *hypostasis* through the Cappadocians. According to him, the Cappadocians used *hypostasis* so as to refer to the concrete particularity of Father, Son, and Spirit in relation to one another and thus persons are regarded as concrete particulars or "beings whose reality can only be understood in terms of their relations to each other, relations by virtue of which they together constitute the being (*ousia*) of the one God." For Gunton this conception used by the Cappadocians brings us two theological understandings: (1) a distinction between the threeness and the oneness of God without losing his unity as the triune God and (2) a new ontology in which the being of God consists in personal communion of the divine persons (Gunton, *Promise of Trinitarian Theology*, 39).

In contrast to the Cappadocians, as Gunton states it, Augustine understood *hypostasis* as "a relation," for "persons," understood as *hypostases*, lack their distinguishable identity, an understanding which is derived from Aristotelian subject-predicate logic where "accidents" which are identified with "relations" are described as being

is a movement following the Augustinian starting point in trinitarian ontology, in which the oneness of God so outweighs the threeness of God that it "makes the persons functionally indistinguishable to all intents and purposes."[53]

The critique of Gunton is closely related to his trinitarian understanding and vision where the trinitarian personhood must be seen to show its practical significance, particularly its anthropological significance with regard to "what it might mean for human personhood."[54] He believes that for Torrance the oneness of God becomes a trinitarian priority, derived from the Augustinian impact on him which led him to belittle attention on the particularity of the divine persons. Thus, for Gunton the Augustinian or western ontology of God that Torrance follows deforms the real meaning of *perichoresis* and undermines not only the particularity of the persons of the Trinity, but also the ontological compatibility of the one and the many.

In this respect, Gunton follows the Cappadocians (particularly Basil) and Zizioulas who regard a person not as a relation, but as one who has his or her being in relation to others, a perspective which for Gunton provides the insight of a trinitarian and ethical understanding in which both the one and the many are given due and equal weight.[55] This is a movement from "person" to "being," a movement which Gunton regards as a theological remedy for the limitation of Torrance and western ontology of God in general.

---

dependent on "substances" for their existence (Gunton, *Promise of Trinitarian Theology*, 40–42). For Aristotle's understanding of substances and accidents, see Ebert, "Aristotelian Accidents," 133–60. Gunton therefore argues that although Augustine recognized the distinction between *ousia* and *hypostasis* (or their Latin equivalents, *essentia/substantia* and *persona*), the dualistic logic in his thought defined "person" as a "relation" which is a logical rather than ontological or substantial way of thinking in relation to *ousia*, such that the particular persons come to disappear into "the all-embracing oneness of God" (Gunton, *Promise of Trinitarian Theology*, 40–42). The Augustinian priority on the *ousia* of the one God was unfortunately passed on to most western theology after him with the result of modalism and has had a damaging effect on the understanding not only of God (ontology), but also of the world (cosmology) with its implications for our understanding of society, church, and humanity (39–42, 58–82, 92–100). This is why Gunton follows the Cappadocian ontology in which "the three persons are what they are in their relations, and thus the relations qualify them ontologically, in terms of what they are" (41).

53. Gunton, "Being and Person," 124.
54. Gunton, "Being and Person," 131.
55. Gunton, "Being and Person," 125.

In reference to this, here it is necessary to answer Gunton's critique and examine whether the Cappadocian ontology does offer a better way to correct Torrance's trinitarian ontology. First, Gunton's critique shows a misreading of Torrance's trinitarian thought. As to the starting point from the *ousia* of the one God, for Torrance it is impossible to begin with and then think out either the oneness or the threeness of God, for the Trinity is fully and perfectly homogeneous and unitary both in the oneness and the threeness of God's activity and of his eternal being.[56] *The oneness and the threeness* and *the threeness and the oneness* are "the obverse of one another."[57] In Torrance's thought on the *homoousion* and *perichoresis*, God is fully three and one simultaneously, and hence the trinitarian formulation of "one being, three persons" where God exists as three distinctive objective *hypostases* as Father, Son, and Spirit in the one eternal being of God.[58]

Of course, it cannot be denied that Torrance has a theological tendency to begin with "one being" instead of "three persons."[59] But this order does not lapse into what Gunton critiques as the "Augustinian starting point of trinitarian ontology," for Torrance's starting point of "one being" follows the order of Nicene trinitarian theology where "the *oneness in being* between the incarnate Son and the Father" was precisely stated as "the central issue upon which the whole Confession of Faith finally depended, not least faith in God the Father Almighty."[60] This clearly shows

---

56. Torrance, *Trinitarian Perspectives*, 67. Here Torrance follows Calvin's trinitarian thought in which the persons cannot be detached from the being of God.

57. Torrance, *Christian Doctrine of God*, 112.

58. Torrance, *Christian Doctrine of God*, 92.

59. This is evident in his book *The Christian Doctrine of God* in which Torrance deals first with the theme "one being, three persons" in chapter 5 and then addresses the theme "three persons, one being" in chapter 6.

60. Torrance, *Trinitarian Faith*, 49. While Gunton asserts that the Augustinian focus on the oneness of God is rooted in Aristotelian dualist ontology, Torrance understands that Augustine based his doctrine of the Trinity on the Nicene *homoousion* and that Gregory Nazianzen's concept of Father, Son, and Holy Spirit as *"eternal subsistent relations* in God" has been further developed by Augustine (Torrance, *Trinitarian Faith*, 49; *Reality and Scientific Theology*, 168). This means that for Torrance Augustine is not a theologian who began with "one God" and defined "person" as "a relation" which subsists merely in a logical and modalistic way because he based his thought of the relation between *ousia* and *hypostasis* upon Aristotelian subject-predicate logic. Ayres too insists that Augustine did not begin with the unity of God "in a way that promotes the divine essence as prior to the persons" and that in his thought the unity of God's being cannot be thought of apart from the relationships of distinct persons as

the reason why Torrance begins with the Nicene emphasis on the oneness in being between Christ and the Father and therefore why he goes on to use *perichoresis* to unfold and shed light on the way in which "one God" has relationality as the divine persons.

In this sense, it can be argued that Torrance's priority on "the oneness in being" in the concept of *perichoresis* does not follow the Augustinian logic as Gunton critiques but the confessional, christological, and soteriological significance of the Nicene trinitarian formula. Further, this evangelical starting point enables us to apprehend "the self-revelation of God to us in his indivisible wholeness as *one Being, three Persons, three Persons, one Being*,"[61] an understanding which does not allow our concept of "one God" to downplay the particularity of the three persons.[62]

Second, in terms of the Cappadocian trinitarian ontology Torrance states that the Cappadocian theologians, such as Basil and Gregory of Nyssa (not Gregory Nazianzen), helped the early church to have "a richer

Father, Son, and Spirit. Thus, it can be argued that for Augustine "the persons are not just relations," but "relations" which are "essential to being God" (Ayres, *Nicaea and its Legacy*, 374–80).

61. Torrance, *Christian Doctrine of God*, 113.

62. As elucidated in "*Homoousion*" of this chapter, this is also evident in Torrance's understanding of *hypostasis*. But Gunton argues that when Torrance defines "persons" as "relations," his definition follows the Augustinian definition of "person" as "a relation" without ontological identity, so that the distinctiveness of the persons is undermined. In this regard, he asks whether "relation is an adequate way of describing the person" and follows Basil who states that "the persons are not relations; rather, persons are constituted by their relations to one another" (Gunton, "Being and Person," 126–27). However, Gunton's understanding of Torrance is a misreading because for Torrance (1) the divine persons are to be thought of as more than distinctive or objective relations, for they really subsist and coexist, hypostatically in their consubstantial relations yet without being confused with one another (Torrance, *Trinitarian Perspective*, 28). This means that (2) the persons are distinctive realities or beings in their objective otherness within the one being of Godhead (Torrance, *Trinitarian Faith*, 10). In this regard, when Torrance states that "the persons are objective relations," this is to be seen as simply unfolding the *onto-relational characteristic* of the Trinity.

Moreover, Gunton's argument is *wrongly* derived from the source that he used in Torrance's book *Trinitarian Perspectives*. Here Gunton thinks that Torrance defines "persons" as "relations," which is the Augustinian way of thinking of "persons," but what Gunton must see is why Torrance, following Calvin and Gregory Nazianzen, does not regard "the Father" simply as the name for a being (*ousia*), but as the name for a relation (*schesis*) *in terms of* which the Father is to be seen as the principle or source of the divinity (*arche theotetos*). The particular context of the debate here in *Trinitarian Perspectives* does not properly address the relation between *ousia* and *hypostasis* in Torrance's thought (Torrance, *Trinitarian Perspective*, 28–29; cf. Gunton, "Being and Person," 127).

and fuller understanding of the three persons of the Holy Trinity in their distinctive modes of existence."[63] But for Torrance, the problem which arose in them was to treat *ousia* as *impersonal*. When the Cappadocians argued for "three persons, one being" and spoke of the three divine persons as having the same being, they understood *ousia* as the general property common to *hypostasis* and were apt to identify *ousia* with *physis* or nature.[64] In this category of thought, *ousia* is understood in an abstract generic sense and thus *ousia* or *physis* is regarded as an impersonal concept, which plays down the personal, dynamic, and relational meaning of *ousia* found in the Nicene *homoousion*.

Moreover, when according to Torrance the Cappadocian thought of God was charged with thinking in "a partitive or tritheistic way, three Gods with a common nature," they attempted to meet this charge by confessing their belief in the *oneness* of God and by arguing that the Father is "the one Origin or Principle or Cause," but "the Father" here meant *hypostasis* not *ousia*, with the implication that it was the person of the Father who "causes, defies and personalises the Being of the Son and of the Spirit and even the existence of the Godhead."[65] This for Torrance is a sharp divergence from the Nicene trinitarian theology and implies "a relation of superiority and inferiority or degrees of Deity in the Trinity."[66]

For this reason, Torrance follows Gregory Nazianzen who used the Greek notion of "*pros ti*," i.e., "*being for*" to express hypostatic interrelations,[67] which "belong intrinsically to what Father, Son and Holy Spirit are *coinherently* in themselves and in their mutual objective relations with and for one another."[68] In their perichoretic relations, the divine persons are not understood as modes of being, but as *ontorelational persons*. As Torrance puts it:

---

63. Torrance, *Christian Doctrine of God*, 177. This is related to the Cappadocian debates with Eunomius who argued that the being of Son is dissimilar (Greek, *anomoios*) to that of Father in virtue of Son's bodily generation. In Eunomius's thought, the Son as well as the Spirit are regarded as products of the divine will, a perspective which brought about subordinationism.

64. Torrance, *Christian Doctrine of God*, 178. Here, as the Cappadocians pointed out, we can think of the way three different people have a common nature or *ousia*.

65. Torrance, *Christian Doctrine of God*, 178.

66. Torrance, *Christian Doctrine of God*, 178–79.

67. Torrance, *Christian Doctrine of God*, 163.

68. Torrance, *Christian Doctrine of God*, 157 (italics added).

> Thus the Father *is* Father precisely in his indivisible ontic relation to the Son and the Spirit, and the Son and the Spirit *are* what they are as Son and Spirit precisely in their indivisible ontic relations to the Father and to One Another. That is to say, the relations between the divine Persons belong to what they are as Persons—they are constitutive onto-relations. "Person" is an onto-relational concept.[69]

It is notable, however, that as Stead argues, although the Cappadocians understood the *ousia* of God in terms of generic oneness, they did not undermine the Nicene *homoousion* of the oneness because the council of Nicaea did not deal with the way in which the unity of God should be understood when it declared the *homoousion to Patri*.[70] While adhering firmly to the Nicene *homoousion*, they were interested in the way of understanding the unity of God and in turn suggested a theological category of thought that was not fully addressed in the council.[71] Hanson also insists that as it is the Nicene *homoousion* that excluded Arianism by emphasizing the equality of divinity between the Father and the Son, the Cappadocians' understanding of *ousia* does not downplay the oneness of God in the Nicene *homoousion*. In this respect, he rejects the interpretation that the Cappadocians deviated from the tradition of the council by understanding *ousia* or the unity of God in a generic sense.[72]

It could be argued that the Cappadocians did not entirely maintain the unity of God by relating *ousia* and *hypostasis* properly (at least in the case of Basil and Gregory of Nyssa). By treating *ousia* in an abstract and generic sense, they tended to maintain the unity of God by reference to the monarchy of the Father, thus avoiding the charge of tritheism. For Torrance, this is detrimental to the living and personal concept of *ousia* accepted by the 381 Council. Their putting forward the monarchy of the Father in response to the critique of tritheism, undermines the meaning of the homoousial and perichoretic relations of the persons of the Trinity which brings about a theological split between the East and the West.[73]

---

69. Torrance, *Christian Doctrine of God*, 157.
70. Stead, *Divine Substance*, 224–66.
71. Stead, *Philosophy in Christian Antiquity*, 162, 183.
72. Hanson, *Search for the Christian Doctrine of God*, 735–37, 817–20.
73. The monarchy of the Father offers a theological basis for the eastern church with regard to the *filioque* debate. It is widely known that the *filioque* clause was added unecumenically to the Nicene Creed by the western church which created the problematic relations between the East and West. As Molnar points out, when the eastern

Hence, it is difficult to say that the Cappadocian ontology of God can be a theological remedy for the limitations of Torrance by its offering due and equal weight not only to the trinitarian balances between the one and the many, but also to the anthropological balances necessary when the trinitarian model is applied to human society. This became a source of disagreement between Torrance and Zizioulas, his erstwhile Edinburgh colleague.

In sum, for Torrance both *homoousion* and *perichoresis* have doctrinal and anthropological significance. The homoousial and perichoretic relations of the divine persons reject any sort of modalism, tritheism, and subordinationism and unfold the personal, dynamic, and onto-relational being and life of the triune God in his uncreated being which for him is the creative source of human person and personhood. The homoousial and coinherent relations enable us to understand the triune God as "*Being for others, Being who loves*" which becomes the very content of the onto-relational concept of the person as applied to God and then to humanity.

Practicality of Trinitarian Personhood

For Torrance, the terms *homoousion* and *perichoresis* unpack the personal, dynamic, and loving being and life of the persons of the Trinity. This refers in particular to the communion of the triune God who does not enjoy communion alone in isolation from his creatures, but rather

---

church understood that the Spirit proceeds from the person of the Father, this for the western church was something that not only opens the door to "subordinationism" within the Trinity, but also downplays the *homoousion* of the Spirit with the Father and Son. But when the western church thought out that the Spirit proceeds from the being of the Father who is homoousial with that of the Son, that is by implication, from the Father *and* the Son, this for the eastern church meant "two ultimate principles" in the Godhead (Molnar, *Thomas F. Torrance*, 65–66).

Torrance finds a theological solution to the problem of the *filioque* debate between East and West within the concepts of the *homoousion* and *perichoresis*, for both together reject the understanding that (1) "the monarchy is limited to the Father which both the Western and the Eastern Church have held in their different ways," (2) "there is a distinction between the underived Deity of the Father and the derived Deity of the Son and the Spirit," and (3) the Spirit does not belong "equally and completely homoousially with the Father and the Son in their two-way relation with one another in the divine Triunity." On this basis, as a doctrinal solution to the problem Torrance suggests that "the Holy Spirit proceeds from the one Monarchy of the Triune God" (Torrance, *Christian Doctrine of God*, 190).

invites us to enjoy it in unity with him. The anthropological and ethical significance of all this is clearly shown in the way that the personal being of God is the creative source of the personal communion which he wants to establish between himself and us.[74] Inasmuch as the onto-relational characteristic of God's being and life was revealed in and through his self-revelation, for Torrance Christ is the epistemic and ontological hinge to not only our understanding of the trinitarian personhood, but also our participation in the divine communion and thus we are to begin with Christology, not the Trinity *itself* with regard to Christian anthropology and ethics. This is a *Christocentric approach* to the practicality of the doctrine of the Trinity, a perspective which presents a different aspect from that of social trinitarians such as Moltmann and Zizioulas.

Dialogue with Jürgen Moltmann: Political and Social

In his book *The Crucified God* (1972), Moltmann states that the Trinity is to be construed as God who has been crucified with the world in human history.[75] Put another way, the doctrine of the Trinity is not to be regarded as metaphysical and speculative, but as practical and dynamic, an understanding in which the important movements and relations of the Trinity, i.e., the inner logic of the Trinity, the human-God relation, and the being and work of the Trinity are not simply vertical, but more horizontal. As Ford argues, the conception of the crucified God with its dynamic relationality underlies Moltmann's doctrine of the Trinity in which God is not only three divine persons in a communion of love, but also a God influencing the world and at the same time influenced by the world in virtue of his intimate interrelation with our creaturely world.[76]

---

74. Torrance, *Christian Doctrine of God*, 133.

75. Moltmann, *Crucified God*, 328–29.

76. Ford, *Modern Theologians*, 211. In other words, as Hunsinger argues, Moltmann's trinitarian theology rejects not only Barth's idea of "a self-identical divine Subject" subsisting in three modes of being, but also any strong distinction between "God for us" and "God in himself," that is, between the economic and the immanent Trinity. This rejection of Moltmann reveals his panentheistic and Hegelian view in terms of the relation between God and the world. In this, it is understood that God's eternity is not an independent realm against history, but rather a transcendent dimension of history in which time and eternity are "objectively constituted by their mutual relations in dialectical identity." However, as we have seen, Torrance opposes the logical necessity or dialectical structure between the economic and the immanent Trinity. Although God is revealed in the incarnation and involved in history, this is only contingent. In

Moltmann understands the divine persons of the Trinity through the concept of *perichoresis* as it refers to their interpenetration and mutual indwelling.[77] With the help of *perichoresis*, he elucidates the way in which the distinctiveness of the persons of the Trinity is united in the divine communion and he then relates the perichoretic relation between each person of the Trinity to human socio-political orders.[78] In this sense, he argues that while Christian monotheism advocates political monarchism and absolutism, the doctrine of the Trinity wholly opposes monarchism and modern absolutism.[79]

Further, for Moltmann the concept of *perichoresis* offers a kind of analogy that can be seen to be embodied in both the divine and the human community. The relationality of the divine persons in their perichoretic relations shows horizontal, dynamic, and relational direction and movement that can be applied to human relationality. This for him unfolds egalitarian and relational implications and applications of practical significance and thus the perichoretic life of the Trinity is regarded as the

---

this sense, Hunsinger asserts that, for Torrance, the relationship of the economic Trinity to the immanent Trinity is one of "correspondence," not one of "dialectical identity," a perspective that follows the Greek fathers rather than Hegel and is much closer to Barth than other theologians, including Moltmann, Pannenberg, and Jüngel (Hunsinger, *Evangelical, Catholic, and Reformed*, 21–28).

However, it is important that although Pannenberg and Jüngel, like Moltmann, surrender the eternal antecedence of the divine essence and attributes as something self-subsisting and absolute, thereby attempting to bring together the divine aseity or ontological independence and God's relationality with the world in their different theological ways, they nonetheless, unlike Moltmann, (1) do not establish their trinitarian theology at the expense of the unity or oneness of God, and (2) do not use or develop direct language that speaks of a social doctrine of the Trinity (Jüngel, *God's Being is in Becoming*, 42–47; Pannenberg, *Systematic Theology*, 1:335). In this respect, it can be said that despite the similarity between them in terms of the relationship of the economic to the immanent Trinity, the significance of the unity of God in the trinitarian logic of Pannenberg and Jüngel deviates from and can be used as a rejection of Moltmann's social trinitarianism (or the social doctrine of the Trinity in general), in which the primacy of the divine three persons constituting their perichoretic relations and then one divine reality has wide-ranging ethical, social, and political implications. We will see in greater depth in the following dialogue with Zizioulas how Torrance is contra the ontological priority of the "person" in social trinitarianism, but it is important to note here that Pannenberg and Jüngel side with Torrance against Moltmann at this point. For further understanding of the emphasis on the unity of God in Pannenberg and Jüngel, see Chiavone, *One God*, 166–69; Peters, *God as Trinity*, 92–93.

77. Moltmann, *History and the Triune God*, 86.
78. Moltmann, *Trinity and the Kingdom*, 211–14.
79. Moltmann, *Trinity and the Kingdom*, 191–200.

"best model of our social programme."[80] As the relationality of the divine persons in the perichoretic communion and love offers an ideal model for human society or social life, humanity is summoned to practice democracy, freedom, sharing, and communion in accordance with the trinitarian life, a whole conception of society which is generally informed by the social doctrine of the Trinity.[81] Thus, for Moltmann the concept of *perichoresis* does provide a theological foundation for trinitarian praxis.[82]

It is notable that while Moltmann employs the concept of *perichoresis* for his political and social theology, Torrance does not draw upon the concept as a theological application for human society. In other words, Torrance does not derive trinitarian praxis from the doctrine of *perichoresis* so as to answer the wide-ranging anthropological, ethical, and socio-political conflicts that Christians are facing today. Rather, Torrance's utilization of *perichoresis* functions together with the *homoousion* and then unpacks the onto-relational concept of the divine persons, an understanding which is derived from Athanasius and Gregory Nazianzen. This for him is the explicit language of *perichoresis* which sheds a fuller light on the mysterious communion of the eternal persons in the Godhead.[83] In this respect, one could charge Torrance with making trinitarian theology speculative and static which is not relevant to Christian life and praxis and thus he could be regarded as a theologian who is merely interested in dogmatic theology or does not seriously take into account numerous practical implications that trinitarian theology might have.

Yet, for Torrance trinitarian theology cannot but have practical implications *in virtue of* its triadic structure in which, as elucidated in chapter 1, God/ourselves/world relations are not independent or

---

80. Moltmann, "Some Reflections," 110–11.

81. Moltmann, "Some Reflections," 21, 145, 198–99.

82. According to McDougall, there are very diverse reflections on what exactly constitutes trinitarian praxis. For instance, Gregory Jones interprets the practical relevance of the doctrine of the Trinity in the category of personal ethics, while Colin Gunton employs it as the basis of a theology of culture. Catherine Mowry LaCugna reads it as a charge to social action, while Miroslav Volf uses it for ecclesial reform. Despite extensive applications of the doctrine, it cannot be denied that for social trinitarians the Trinity *per se* has a wide range of implications for "notions of the human person, interpersonal relations, and the social structures and institutions that join human beings together in community" (McDougall, "Return of Trinitarian Praxis?" 177–78).

83. Torrance, *Trinitarian Perspectives*, 34–36.

isolated from one another but correlated together.[84] When the relations and movements of the triune God are addressed in trinitarian theology, the *homoousion* and *perichoresis* do not merely function as a dogmatic exposition of the inner logic or structure of the Trinity, but reflect on the personal and relational nature of God who is freely in interrelation with humanity and the world.

In the language of *perichoresis*, the divine communion is not metaphysical but *participatory* so that in and through Christ who is the one and only mediator human beings are drawn into the divine communion that he enjoys with the Father and the Spirit. Through this *mediated participation*, the restoration of the relational *imago Dei* takes place which for Torrance means the personal and relational transformation of our being and relation with God and other persons, and the true starting point of our anthropological and ethical concerns.[85]

This is the way in which Torrance derives human personal life, relation, and praxis precisely from trinitarian theology. For him it is *impossible* for a person to live out the perichoretic life among other persons without "the mediated participation" in the divine fellowship and communion. This draws our attention to the two simple but significant evangelical aspects, "the nature of sin" and "the mediation of Christ." The

84. See footnote 7 of chapter 1.

85. See Torrance, "Goodness and Dignity of Man," 315–17; *Christian Frame of Mind*, 39. With regard to Torrance's thought about "the mediatorial role of Christ in creating personal life and relations," this is similar to the logic that Eberhard Jüngel displayed in his theological anthropology. According to Jüngel, a new ontological and relational beginning is *only* embodied in the person of the crucified and risen Christ, bearing in himself our relationlessness and creating new relationships in love. As Christ in his substitution for us "*creates peace in the midst of strife* of a damaged relation to God, of a damaged relation to one's contemporaries and to oneself," for Jüngel the person of Christ is "key" to humanity and thus it is in our "participation" in his person that the well-ordered richness of relations with God and others (which are destroyed by "sin" making everything disconnected and relationless) is healed and restored (Jüngel, *Theological Essays II*, 112–13, 252–54).

However, in his account of sin as "relationlessness," Jüngel does not focus on Christ's reconciling life and work in his whole vicarious humanity as fully as Torrance does. In this sense, Kilcrease argues that when the focus in Jüngel's doctrine of atonement does not properly consider Christ's objective fulfilment of the law for sinners, the sinner's appropriation of the new relationship of faith is emphasized more (Kilcrease, *Doctrine of Atonement*, 92–100). Thus, it can be said that in his theological anthropology Jüngel has less focus on Christ's soteriological fulfilment for humanity than Torrance. In chapter 3, we will see Torrance's articulation of the ways in which Christ, particularly in his vicarious and new humanity, atones, restores, and personalizes our sinful humanity with regard to anthropological and ethical implications.

fact that no one can enjoy and live out a perichoretic life before being united with the divine communion shows the necessity of restoring the "ontological dehumanisation" lodged in the depths of our being by virtue of sin.[86] This is the reason why Torrance emphasizes the mediatorial work of Christ and our *living union* with him who not only brings us into reconciling relation with God and who shares his divine fellowship and communion with us,[87] but also personalizes and humanizes our sinful and distorted humanity that obstructs personal vertical and horizontal relations.[88]

Moltmann, of course, insists that Christ is the revealer of the Trinity and of their communion in disclosing his dynamic relations with the other divine persons.[89] He also does recognize that the significance of Christ's death *for our sins* affects our vertical and horizontal realm.[90] However, his theological focus on applying trinitarian praxis to human political and social conflicts leaps too swiftly into the practical meanings and applications of trinitarian theology without paying sufficient attention to the ontological and living union with Christ that restores our impersonal humanity and thus facilitates personal life and praxis. As a result, the balance between vertical and horizontal movements is disrupted and absorbed into one of predominantly horizontal significance. Although he states that Christ and the Spirit's presence enable us to fulfill "the messianic hope for the kingdom of freedom" by making new creation in humanity and bringing us into the divine communion, there is no adequate reasoning of and focus on how humanity can be transformed into new creation and drawn into the communion which

---

86. Torrance, *Mediation of Christ*, 69–71. In terms of Torrance's understanding of the nature of sin as the ontological contradiction of our humanity and as the breach of vertical and horizontal relations with God and others, see "*Imago Dei* in the Christian Tradition" of chapter 1.

87. Torrance, *Christian Doctrine of God*, 132.

88. Torrance, *Christian Frame of Mind*, 39.

89. Moltmann, *Trinity and the Kingdom*, 65. In particular, the cross event, like *perichoresis*, unfolds the mutuality of trinitarian fellowship and the depths of God's self-giving for humanity (Moltmann, *Trinity and the Kingdom*, 83).

90. Moltmann, *Crucified God*, 147–48, 169, 181–82. According to Kelsey the doctrine of sin in Moltmann's thought is mainly interpreted in the liberationist perspective in which sin refers to unjust social and political structure or contradiction (Kelsey, "What Happened to the Doctrine of Sin?" 169–78). Despite his recognition of the vertical meaning of the cross for our sins, it is true that Moltmann does lay more stress on the horizontal significance of Christ's death on the cross.

for Torrance is definitively actualized only in and through union with Christ.[91]

In this regard, it can be said that Moltmann emphasizes *how* trinitarian theology entails its practical significance and provides trinitarian praxis for Christian life, while Torrance focuses more on *where* Christian anthropology and ethics occur and derive their motive force which for him is definitively the person of Christ alone. In Torrance's thought, any morality of individual or social significance is only possible in the union and communion of the human person with the person of Christ. Hence, although the divine communion might offer social implications for right socio-political order and for the structure of human community, for Torrance, unlike Moltmann, the nature of the trinitarian communion as such is not to show how it affects and transforms distorted and impersonal human society. This is the *participatory* communion that we are brought into by living and continuing union with Christ in grace, a perspective which then underlies and transforms all Christian personal life and praxis.[92]

Dialogue with John Zizioulas: The Ontology of Person

Zizioulas is widely recognized as the most influential Orthodox theologian of recent times.[93] He treats trinitarian theology within the boundary of an ecclesiology in which the concepts of "the ontology of person" and "being as communion" are placed in the center, an understanding which

---

91. Moltmann, *Crucified God*, 127, 203. For Moltmann, the embodiment of the human being's messianic identity as the *imago Trinitatis* is mediated through the reciprocal agency of Christ and the Spirit and thus the trinitarian life and praxis that develop among human beings are Spirit-filled works of fellowship (McDougall, "Return of Trinitarian Praxis?" 195).

92. We can find a similar theological logic in Alan Torrance's critique of Moltmann with regard to his "Pelagian tendencies" in which human "doxological participation in the transcendent triune life" is regarded as a task that is to be achieved for Christian praxis rather than an "event of grace" actualized in and through Christ (Torrance, *Persons in Communion*, 310–13).

93. According to Torrance, despite some of Zizioulas's fine theological works there are opponents of his in the Greek Orthodox Church which derives from their theological disagreements with regard to Cappadocian theology (Torrance, "Thomas Torrance Responds," 314). For further details of objections among Orthodox theologians to Zizioulas in terms of his interpretation of the Cappadocian Fathers and their relevance to social trinitarianism, see Brown, "On the Criticism of Being as Communion," 35–78.

is rooted in the Cappadocian patristic theology. This offers a theological rejection or corrective not only to Greek impersonal and metaphysical ontology, but also to the western (Augustinian) priority of substance over person, which entails theological and anthropological implications.

As Zizioulas states, it is the Cappadocians who played a decisive role in breaking the ontology of Greek and Roman traditions, e.g., the static nature of the self-existent substance in Aristotelian ontology and its damaging effect on the ontology of God in the early church, particularly western church in which the unity of God was regarded as consisting in the *substance* of God.[94] By unfolding the relational characteristic of being that is constituted only by persons, they argued that "the unity of God, the one God, and the ontological principle or cause of the being and life of God does not consist in the one substance of God but in the *hypostasis*, that is, *the person of the Father*."[95]

This, for Zizioulas, is an order which reverses the order of "being to person" to that of "person to being" and which is a revolutionary movement from a closed ontology to an open ontology resulting in "the *ek-stasis* of being, i.e., a movement towards communion."[96] It is the personal freedom of the Father that underlies the trinitarian communion by becoming the cause of the generation of the Son and the procession of the Spirit. In this regard, the divine communion is the consequence of a free person's relation with other persons, a perspective which provides "an ontology" in which "true being comes only from the free person, from the person who loves freely—that is, who freely affirms his being, his identity, by means of an event of communion with other persons."[97]

---

94. Zizioulas, *Being as Communion*, 40. Following the Cappadocians, particularly Basil and the Gregory of Nyssa, Zizioulas understands "substance" or "being" as the common nature of the particulars. On this basis, the priority of *ousia* found in western theology is regarded by him as bringing us back to "the ancient Greek ontology" where the order is that "God first *is* God (His substance or nature, His being), and then exists as Trinity, that is, as persons," and thus the unity of God refers to "the one divine substance, the one divinity" (Zizioulas, *Being as Communion*, 40). This line of thought argues that the ontology of God in western theology cannot produce a personal concept of God without the help of *hypostasis* and therefore that the being of God needs to be understood in accordance with his personal freedom, loving well, and dynamic movement in the communion of persons (Zizioulas, *Being as Communion*, 97, 106).

95. Zizioulas, *Being as Communion*, 40.
96. Zizioulas, "Human Capacity and Human Incapacity," 408.
97. Zizioulas, *Being as Communion*, 18.

In Zizioulas's trinitarian thought, person and communion have ontological priority over substance which offers the theological and anthropological implications that (1) "there is no true being without communion" and thus nothing exists as an individual without communion as an ontological category, and that (2) communion which does not come from a *hypostasis*, i.e., a concrete and free person, and does not lead to *hypostases*, i.e., concrete and free persons, is not "an image of the being of God."[98] The primacy of person and the understanding of being as communion provide Zizioulas with a safeguard for the "coincidence between the One and the Many in divine being,"[99] which also becomes a trinitarian remedy to "oscillating between collectivism and individualism" in human society by identifying a person with his or her being in relation to others.[100]

In this regard, Torrance is accused of not participating more in the work of Zizioulas with regard to *what trinitarian personhood means for human personhood*.[101] This line of thought postulates that as Torrance follows the western (Augustinian) focus on the unity of God with its substance-based ontology, the particularity of the persons is undermined in his ontology which makes it difficult to give due and equal weight to the necessary trinitarian and anthropological balances between the one and the many. In other words, since Torrance's ontology of God—western theology in general—cannot produce a personal and relational concept of God's being without the help of *hypostasis*, the being of God must be understood in accordance with his personal freedom, loving will, and dynamic movement in the communion of persons, all of which offers better anthropological and ethical insights.[102]

However, Torrance's ontology is not derived from the substance-based ontology that Zizioulas critiques, for the Nicene *homoousion* and *perichoresis* that he follows do not speak of the ontological priority of "being" over "person." As elucidated, in the *homoousion* and *perichoresis* the divine persons *are* objective realities in distinction from one another as Father, Son, and Spirit in the communion of the eternal Godhead. The persons are *not* understood only as different aspects of the one divine

---

98. Zizioulas, *Being as Communion*, 18.
99. Zizioulas, *Communion and Otherness*, 38.
100. Gunton, "Being and Person," 131.
101. Gunton, "Being and Person," 131.
102. Zizioulas, *Being as Communion*, 97, 106.

being or adjunct relations that merely reflect the eternal being of God, but also as inbuilt constituent features of the *ousia*. Both *ousia* and *hypostasis* signify "being" in internal and objective relations which does not allow *ousia* to constitute *hypostasis*, nor the reverse, so that we cannot begin with either the oneness or the threeness of God.[103]

It is of course evident that despite the inseparability of God's oneness and threeness, for Torrance, the oneness or the unity of God in eternity is regarded as the ultimate level of the Trinity. This does not mean, however, that substance-based ontology is at the center of his trinitarian formulation, but rather that it shows "the ontic and the epistemic link between the evangelical revelation of God as Father mediated to us in the incarnate economy of his saving acts in the Son and the Spirit, and the revelation of God as the eternal Father of the eternal Son."[104] It is a movement from the economic to the immanent Trinity through which we are given to know that the dynamic and personal Fatherhood in the incarnate economy is identical with the Fatherhood in eternity. This follows the Athanasian and Nicene emphasis (with all its implications) on "the dynamic and personal nature of God's being" which is to be understood in a *christological* and *soteriological* dimension, not an ontological and philosophical one.[105] Therefore, it is a misreading to think that the ontology of God's being and the movement to the unity of God in Torrance is a regression to the ancient Greek ontology with the consequent result of an insufficient weighting between being and person.

---

103. Torrance, *Trinitarian Perspectives*, 117. In this sense, Torrance argues that we must begin with "God's self-revelation" in and through Christ in which God is known as one being, three persons simultaneously. Therefore, for him it is Christ alone who enables us to know the triune God and to participate in the communion of the divine persons through union with him.

104. Torrance, *Christian Doctrine of God*, 141.

105. It is important to note that the central issue at Nicaea was about Christ's ontological identity, that is, the identity of his *ousia* with that of the Father, not his *hypostasis*, so that Athanasius focused on the wholeness of the Godhead and viewed each person of the Trinity in that light. His approach to the doctrine of the Trinity took its start and controlling norm from the oneness of the triune God in time where the revealing and saving acts of God in the incarnate *parousia* of Son moves from the *homoousios to Patri* to its ultimate ground in the eternal Godhead. This for Torrance is what Athanasius gave attention to in the *homoousion* by which the oneness of God in being and act was emphasized christologically and soteriologically. Yet, this does not mean that Athanasius argued for the ontological primacy of *ousia* in an existentialist way, for in his trinitarian thought each person is "whole of the whole" in their coinherent and undivided wholeness (Torrance, *Trinitarian Faith*, 304–5).

Moreover, Torrance's understanding of the triune being of God does not break the ontological compatibility between the one and the many, but rather undergirds it. While Zizioulas interprets "being" as the general or the common nature of the particulars, Torrance views "being" in a dynamic and personal framework which follows the new meaning of *ousia* promulgated at Nicaea where the triune being of God is understood as essentially dynamic, personal, and relational being.[106] In this sense,

106. Torrance, *Christian Doctrine of God*, 124–25. As elucidated, this illustrates one of the reasons why Torrance rejects the Cappadocians's interpretation of "being," for in the abstract generic sense of "being" the personal and relational meaning of *ousia* is belittled. But in terms of the other reason, that is, the danger of subordinationism, Gunton argues that although Zizioulas's description of the Father as the cause of the triune being appears to bring about subordinationism, this is not the teaching of subordinationism because the Son and the Spirit are fully divine "as obedient to and sent into the world by the Father and therefore as such are economically although not ontologically subordinate." For Zizioulas, "the Father"—like "person" in general—refers to an inherently relational term which means that "there is no, ontologically speaking, Father without the Son or the Spirit, in other words that there is ontological interdependence between the persons." In this regard, when we say that the Father is the cause of the Trinity this does not signify "substantialistic" causation as understood in the modern west, but rather has connotations of "personal origination." Any objection to this is regarded by Zizioulas as a misunderstanding based on a presupposed individualism (Gunton, "Person and Particularity," 98–99).

However, even if the ontology of person does not entail a substantialistic causation by the person of the Father, this line of thought *overlooks* the transformed meaning of *ousia* at Nicaea where the unity of God is constituted by the triune being of God which is to be understood with christological and soteriological implications. When Torrance critiques the Cappadocian ontology, the key point rests not on a philosophical basis, i.e., a presupposed individualism, but on a historical and evangelical one. In this sense, it can be argued that Zizioulas shows inadequate comprehension of trinitarian doctrines, reducing doctrines to *philosophical* contents.

In this context, Coakley's argument is notable that Zizioulas's ontology of person, which makes a "person" an individual linchpin of consciousness, belongs to modern and *not* to patristic triadology, an understanding which is used to reject Latin trinitarianism, although it does not originate in Greek trinitarianism but in studies of the Trinity by Théodore de Régnon who invented the Greek/Latin paradigm and geometrical diagrams (Coakley, "Introduction," 2–4; "Person in the Social Doctrines," 126–37). See also Barnes, "Augustine in Contemporary Trinitarian Theology," 237–50. Here Barnes argues that some critiques of Augustine—western trinitarianism in general—who divorced the immanent Trinity from the economic Trinity are heavily dependent on de Régnon's characterization of western theology as demonstrating "a tendency towards a logic of ideas, including a lust (operative even when unfulfilled) for encyclopedic comprehensiveness at the conceptual level coupled with a reductive use of primary sources, a retreat from the polemical genre, with an emphasis on *philosophical content of doctrine*" (Barnes, "Augustine in Contemporary Trinitarian Theology," 250 [italics added]).

ousia does not refer to abstract generic nature but "the divine *Parousia*" in both the economic and immanent relations. In the economic history God's *parousia* shows the real meaning of the being or the *I am* of God to be such that he freely establishes a living and dynamic fellowship/communion with us which reflects his very nature, that he is a communion in himself as Father, Son, and Spirit.[107] Accordingly when "being" is interpreted in dynamic, personal, and relational terms in the communion of the divine persons, it can be argued that the trinitarian tensions between the one and the many are balanced and maintained without either being given undue weight.

In reference to the above, it is evident that although Zizioulas's critical recognition of the closed and static ontology pervading western theology and anthropology is in partial agreement with Torrance, Torrance does not situate "person" in the center of trinitarian ontology in order to create an open ontology.[108] Rather, he develops "an ontology of God's being" from the Nicene *homoousion*. Here the unity of God, the one God, the principle or cause of the dynamic and personal being and life of the Trinity are not constituted by the person of the Father but by the triune being of God revealed to us in Christ.

This effects a *Christocentric* approach to the practicality of trinitarian personhood in which the mediatorial role of Christ and union with him play the decisive role in human beings knowing the triune God and participating in the communion of the divine persons, which for Torrance underlies the way in which trinitarian personhood penetrates and transforms human sinful and alienated personhood. In relation to this, it is important to take note of the concept of the *personalizing person* of Christ where we find how Christ heals and restores in himself our dehumanization and through continuing union with him, and overcomes our individualism and collectivism.[109]

---

107. Torrance, *Christian Doctrine of God*, 123–24.

108. Like Torrance, Zizioulas critiques the Boethian and Augustinian understanding of the human person as "the self" for being rooted in two basic components, i.e., "rational individuality" and "psychological experience and consciousness" (Zizioulas, "Human Capacity and Human Incapacity," 405–6). In terms of Torrance's criticism of ancient and modern impersonal thought of the human person, "Torrance's understanding of human being as persons in relation: an historical overview" of chapter 1.

109. Torrance, *Mediation of Christ*, 67–72. In chapter 3, we will address in more detail the ways in which the person of Christ and union with him offer significant anthropological and ethical implications.

In this sense, for Torrance it can be asserted that when Zizioulas focuses on the meaning of baptism and the Eucharist without sufficient attention to how our hypocritical and alienated humanity is restored and transformed as a new humanity in and through Christ, the mediatorial life and work of Christ and our living union with him *per se* is obscured.[110] This tendency may arise from Zizioulas's ontology of person that is rooted not in christological and soteriological but in *ontological* and *philosophical* grounds. Further, in the inadequate christological focus of his ontology, practicality of trinitarian personhood becomes merely an abstract theological idea, for there is no ontological and epistemological possibility for humans to know what trinitarian personhood is and to participate in the communion of the persons of the Trinity without Christ, the one mediator of God and humanity.

Critical Appreciation of Torrance's Christocentric Approach to Trinitarian Personhood in Relation to Social Trinitarianism

In the dialogue with Moltmann and Zizioulas, we have seen how Torrance understands trinitarian personhood in the concepts of the *homoousion* and *perichoresis* and derives the practicality of trinitarian theology. This points to the centrality of Christ where his ontological and epistemological role underlies the knowledge and practicality of trinitarian personhood, and this explains why Torrance argues for a Christocentric approach and rationality with regard to trinitarian praxis.

This appears to be very different from the social trinitarian approach—including that of Moltmann and Zizioulas—in which it is trinitarian personhood and communion *per se* which plays the crucial role so that the ontological and epistemological significance of Christ is relatively diminished. But in view of the as yet limited dialogues above

---

110. It is evident in Zizioulas's understanding of baptism in which his main focus is not on "union with Christ"—though this is indeed significant for Torrance—but on "a radical conversion from individualism to personhood," that is, a conversion from "the *hypostasis* of biological existence" to "the *hypostasis* of ecclesial existence" (Zizioulas, *Being as Communion*, 50–62, 113; cf. Torrance, *Mediation of Christ*, 89–92). It is baptism (and the Eucharist) of course that signify an ontological transformation from sinful and self-centered humanity, but this must be thought of as a result of union with Christ in baptism. Therefore, as Russell rightly points out, it can be argued that Zizioulas stresses "the signifier not the thing signified" (Russell, "Reconsidering Relational Anthropology," 179).

and the numerous proponents of social trinitarianism who utilize plausible theological sources in relation to the doctrine of the Trinity and its practical significance, we cannot at the moment reach the conclusion that Torrance has a theologically preferable approach. It is therefore required to first have a wider range of discussions with social trinitarians so as to judge whether Torrance's Christocentric approach can have a more appropriate theological validity and thus be a corrective or supplement in provision of profounder theological implications to practical concerns today.

Although it is difficult to explicitly identify all those who are social trinitarians because one of the general features of contemporary trinitarian theology is to focus on the relationality of the Trinity, here we could typically regard the following as social trinitarians: Moltmann and Cornelius Plantinga Jr in the Reformed tradition,[111] Zizioulas as an Eastern Orthodox theologian,[112] Catherine Mowry LaCugna on the Roman Catholic side,[113] Leonardo Boff as a liberation theologian,[114] Anne Carr

---

111. According to Moltmann, "the Trinity corresponds to a community in which people are defined through their relations with one another and in their significance for one another, not in opposition to one another, in terms of power and possession" (Moltmann, *Trinity and the Kingdom*, 198). For Plantinga, the criterion of a social doctrine of the Trinity is to distinguish between the Father, Son, and Spirit and at the same time to present the three persons as "a social unit" in cohesion (Plantinga Jr., "Social Trinity and Tritheism," 22, 31).

112. As Brink points out, Gunton, Robert Jenson, and Christoph Schwöbel, all influenced by Zizioulas, strongly advocate a similar relational and communal understanding of God's being constituted by "person" and explore some of its consequences for other theological and cultural issues (Brink, "Social Trinitarianism," 334).

113. LaCugna adopts Zizioulas's preference for the eastern or Cappadocian thought of the Trinity and identifies *oikonomia* with *theologia* in order to let the doctrine of the Trinity transform our lives as schematized in her "ontology of relation or communion." In her ontology, both God and the creature exist and interact as persons in communion and thus God's being in relationship to us is what God *is* (LaCugna, *God for Us*, 221, 249–50). This for her is a rejection of the western theology which makes the immanent Trinity a speculative and metaphysical formula. For her God is to be regarded as "God for us" who brings us to communion with himself in his triunity and with one another.

114. Boff insists that the mystery of the Trinity is "a pointer toward social life and its archetype" such that the doctrine of the Trinity produces a theological vision that supports egalitarian communities in human society, an understanding which rejects not only any western theological tendency which undermines the full distinct personal existences of the persons, but also socio-political oppression and exploitation as in Latin America (Boff, *Trinity and Society*, 119).

as a feminist theologian,[115] Stanley Grenz as an evangelical[116] and Joseph Bracken as a process theologian.[117] Despite seemingly different focuses and applications, there are four insights, as Brink expounds it, that social trinitarians have shared which form the social doctrine of the Trinity: a "three personal God," "relational ontology," "historical re-orientation," and "practical relevance."[118]

In social trinitarian doctrine, Father, Son, and Spirit are conceived of as *three* distinct persons and fully equal centers of consciousness who constitute the one God. Their eternal perichoretic *relationality* for one another constitutes their personal subsistence. This requires a careful *re-examination* both of our theological tradition as led by western (Augustinian) theology and of its normative sources, the scriptures of the bible. This leads to the conclusion that the doctrine of the Trinity is no longer regarded today as an obscure and speculative piece of theological mathematics but rather as a basic doctrine of the church, a *practical* doctrine that guides and informs Christian ways of viewing, experiencing, and acting in relation to God, ourselves, and the world.[119] Hence for social

---

115. For Carr the Trinity as ultimate and perfect sociality embodies "mutuality, reciprocity, cooperation, unity, peace in genuine diversity that are feminist ideals and goals derived from the inclusivity of the gospel message" and this provides women with "an image and concept of God that entails the qualities that make God truly worthy of imitation, worthy of the call to radical discipleship that is inherent in Jesus' message" (Carr, *Transforming Grace*, 156–57).

116. Grenz states that as "God is the social Trinity, a polarity in unity, the ideal for humankind does not focus on solitary persons, but on persons-in-community." In this understanding, God is regarded as the ultimate model or standard for humankind, forming a paradigm for the life of the Christian and the Christian community (Grenz, *Theology for the Community of God*, 76).

117. Bracken understands the Trinity as personal community and society in the light of which he criticizes traditional trinitarian theology as an impersonal model and proposes social trinitarianism as a social model for human societies (Bracken, *Triune Symbol*, 7).

118. Brink, "Social Trinitarianism," 336.

119. Brink, "Social Trinitarianism," 336. As to "historical re-orientation" in particular, social trinitarians have levelled the charge against western or Augustinian trinitarian theology that their theological focus is placed on the "being" or oneness of God and that this leads to modalism such that the particularity of the persons is belittled. It can be argued to the contrary that social trinitarians' stress on the "three personal God" is at risk of a tritheism which lead them to draw upon certain theological sources, e.g., the concept of *perichoresis*, the interrelation between the economic and the immanent Trinity in the event of revelation, and biblical passages such as John 1:1 and 14–17, to explain "the way in which distinct divine persons constitute one God." Social trinitarians turn these objections completely around and argue that far

trinitarians "what the trinity is like is thought to establish how human societies should be organized; the trinity is taken to be the best indicator of the proper relationship between individual and community; and so on."[120]

The inner logic and approach of social trinitarianism do seem to contribute to our understanding of the triune as not a metaphysical and philosophical principle but as a personal and relational God in the communion of the divine persons, an understanding which underlies a trinitarian focus on an inherent "relationality" between persons not only in the divine but also in human communion and community. This requires a "radical transformation" of the role of theology and the church from merely speculating about God to letting the relationality and dynamic of trinitarian personhood and communion flow into our society. In this respect, one could argue that social trinitarianism offers and injects a more plausible practicality into trinitarian theology today which implies that the starting point from and focus on the unity of God in western theology must be modified and even discarded for a proper trinitarian praxis.[121]

Although social trinitarian teaching has resonated with the church as to the theological applicability of trinitarian theology to wide ranging anthropological, social, and political issues, it has been critiqued by theologians such as Karen Kilby, Kathryn Tanner, and Stephen Holmes. Put simply, they reject social trinitarianism on the grounds that, (1) theological attempts to derive moral, social, and political ideas from the Trinity are not consonant with the trinitarian theology of the church fathers,[122]

---

from these objections being used validly against them, they are actually in their favor. Interestingly, this kind of defence from the charge against them has been used as the most important rationale to prove the theological legitimacy of social trinitarianism in several theological works. See Hasker, "Objections to Social Trinitarianism," 421–39; Davidson, "Logical Space of Social Trinitarianism," 333–57; Horrell, "Toward a Biblical Model," 399–421.

120. Tanner, *Christ the Key*, 207.

121. This is evident in numerous social trinitarians' thought, particularly Gunton and LaCugna.

122. Holmes, "Three Versus One?" 85–88; *Quest for The Trinity*, 82–120. "The church fathers" here refers to the apostolic fathers, ante-Nicene church fathers, and post-Nicene church fathers in general. Holmes points out that for them the most important issue was related to Christology and thus that if social trinitarians use the doctrine of the Trinity from patristic tradition to answer questions of ontology, soteriology, and ethics including political and social theory, then their usage of it should be identical with that the fathers answered by *Christology*.

(2) the social doctrine of the Trinity is merely "the projection of human aspirations onto God" in the sense that what is projected onto God is immediately reflected back not onto God but onto the world, so that "this reverse projection obscures what is in fact *important* about trinitarian theology,"[123] and (3) to apply the ineffable nature and content of trinitarian personhood and communion to human society directly without theological focus on Christ is at risk of engendering "epistemological and ontological abstraction."[124] Holmes and Kilby particularly point out the inadequate comprehension and claims of social trinitarians about their use of theological terms ("person" and *perichoresis*), their interpretation of the history of theology (particularly the theology of the fathers), and their account showing how three persons are one.[125] All this implies that social trinitarians have put certain theological insights and sources to improper use for achieving their social vision.

There are of course some defences against the objections above. But it is notable that numerous proponents of social trinitarianism do not regard these kind of critiques as one of real *christological* import.[126] Accordingly, they try to defend the legitimacy and rationality of their doctrine by mitigating the concern beyond the objections to it. Responses from the understanding might offer some validity for social trinitarianism but from their responses, however, it is difficult to find whether the theology of social trinitarianism as a whole can sufficiently unfold and deal with

---

123. Kilby, "Perichoresis and Projection," 442. Kilby insists that "the doctrine of the Trinity arose in order to affirm certain things about the divinity of Christ, and secondarily, of the Spirit, and it arose against a background assumption that God is one." Thus for her the doctrine is a kind of "structuring principle of Christianity" that specifies "how various aspects of the Christian faith hang together," rather than "an exciting resource" which provides the wider world with relational implications (love, empathy, etc.) of the Trinity in its reflections on relationships and relatedness (Kilby, "Perichoresis and Projection," 442–43).

124. Tanner, *Christ the Key*, 222.

125. For detailed discussions about the issues, see Holmes, "Three Versus One?" 82–89; Kilby, "Perichoresis and Projection," 433–44.

126. It is evident in Brink's understanding of recent theological objections to social trinitarianism, he fails to take seriously the meaning, importance, and validity of the christological concern. Instead he counters the validity of the concern with discussions about the following merits of social trinitarianism, its "the practical usefulness," "relation to the theology of the Father," "assumed background in Scripture," and "claims about the inner being of God and the unity of God." Brink then concludes that social trinitarianism is true to "the sources of Christian faith" (Brink, "Social Trinitarianism," 337–50). As already elucidated, this kind of defence is fashionable among proponents of the doctrine.

the epistemological and ontological role of Christ, the one and only mediator between God and humanity, who enables us to have the knowledge of the triune God and participate in communion with him. This is the very content of Tanner's critique[127] and she interestingly cites Torrance in order to assert that Christ in his mediatorial ministry provides "a clue to the pattern or structure that organizes the whole even while God's ways remain ultimately beyond our grasp."[128] This again draws our attention to Torrance's Christocentric approach to trinitarian personhood and praxis and its theological validity in comparison to that of social trinitarianism.

As we have seen, there are some significant points from Torrance's approach to trinitarian theology which are to be considered in relation to social trinitarianism. First, Christology underlies his overall trinitarian theology. In his thought all dogmatic theology should start and end with the incarnate, risen, and ascended Christ, for only the being and work of Christ, i.e., the *homoousion*, hypostatic union, atoning incarnation, reconciliation, and the vicarious humanity, etc., reveal the ineffable nature and relations of the triune God to us.[129] Second, the centrality of Christ in trinitarian theology matters not only for its soteriological, but also its anthropological and ethical significance. Through Christ the personal, dynamic, relational being, life, and communion of the triune God become known to us and we are drawn into his communion. This effects a true reconciliation with God and our fellow humans. Third, it is Christ to whom we turn for our understanding of God and the *imago Dei*, for it is only Christ, the one and only mediator who has both full divinity and full humanity. Therefore, it is Christ who has to be considered as the ontological and epistemological fulcrum of trinitarian personhood and praxis which underlies all soteriology, anthropology, and ethics.

This line of thought enables us to explicitly recognize who God is, not in "some mystical existential experience" but only in and through

---

127. In a similar sense, Holmes points out that social trinitarianism's focus on the Trinity so interprets New Testament narratives and theological sources in relation to "trinitarian" questions that it gives rise to an inadequate focus on "the person of Christ," the very issue chiefly addressed by the patristic fathers in the relation between the Trinity and Christology. Holmes argue that this concern was also shared in every detail by the fathers of the Reformation (Holmes, "Three Versus One?" 88–89).

128. Tanner, *Christ the Key*, viii. For Tanner like Torrance "Christ is the key" to human knowledge of and participation in God and his communion. See Torrance, *Theology in Reconciliation*, 258–60; *Divine Meaning*, 121–23.

129. Torrance, *Space, Time and Resurrection*, 74.

Christ.[130] As already elucidated in chapter 1, it is evident that in Torrance's realist theology we are given to know the *reality* of God only in the incarnation in the time and space of real human history.[131] Hence we must find any interrelation or relatedness between the triune God and human beings only in and through Christ. Further, this offers a *participatory* understanding of salvation that effects Christian praxis. In union with Christ through his Spirit, we are bound together to be "a community with a trinitarian form of life in service to others."[132] Thus, soteriology leads to anthropological, ethical, and social practice that is embodied in our new relation to God only in and through Christ.

This does not mean, however, that social trinitarianism itself does not acknowledge the mediation of Christ in relation to trinitarian personhood and its practicality. It is not surprising that social trinitarians do recognize the significance of Christ, particularly in relation to the inseparability between the economic and the immanent Trinity. For instance, LaCugna argues that Jesus Christ is the reason why the immanent Trinity cannot be separated from the economic Trinity, for who and what God is becomes known to us by having a "history" in Christ.[133] Yet when she asserts that theology has to ask "who this God is, who acts in this history, with these people," the theological focus is swiftly moved to the relation between the triune God and the world.[134] This movement creates the serious problem that the epistemological and ontological role of Christ is not considered with sufficient attention or adequate reasoning. If Christ is indeed he who reveals the divine persons' loving and relational being and life in his interrelation with Father and Spirit and this underlies human interpersonal life and society, the ways in which God's self-revelation and reconciliation are known to us and actualized in Christ must be fully unpacked.

This is the reason that Torrance draws so heavily upon Christology, particularly the concepts of the *vicarious* and *new humanity* of Christ in which his life, death, resurrection, and ascension to the Father are understood vicariously as in our place, for our sake, that is, for our new

---

130. Molnar, *Thomas F. Torrance*, 331.

131. See Torrance, *Mediation of Christ*, 55.

132. Tanner, *Christ the Key*, 281.

133. LaCugna, "Philosophers and Theologians on the Trinity," 173. See also LaCugna, "Practical Trinity," 678; Janson, *Triune Identity*, 139.

134. LaCugna, "Philosophers and Theologians on the Trinity," 173.

humanity.[135] As we will see, the ways in which the humanity of Christ lead not only to revelation and reconciliation, but also to new moral/social life and relations. But what it is important to mention here is that the knowledge of God's self-revelation mediated through Christ draws our attention to the ultimate purpose of revelation, which is God's reconciliation with humanity in Christ who healed and restored our sinful humanity, transforming it into a new humanity in his person and uniting us to his new humanity through the Holy Spirit and so leading us to new moral life and order.

This requires a theological change in social trinitarianism, i.e., a movement from trinitarian praxis to *Christopraxis*. As Anderson rightly points out, since Torrance's christological theology binds revelation as true knowledge of God to reconciliation as the saving praxis of God, "without the saving praxis of Christ's ministry of reconciliation, knowledge of God becomes partial and abstract, leading only to theory without practice and, in fact, no longer truth."[136] Therefore, inasmuch as there is inadequate attention to the epistemological and ontological role of Christ as to revelation and reconciliation in social trinitarianism, Torrance's *Christopraxis* has to be seriously considered as a complement or corrective to social trinitarian thought.

Conclusion

This chapter has explored Torrance's understanding of trinitarian personhood and its practical relevance. Through the exploration we have found that for Torrance the concepts of the *homoousion* and *perichoresis* serve to reveal the ontic relations of the divine persons in which the dynamic, personal, and relational being and life of the triune God are clearly unpacked. The being and life of God focus our attention on the very nature and content of trinitarian personhood, thereby allowing and enabling us to know the triune God as a *Being for others, a Being who loves*, which offers a trinitarian foundation for human person and personhood.

Since the personal and relational characteristics of trinitarian personhood as the creative source for all created personal being and community are revealed to us only in and through Christ, Christ is the one and only mediator between God and us. God's self-revelation in Christ

---

135. See Torrance, *Incarnation*, 31; *Trinitarian Faith*, 267.
136. Anderson, "Reading T. F. Torrance," 178.

leads to his reconciliation with us which underlies the new moral and social life among human persons and thus for Torrance Christ is the epistemological and ontological linchpin of the knowledge of and participation in trinitarian personhood and communion.

This chapter has also found some critiques of Torrance's trinitarian theology. The various charges, the inadequate focus on the elements of subordination in the economy with its downplaying of the distinctiveness of the divine persons, and a modalist tendency were all posed, arguing that his trinitarian thought is rooted in a western or Augustinian focus on the being of God, that is, in substance-based ontology. Yet this was clearly identified as a misreading, for the distinctive characteristic of the persons is not either isolation from or absorption into the unity of God in his trinitarian logic, particularly as highlighted in the concepts of *homoousion* and *perichoresis*.

Further, Torrance's christological approach to trinitarian personhood and praxis was compared with that of Moltmann, Zizioulas, and other social trinitarians so as to identify how his approach has practical implications without remaining merely dogmatic. Through this we have found that when the ontology of persons and the personal and relational content of the trinitarian communion are used in social trinitarianism as our social model, there is inadequate reasoning about the way in which we are capable of knowing the triune God and participating in his communion, something for Torrance is realized only in and through Christ. His trinitarian thought focuses our attention on the epistemological and ontological role of Christ not only for the knowledge of God, but also for true Christian praxis which can only begin from our reconciliation with God in Christ, the personalizing person who heals and restores our dehumanization and creates new moral life, order, and relations. This, therefore, can be a theological corrective to social trinitarianism.

An important question to consider at this point is whether Torrance's christological approach can be regarded as a corrective, and indeed whether it can therefore escape all the critiques that we have seen levelled at the social trinitarians in relation to the limits of theological speech. If so, we should carefully consider whether Torrance has a more proper theological system and logic in the correct and incorrect versions of the trinitarian dogma and praxis.

In response to the above question, it could be suggested that when Torrance focuses on the epistemological and ontological role of Christ for revelation and reconciliation and its *resultant* reconciling and personalizing impact on human life and relations, this *profoundly* reveals how the trinitarian communion and praxis *in* and *through* Christ affects "ethics" in our midst. Following this line of thought, Torrance seems to avoid all the critiques levelled at social trinitarianism, that is, the wrong derivation of moral, social and political visions from the Trinity *per se* (Holmes), the projection of human aspirations onto God (Kilby), and the epistemic and ontological abstraction in relating the ineffable trinitarian personhood and communion to human society directly *without* sufficient focus on Christ (Tanner). Hence, it can be argued that Torrance establishes and develops a christological criterion in the trinitarian theology as the epistemic and ontological hinge, an understanding that offers a more effective approach to the trinitarian praxis.

However, it can be questioned how exactly Christ brings about true reconciliation with God and how his reconciling ministry does effect new human moral and social life and patterns. It is a significant theological question inasmuch as commentators on Torrance have argued that his christological and incarnational theology falls shorts of the practical concerns.[137] Thus, in chapter 3 we will see, in discussions about the concept of the humanity of Christ and its anthropological and ethical significance, how Torrance might respond to the question and the ways in which he might do so.

---

137. According to Anderson, Torrance follows Barth's concern for "a trinitarian exposition of dogma" rather than Bonhoeffer's concern for "a practical application of theological ethics." Bonhoeffer assumed Barth's christological theology as the very revelation of God, but he pressed the theology of Christ for a more contemporary answer to the question "What is Christ in the world today and what am I to do as an obedient disciple?" In this sense, Anderson argues that "the ethical question is there in Torrance's theology of the vicarious humanity of Christ, but it lies undiscovered and unappreciated in his major writings" (Anderson, "Reading T. F. Torrance," 177). Fergusson too argues that as the most significant movements and relations found in Torrance are vertical, not horizontal, the wider socio-political significance and implications cannot help but be confined to the individual and ecclesial areas, without reaching the wider social dimension (Fergusson, "Ascension of Christ," 101).

3

The Humanity of Christ

The Onto-Relational Restoration of the Human Person and Personhood

Introduction

As we have seen in chapter 2, for Torrance, as the creative source of all created personal being and community, the personal and relational trinitarian personhood and communion are only revealed to us in and through Christ. Importantly, Torrance focuses on and expands on "the humanity of Christ" in terms of the way in which Christ can be the epistemological and ontological linchpin of knowledge of and reconciliation with God.[1]

---

1. In Torrance's theology, the humanity of Christ is regarded just as significant as the deity of Christ. Although the humanity of Christ as co-existing with divinity in his one person seems to be difficult for the finite mind of humankind to comprehend, it is a biblical fact—for instance, John 1:14 and Colossians 2:9—and has a theological significance that is in total opposition to Ebionism and Docetism. As Torrance expounds it, Ebonite Christology accounts for Christ's nature as Jesus the man given divine sonship when he was baptized through the Holy Spirit's descent upon him. This approach from below upwards explained "*how* God was in Jesus Christ in such a way as to give full value to his unique place within Christian faith, and yet in such a way as not to compromise the absolute oneness and transcendence of God." Docetic Christology regards the humanity of Christ as being not real but only as seeming to be real, explaining "on a dualist basis *how* God became man in Jesus Christ in such a way as not to compromise his eternal immutability and impassibility through union with the flesh." For Torrance, Ebonite and Docetic Christology undermine the "undivided wholeness of his [Christ's] divine-human reality" that underlies his understanding of revelation and salvation (Torrance, *Trinitarian Faith*, 113–14). See also Torrance, *Incarnation*, 10, 186.

85

In Torrance's thought, on the one hand, the humanity of Christ sheds light on how God can be accessible to us epistemologically and ontologically and, on the other hand, the humanity of Christ elucidates how human beings are united and reconciled to God and with other fellow humans in Christ so that a new moral and social life occurs. Put another way, the humanity of Christ is essential not only for God's self-revelation to and reconciliation with human beings through the hypostatic and atoning union, but also for healing the ontological split within all humanity in relation with God and others.[2] As such, for Torrance the humanity of Christ plays a pivotal role in our understanding of revelation and reconciliation and its resultant personal and ethical life which is in accordance with God's redemptive purpose.[3]

In this regard, the understanding of the humanity of Christ is inevitably linked to Torrance's anthropological and ethical thought, providing the source which gives rise to theological principles of true and genuine restoration and transformation of our person and personhood. Thus, it is important to unpack the humanity of Christ so as to properly understand where and how anthropological and ethical foundations of significance are revealed in Torrance.

However, some questions arise as to the understanding and role of the humanity of Christ: (1) in general, how can the humanity of Christ reveal the epistemological and ontological accessibility of God and offer the grounds for the onto-relational restoration of the human person and personhood, (2) more specifically, how can the humanity of Christ lead persons to true God/human and human/human relations and a new moral and social life, and (3) does such a Christocentric understanding of and approach to anthropology and ethics make the human agent inactive in ethical practice and unpack not only dogmatic (doxological or vertical), but also practical (relational or horizontal) significance in dealing with public issues in a wider social and political dimension?[4]

2. Torrance, *Mediation of Christ*, 68–69.
3. Torrance, "Goodness and Dignity of Man," 309.
4. The third question in particular reflects Webster's critique of and Fergusson's critical evaluation of Torrance. According to Webster, in Torrance's account of the humanity of Christ, particularly the vicarious character of Christ's atoning and reconciling being and act in relation to humanity, Christ's humanity is seen to absorb that of others, so that human faith and response is at risk of being dissolved in Christ's vicariousness and thus passive human ethical activity takes place (Webster, *Barth's Ethics of Reconciliation*, 171; "Christian in Revolt," 126; "Editorial," 371).

In terms of the practicality of Torrance's christological theology, Fergusson argues

With the above questions in mind, this chapter will address first the significance of the humanity of Christ for revelation and reconciliation in discussion of Torrance's critical realism and the *homoousion* and the hypostatic union. It will then deal with the different aspects of Christ's humanity (fallen, vicarious, new) to clarify the ways in which his humanity has onto-relational connection to and the practical effect on our humanity. Restoration and transformation of the human person and personhood in the new humanity of Christ will be outlined in the following section. Lastly, some ethical issues, i.e., women in ministry, man-woman relations in marriage/divorce, abortion, and the priestly role of humanity in ecology addressed by Torrance's christological view will be presented.

Through this process, it will be argued that for Torrance the humanity of Christ is the epistemological, ontological, and soteriological fulcrum in relation to revelation and reconciliation and its resultant anthropological and ethical implications. When we participate and share in justification and reconciliation, which is what Christ has done in his vicarious and new humanity, we are *personalized* or *humanized* as persons who are in true relations with God and other persons and we live out a new moral life and order before God and others. This illustrates that the vicarious characteristic of Christ's person and work does not undermine, but instead upholds and underpins individual faith and response, and that union with Christ in his vicarious and new humanity (vertical movement) affects new moral life and order (horizontal movement). Moreover, the ethical issues addressed by Torrance suggest that his Christocentric anthropology and ethics do in fact have a practical significance in a horizontal direction, but as far as the *scope* of the issues is concerned, wider social and political concerns and discussions are needed in order for the theological expansion of a Christocentric anthropology and ethics.

---

that while Torrance does focus on and articulate vertical and doxological relations and movements, he pays relatively little attention to developing the wider practical implications of the gospel and thus his theology displays insufficient horizontal attention to issues of social and political significance (Fergusson, "Ascension of Christ," 101). See also Anderson, "Reading T. F. Torrance," 177–78.

The Ontological and Epistemological Significance of Christ's Humanity

For Torrance, the humanity of Christ is "the objective actuality of God to us in revelation and redemption."[5] This means that Christ in his humanity enables us to have knowledge of God himself revealed in the incarnate Word in space and time and to be reconciled to God and with others in his redemptive purpose. Therefore this does not only mean that the humanity of Christ plays a pivotal role in understanding Christ's soteriological and mediatorial life and work, but also that, through the ontological and epistemological understanding of and emphasis on Christ's humanity, it discloses the fact that knowledge of God is accessible and attainable to us in and through Christ's human nature.[6] In the humanity of Christ, knowledge of God is ontologically accessible to us in our own human form and human language and human persons are united, healed, and restored through participating in the humanity of Christ.

Ontological and Epistemological Significance of the Humanity of Christ for Knowledge of God (Revelation)

In order to properly understand the reason why the humanity of Christ is ontologically and epistemologically integral to *knowing God* through *revelation*, it is important to spell out first Torrance's "realist" or "interactionist" perspective. Torrance's realist theology leads him into collision with both ancient and modern forms of "dualism," that is, the division and separation of reality into two independent and incompatible areas.[7] He states that the church has faced an ongoing struggle with a

---

5. Torrance, *Doctrine of Jesus Christ*, 133.

6. For Torrance the humanity of Christ is to be understood as being indivisible and inseparable from his divinity: "We cannot separate the humanity of Christ from his Divinity for his humanity as such has no separate existence or self-existence." In this regard, "both these truths, the Divinity and the Humanity of Christ, must be held inseparably together" (Torrance, *Doctrine of Jesus Christ*, 100, 113).

7. Watson, "Dualism," 244. According to Colyer, Torrance does not begin by critiquing dualism, and then by elucidating his God-world relation (ontology) and epistemology. Rather, his ontology and epistemology of the God-world (or human) relation are derived from his theological investigation of Christology and soteriology and draw him into his rejection of dualism (Colyer, *How to Read T. F. Torrance*, 58).

dualist mindset, particularly cosmological and epistemological dualism in the early centuries and modern era.[8]

Dualism generally posits "a separation between the reality or essence of something and the empirical sources of our knowledge about it—between substance and appearance."[9] According to Torrance, cosmological dualism typically originates in Plato and Aristotle not in the biblical perspective reflected by the cultural milieu of the early church.[10] Plato separated the sensible world and intelligible world and Aristotle detached event from idea, becoming from being, material from spiritual, visible from invisible, and temporal from eternal, which have both had such a dualist philosophical and scientific effect on European thought for more than a millennium.[11] Cosmological dualism was revived in modern science by Newton. Newton's system of the world (or cosmology) was characterized by Torrance as "a thorough-going dualism between absolute space and time and the contingent events that took place within their embrace."[12] In other words, we find a radical disjunction between "the philosophical backdrop of absolute, eternal and unchanging space and time" and "the dynamic world of objects and appearances" which is reflected in "an equally radical disjunction between the creator God and the independent, ongoing processes and activities of the created order."[13]

Both ancient and modern philosophical and scientific forms of cosmological dualism have affected Christian theology.[14] In the theological

8. Torrance, *Mediation of Christ*, 1–4.
9. Achtemeier, "Natural Science and Christian Faith," 273.
10. Torrance, *Trinitarian Faith*, 47.
11. Torrance, *Trinitarian Faith*, 47.
12. Torrance, *Theology in Reconciliation*, 268.
13. Achtemeier, "Natural Science and Christian Faith," 285–86. For further understanding of Newton's absolute time and space, see Torrance, *Christian Frame of Mind*, 67–69; *Theology in Reconciliation*, 268–69.
14. Arian and Gnostic dualism, for instance, illustrate how cosmological dualism had a damaging effect on the early church. In Arianism, the realms of the uncreated and divine and of the creaturely and human are to be divided from one another and the person of Christ belongs to "this world of created being and not to the other world of divine Being." The Gnostic perspective displays the utter separation between the world of the divine and the world of the creature and here any thought and form of interaction between the two worlds is to be understood in a mythological way. Thus, for Torrance the biblical account of the act of God in time and space, i.e., the incarnation, crucifixion, and resurrection are regarded and rejected by gnostic interpretation as myth. Torrance critiques that the dualist thought engenders ontological division and separation between Christ and God and between the message of Christ and the person

sense, cosmological dualism posits an ontological division between God and the world. In both ancient Graeco-Roman philosophy and in any modern dualism such as Newtonian, deistic, and other dualist perspectives, there is a deep chasm between God and the world which engenders an ontological impossibility of any activity by God in the world.[15] Here it is impossible to recognize and embrace God's interrelation and interaction with the world. Then God's agency in the world is likely to be interpreted as "nonliteral symbolism or premodern mythology" and thus the biblical accounts of God's reality and action in interrelation with the world are regarded as being allegorical or mythological.[16]

In contrast to cosmological or ontological dualism separating God's reality and presence from the world, Torrance adopts a realist or interactionist perspective. In his realist perspective, Torrance asserts that the relation between God and the world should be understood in terms of personal interaction although God is a distinct reality from the world of nature and history.[17] In the light of his self-revelation, God has personal, ontological, and dynamic interrelation with our creaturely world through the incarnation in which the humanity of Christ is essential and pivotal. As Torrance puts it:

> Christ's humanity signifies that objective actuality of God's coming and presence in the very same sphere of reality and actuality to which we human beings belong. If Jesus Christ were not man as well as God, that would mean that God had not actually come all the way to man, that he had not really got a foothold in our creaturely world, as it were, within the time series in which we are. It would mean that God was still far away from us, as far as the heaven is from the earth, as far as creator is from creature.[18]

As such, for Torrance, human beings have ontological relationship with the eternal reality of God in the person of Christ who as man is one of

---

of Christ (Torrance, *Ground and Grammar of Theology*, 38). See also how Torrance critiques Cartesian-Kantian dualism since the Reformation (Torrance, *Space, Time and Resurrection*, 40–45).

15. Colyer, *How to Read T. F. Torrance*, 58.

16. Colyer, *How to Read T. F. Torrance*, 58.

17. Torrance, *Karl Barth*, 136–41; *Reality and Evangelical Theology*, 97–99.

18. Torrance, *Incarnation*, 185. For further understanding of the significance of Christ's humanity with regard to the ontological relation between God and the world, see Torrance, *Doctrine of Jesus Christ*, 133; *Theology in Reconciliation*, 101–2; *Space, Time and Resurrection*, 71; "Predestination in Christ," 140.

us in time and space. The ontological penetration of God's reality and real presence into the world and history by assuming human form in and through Christ's humanity discloses not only the fact that "we have God among us" but that "the full measure of Christ's humanity is the full measure of God's reality for us, God's actuality to us, in fact the measure of God's love for us."[19] Thus, all biblical statements on the humanity of Christ can be taken as ontological statements about the ontological relation that God has with the world and humankind in and through Christ's humanity.

Epistemological dualism presupposes that an epistemological disjunction exists between the human subject and the reality. This has to do with the disintegration of form in human knowing and is derived from the thought of René Descartes, John Locke, and Immanuel Kant.[20] According to Kant, for instance, it is impossible to know God in human knowledge. Since human knowing is heavily conditioned by the nature and structure of the human mind, we cannot know objective reality, namely, *Das Ding an sich*, i.e., the thing in itself. The human knower only knows how the thing appears through our "cognitive grid, the categories and mental structures of the mind."[21] Thus in this epistemological dualistic framework, it is difficult or impossible to know about God in himself inasmuch as anything about God found in the Old and New Testaments has been colored by human interpretation and categories of thought.

Protestantism has had severe struggles with the deistic disjunction between God and the world which was derived from "the new cosmological dualism of Newtonian science" and which was reinforced by "the epistemological dualism of Cartesian-Kantian philosophy."[22] Torrance

---

19. Torrance, *Incarnation*, 185. In and through revelation not only God *with* us but God *for* us is unfolded to us. This means that revelation through the incarnation inevitably has redemptive purpose, for God's self-revelation in and through Jesus Christ ended up redemption for us. The inseparable relation between revelation and redemption (or reconciliation through atonement) will be more dealt with when this chapter proceeds.

20. Torrance, *Theology in Reconciliation*, 130.

21. Colyer, *How to Read T. F. Torrance*, 58, 329-30.

22. Torrance, *Theology in Reconciliation*, 46. Torrance takes Schleiermacher's understanding of knowledge of God as an example of an epistemologically dualist theology. Schleiermacher accepts "the unknowability of God," for God is so transcendent and different. Thus, though God for Schleiermacher cannot be the object as such of human knowledge, the human knower can have some knowledge of God through human immanent religious consciousness (Torrance, *Space, Time and Incarnation*, 43-44; "Problem of Natural Theology," 121).

elucidates how epistemological dualism, together with cosmological dualism, has its damaging effect on theology:

> The damaging effect of all this [Newtonian-Kantian dualism] nowhere appears more sharply than in the wide gap that opens up between an inert God who cannot be known in himself and the world of phenomena conceived as a closed continuum of cause and effect. . . . It means that even Christian forms of thought and speech about God are uprooted from any objective ground in the being of God himself and float loose in the vague mists of modern man's vaunted self-understanding.[23]

In opposition to epistemological dualism, Torrance embraces "a critical realist epistemology" or "a critical realism" in which reality discloses *itself* in such a way that the human knower is really capable of understanding both God and the world.[24] Emerging in the United States in the early twentieth century according to Padgett, critical realism rejects an idealist overemphasis on human consciousness and experience, particularly the idealist insistence that *esse est percipi*, i.e., "to exist is to be perceived."[25] Critical realism takes note of the Kantian epistemological emphasis on human cognition and perception, arguing that even though the world might be conceptually mediated, it does not signify that human concepts or apperceptions constitute reality.[26]

In his realist perspective, Torrance defines realism as "an epistemic orientation of the two-way relation between the subject and object poles of thought and speech, in which ontological primacy and control are naturally accorded to reality over all our conceiving and speaking of it."[27] In this way, the reality becomes independent of the human experience or perception, which for Torrance means the *knowledgeability of God* beyond our human subjective pole.

It is obvious that in Torrance's critical realist epistemology, it is the incarnation that underlies not only all our knowledge of God as its epistemological center in our world of space and time but God in himself. In and through the incarnation of Christ, the human knower has both

---

23. Torrance, *Theology in Reconciliation*, 269.
24. Torrance, *Reality and Evangelical Theology*, 97–99; *Karl Barth*, 136.
25. Padgett, "Dialectical Realism in Theology and Science," 187.
26. Patterson, *Realist Christian Theology in a Postmodern Age*, 14.
27. Torrance, *Reality and Evangelical Theology*, 60.

"cognitive access to God" and real "knowledge of God."[28] Thus, God's reality and presence can be known and comprehended by human knowing, for it has been disclosed through God's self-revelation. Yet, in Torrance's critical realism, as Hardy rightly points out, there is no necessary or inherent correspondence between human mind/thought and reality, that is, no analogy of being in knowledge of God, but rather an actual correspondence between human thought/language and reality as and when the human knower is conformed to the self-communication of reality in the proper form.[29] As Torrance puts it:

> If we are to know him and speak about him in a way that is appropriate to him, we need to have fitting modes of thought and speech, adequate conceptual forms and structures, and indeed reverent and worthy habits of worship and behaviour governing our approach to him.[30]

In this regard, it is not only God's self-revelation, but appropriate forms of human thought and speech (proper human response and communal reciprocity where God's redemptive purpose is realized in the human world of time and space) which become the epistemic requirement for human beings to know God.

It is remarkable that for Torrance the incarnation of God in Jesus Christ underlies the knowability of God to us and the accessibility of God to human beings in human language and forms.[31] This means that God penetrates into and interacts with our creaturely world (realist ontology) and is personally known to us in his self-revelation (realist epistemology or critical realism). In and through the incarnation, as Torrance puts it, human beings have "a knowledge of the Unknowable."[32] God assumed human form and nature in the humanity of Christ in order that "we who can think only in terms of human forms may really get to know God."[33] In other words, it is only in a human form, such as human language and categories of thought, that human beings may apprehend God and thus the humanity of Christ, as the incarnate and historical form in human

---

28. Torrance, *Ground and Grammar of Theology*, 165.
29. Hardy, "T. F. Torrance," 169.
30. Torrance, *Mediation of Christ*, 6.
31. Torrance, *Doctrine of Jesus Christ*, 98.
32. Torrance, *Doctrine of Jesus Christ*, 98.
33. Torrance, *Doctrine of Jesus Christ*, 98.

space and time attainable and accessible to us, provides the appropriate epistemic forms at human level for us to know God.

In this respect, the rejection of cosmological and epistemological dualism in Torrance's realist perspective is closely associated with God's self-revelation in which Christ's humanity plays a pivotal role in ontological and epistemological mediation between God and the world and between knowing and reality in time and space. Thus, for Torrance the humanity of Christ becomes the ontological and epistemological guarantee of God's revelation to creaturely humanity within "the relatives and contingencies of our historical human existence," so that "revelation is reality, and is actuality accessible to us" at our ontological and epistemological level.[34]

Soteriological Significance of the Humanity of Christ for Reconciliation

As Torrance asserts and stresses, the humanity of Christ, and not just his divinity, has real soteriological significance in *God's act of reconciliation*.[35]

---

34. Torrance, *Incarnation*, 186. The significance of Christ's humanity in Torrance's theology rejects not only ontological and epistemological dualism, but also any kind of anthropocentric or subjectivist starting point with regard to knowledge of God, e.g., Schleiermacher's subjectivist tendency of religious knowledge relying on human consciousness over revelation. Although the humanity of Christ is essential to God's self-revelation and salvation, Torrance recognizes that this is "of *sheer grace*, and not necessity" and thus it is necessary to understand that Torrance's theological system at this point does not reveal the significance of Christ's humanity in determinism (Torrance, *Incarnation*, 184). For Schleiermacher's understanding of religious knowledge, see Adams, "Faith and Religious Knowledge," 35–52.

35. In terms of the terminology of "reconciliation" in the New Testament, as Torrance elucidates it, the Greek word *katallasso* with the noun *katallage* (both derived from *allasso* meaning "to change," and "to exchange") refers to "reconciliation through a substitutionary exchange and involves expiation." *Katallage* refers to "exchange effected by substitution or expiation, that is, atonement or reconciliation through atonement" (Torrance, *Atonement*, 138). In this sense, for Torrance reconciliation between God and humanity is to be understood as deriving from the atoning exchange of Christ, for Christ in his actual human nature took our sin, shame, and death and exchanged them for his holiness, glory, and life in order for us to be reconciled to God "clothed with his righteousness and stand before God in his person" (151). As James Torrance similarly and rightly points out, "the word comes to mean, to reconcile, to exchange friendship for enmity, love and peace for hatred. That, says the Apostle, is what God has done for us in Christ" (Torrance, "Place of Jesus Christ in Worship," 361). Thus, the term "reconciliation" is always used by Torrance in the sense of "atoning reconciliation" (Torrance, *Atonement*, 138, 161, 384, 439). See chapter 5, "Atonement

For since the onto-relational reconciliation between God and humanity is explicitly rooted in the fact that it was in his human nature that Christ mediated the actuality of reconciliation (or atonement) to us, it is clear that for Torrance the humanity of Christ plays an essential role in understanding God's reconciling action on our behalf.[36]

Here, it is important to spell out first the unitary perspective of Torrance in which revelation and reconciliation are indivisible, for it is in the soteriological continuity between God's revealing and reconciling act that we can most properly make sense of the importance of the humanity of Christ for onto-relational reconciliation. As elucidated, Christ's assumption of humanity through the incarnation reveals God ontologically and epistemologically, *with* and *among* us in our creaturely world and existence. For Torrance, this inevitably draws our attention to the *for* us of God in his redemptive purpose, for "revelation does not achieve its end in humanity apart from reconciliation."[37] As Torrance insists:

> The Gospel tells us that God does not choose to live for himself alone, for he has become man in order to seek and save the lost, to bring human beings into reconciling relation with himself and to share his own divine fellowship with them.[38]

It must be said that for Torrance revelation becomes the starting point for reconciliation and that reconciliation is the soteriological purpose of God's self-revelation disclosed in and through the incarnation. In the

---

as Reconciliation" in his book *Atonement* for further understanding of the term and meaning of reconciliation.

36. Torrance, *Incarnation*, 186. It is important that for Torrance reconciliation is not separated from revelation and *vice versa*. This is closely associated in Torrance's thought with the inseparability of Christology and soteriology. The doctrine of Christ, as Walker expounds it, has traditionally and archetypically been divided into two categories, with the doctrine of the person of Christ (who Christ *is*) being known as Christology and the doctrine of the work of Christ (what Christ *did*) being known as soteriology. For Torrance, the two doctrines making up the doctrine of Jesus Christ are not to be understood apart from each other, for "our salvation is in the person of Christ, but the person of Christ includes in itself all that he has done for us and worked out in his life, death, resurrection and ascension" (Walker, "Editor's Introduction," xxxvii). In this light, it can be said that the inseparability of revelation and reconciliation in Torrance's thought reflects the indivisibility of Christology and soteriology, where the person and work of Christ are similarly not separable.

37. Torrance, *Theology in Reconstruction*, 132.

38. Torrance, *Christian Doctrine of God*, 132.

unitary perspective, revelation and reconciliation are fundamentally and soteriologically interwoven.

On this basis for Torrance, as the reality and actuality of Christ's humanity plays an ontological and epistemological role in revelation to us, so his humanity also underlies the onto-relational reconciliation between God and humanity which is evident in the two doctrines: of the *homoousion* and the hypostatic union. Torrance derives the soteriological significance of the humanity of Christ from the two doctrines, for the two together expound how Jesus Christ mediates reconciliation (or the actuality of atonement) not in an external but in an internal act, as it were, in our estranged and sinful humanity.

The doctrine of the *homoousion* unfolds the fact that the humanity of Christ becomes the soteriological pole on the human side for reconciliation between God and humanity, for it signifies that Jesus Christ is "of one being with the Father."[39] Yet, it is not confined only to the Father-Son relation but rather extended to the incarnate Son-human relation for Jesus is of one being with us also in our human existence.[40] Following Athanasius, Torrance insists that "it is precisely as the incarnate Son shares with the Father his eternal being and nature, that he also shares with us our contingent and mortal being and nature."[41]

Torrance understands this "double *homoousion*" or "double consubstantiality" of the incarnate person of the Son as "dominated by a soteriological concern" in which Jesus Christ as Mediator embraces "both sides of the mediating relationship" for reconciliation.[42] Since Jesus Christ is

---

39. Torrance, *Trinitarian Faith*, 122. The term *homoouision*, i.e., from the Greek, *homo-ousios*, meaning same-being or of one being with, was used by Nicene theologians, particularly Athanasius, in opposition to Arianism arguing that "Jesus was not of the same being as God and therefore not God but the highest of creatures, created by God for a mediatory and creative role." The doctrine of *homoousion* was adopted at the council of Nicaea in AD 325 (Walker, "Glossary," 348).

40. Torrance, *Trinitarian Faith*, 110–45; *Incarnation*, 203.

41. Torrance, *Trinitarian Faith*, 136.

42. Torrance, *Trinitarian Faith*, 146; *Mediation of Christ*, 56. Christ's double consubstantiality or double *homoousion* is based on the claim of the Council of Chalcedon in AD 451. According to Cvetkovic, this term developed especially by Cyril and Maximus "is more pregnant with economical than with Trinitarian implications," for it reveals "the reciprocity between the human and divine nature in Christ." He goes on to say that it may be the reason why Torrance reads this later development into the term *homoousion* inasmuch as for Torrance an Athanasian soteriological perspective can hardly be disclosed in a static *homoousion* concept in the fourth century (Cvetkovic, "T. F. Torrance," 82). However, Torrance's interpretation of Athanasius, particularly of

"God of the nature of God, and man of the nature of man, in one and the same Person," "in Jesus Christ we have to do with One who is wholly God and yet with one who is wholly man."[43] In this sense, in order that Jesus Christ can as the Mediator reconcile us to God, he has to be *homoousios* with our humanity as he is *homoousios* with the Father. In other words, "if Jesus Christ the incarnate Son is not true God, then we are not saved, for it is only God who can save; but if Jesus Christ is not truly man, the salvation does not touch our human existence and condition."[44]

In terms of the embodiment of reconciliation, it is explicitly evident that for Torrance "the *homoousion* is inseparably bound up with the *hypostatic union*."[45] The *homoousion* requires the necessity of the hypostatic union, for if the one Jesus Christ does not share *homoousion* with us as well as with the Father (the double *homoousion*), then his humanity is not completely united with his divinity in his one person (the hypostatic union), and atoning reconciliation is not actualized.

For Torrance, "the hypostatic union operates as a reconciling union in which estrangement is bridged, conflict is eradicated, and human nature taken from us is brought into perfect sanctifying union with divine nature in Jesus Christ."[46] This is not merely a static union of the divine and human natures, but "a dynamic atoning union" removing sin and guilt and sanctifying our fallen and sinful humanity in union with divinity in the one person of the incarnate Son.[47] Therefore, in and through

---

the *homoousion* in a soteriological sense, has been criticized as a soteriological reconstruction of Greek patristic theology. This criticism is closely linked to Holmes's criticism of contemporary trinitarian theologians, primarily social trinitarians, drawing unfaithfully upon the fathers by way of their own preconceptions and commitments (Ernest, *Bible in Athanasius of Alexandria*, 17; Copan, "Review of the Christian Doctrine of God," 248; Holmes, *Quest for The Trinity*, 1–32). Nevertheless, as Radcliff argues, Torrance's soteriological reconstruction of the *homoousion* is not to be regarded as misrepresentation and unfaithful interpretation of the Nicene theology. Although Torrance's *homoousion* may not be identical with Athanasius's, this should be seen rather as disclosing a Reformed evangelical perspective of patristic theology in its christological and soteriological significance (Radcliff, *Thomas F. Torrance and the Church Fathers*, 50).

43. Torrance, *Mediation of Christ*, 56.

44. Torrance, *Trinitarian Faith*, 149.

45. Torrance, *Christian Doctrine of God*, 101; *Transformation and Convergence*, 253.

46. Torrance, *Mediation of Christ*, 65.

47. Torrance, *Mediation of Christ*, 65–66. It is important that for Torrance the dynamic atoning union is not actualized only in the hypostatic union, but rather, steadily

the hypostatic union, the atoning reconciliation of humanity becomes embodied in the fallen and sinful humanity of ours which Christ assumed and placed on a "new basis in union with himself," that is, a new humanity.[48]

This is the reason why Torrance follows Gregory Nazianzen's epigrammatic expression, "The unassumed is the unhealed."[49] If the incarnate Son is not fully identified with us in every aspect of our humanity, as Colyer points out, "all that Christ has done would have no connection with our side of the chasm between humanity and God created by human sin, guilt, and alienation."[50] Since Jesus Christ is really and fully man and his humanity is united with his divinity in his hypostatic union, "the actuality of atonement" is accomplished within the humanity of Christ which is not an *external* act upon human nature but an *internal* act within it.[51]

Torrance's insistence on an internal perspective on atoning reconciliation is closely linked to his understanding of "sin." For Torrance sin is not merely a forensic or legal problem but an ontological one in which we find our alienation from God as well as from neighbors in the ontological depths of our fallen humanity.[52] As an ontological problem, sin is to be

worked out "within the structures of human existence all through the course of our Lord's vicarious earthly life from his birth to his crucifixion and resurrection." This leads us not only to the person and life of Christ but to the purpose of the atoning union, that is, union with God in and through Jesus Christ. In this regard, it has to be said that Torrance's understanding of reconciliation is inherently trinitarian as well as christological.

48. Torrance, *Karl Barth*, 179. It is important that for Torrance the concept of the new humanity of Christ underlies Christian anthropology and ethics, for through union with Christ's new humanity, human person and personhood are ontologically healed, restored, and transformed to live out a new moral life and order. This will be dealt with in more detail as the chapter proceeds.

49. Torrance, *Trinitarian Faith*, 164.

50. Colyer, *How to Read T. F. Torrance*, 81.

51. Torrance, *Incarnation*, 186; "Karl Barth and the Latin Heresy," 475–76.

52. In terms of the internality of incarnational atonement, Torrance opposes "the Latin heresy," that is, any form of dualistic Christology separating between the person and work of Christ. This view is characteristic of western theology including Roman Catholicism and Evangelicalism. In the Latin perspective, the atonement tends to be confined to the cross-work of Christ offering his body as an "external transference of penalty" between sinners and God, rather than, as "the culmination of God's incarnational penetration into the alienated roots of humanity in order to cancel sin and guilt and undo the past, and to effect within it once for all atoning reconciliation between the world and himself" (Torrance, "Karl Barth and the Latin Heresy," 461–81; *Mediation of Christ*, 39). This for Habets is the reason, as he points out, why "Torrance has

addressed at the depths of our corrupt humanity.[53] Through the hypostatic union in the incarnation, as already elucidated, God penetrates the ontological depths of our humanity, not only removing sin and guilt but sanctifying our fallen human nature.

In this respect, atoning reconciliation is internally embodied at the very ontological roots of our humanity that Christ assumed in his own person. Thus, it can be said that for Torrance it is the humanity of Christ in the concepts of the *homoousion* and the hypostatic union which becomes the ontological and soteriological linchpin for reconciliation to God from the human side.

The Nature of the Humanity of Christ

We have seen the reason why the humanity of Christ has ontological, epistemological, and soteriological significance for revelation and reconciliation. For deeper understanding of how Christ penetrates human existence and sanctifies it, it is important here to expound the different aspects of the humanity of Christ, namely, fallen, vicarious, and new *per se*. Torrance deals with three important soteriological and christological subjects in these concepts: (1) the fallen humanity of Christ elucidates Christ's onto-relationality with our sinful humanity, (2) the vicarious humanity of Christ enables us to recognize the ontological and soteriological efficacy of what Jesus Christ has done for us in his vicarious life and death, and (3) the new humanity of Christ presents us with the onto-relational transformation of our sinful and hypocritical humanity. For Torrance this has soteriological, anthropological, and ethical implications.

---

written less on the cross and its redemptive significance than he has on the atoning aspects of the life of Christ." Although Torrance fully recognizes the soteriological importance of the cross, he intentionally emphasizes the whole vicarious life of Christ (Habets, *Theosis in the Theology of Thomas Torrance*, 84). For Torrance, Habets stresses, atonement is not something instrumental and external deriving simply from what Jesus Christ "does," which excludes and even ignores the ontological and soteriological necessity of the human life of Christ in his one person. Any doctrine of atonement in this regard, must begin with who Christ "is," which leads us to the internal aspects of atoning reconciliation embodied in his incarnational constitution.

53. Torrance, *Mediation of Christ*, 70.

The Fallen Humanity

The humanity the incarnate Son assumed was our sinful and fallen humanity. This, as elucidated, is significant for the actuality of revelation and atoning reconciliation in our place.[54] For Torrance this ontological and soteriological importance of Christ's fallen humanity derives from two facts: (1) Christ identified himself fully with us, "in complete and utter solidarity with us sinners in our fallen and guilty humanity, under God's wrath and judgement" and (2) without being a sinner he condemned sin in himself, resisting and overcoming "the opposition and enmity of our fallen human nature to God."[55] In this regard, the fallen humanity of Christ provides us with a recognition of how Christ's humanity was both *like* us as well as *unlike* us in a soteriological sense.

The humanity of Christ was not something abstract but *real*, in "the likeness" of our humanity. For Torrance this is evident in the doctrine of "*enhypostasia*." As Torrance expounds it, *enhypostasia* states that "the human nature of Christ is given existence in the existence of God, and co-exists *in* the divine existence or mode of being (*hypostasis*)—hence *en-hypostasis* ('person *in*,' that is, real human person *in* the person of the Son)."[56] This signifies that the incarnate Word of God assumed our

---

54. The soteriological significance of Christ's fallen humanity follows Pauline's understanding of justification. In relation to the fallen humanity of Christ and our redemption, Torrance cites 2 Corinthians 5:2 that "He [Christ] who knew no sin became sin for us that we might be made the righteousness of God in him." Christ assumed our sinful humanity and sanctified it in his vicarious life which underlies justification before God (Torrance, *Doctrine of Jesus Christ*, 121). This will be dealt with more as the chapter proceeds.

55. Torrance, *Incarnation*, 205.

56. Torrance, *Incarnation*, 84. The doctrine of *enhypostasia* forms a theological couplet with the doctrine of the *anhypostasia*. *Anhypostasia*, as Torrance elucidates it, asserts that "Christ's human nature has its existence only in union with God, in God's existence or personal mode of being (*hypostasis*). It does *not* possess it in and for itself—hence *an-hypostasis* ('not person,' i.e., no separate person)." This means that there would be no human nature of Jesus Christ apart from the incarnation. The "theological couplet," *anhypostasia* and *enhypostasia*, is traceable to Cyril of Alexandria who conceived the terms to repudiate "schizoid" or dualistic Christologies, e.g., Nestorianism separating between the human and divine persons of Jesus Christ. In this theological couplet, there are two particular ways of opposing christological heresies. On the one hand, the doctrine of *anhypostasia* rules out adoptionist Christologies in which Jesus, as an independent human person, was united with the eternal Word and adopted as the Son of God at his baptism. This is because the negative term *anhypostasia* clearly points out that Jesus would not have been a man in our time and space *apart from* the incarnation of the *Logos* (or the hypostatic

full and real human form, that is, human body, will, heart, and mind in our flesh. In the New Testament the term "flesh" fundamentally denotes "fallen humanity under the sentence and wrath of God" so that flesh is understood as "the actual form of our humanity" which is to be redeemed and reconciled to God.[57] For Torrance therefore it is clear that the humanity Christ took upon himself from the Virgin Mary was our sinful and fallen human nature and so was just like us.[58]

In spite of full identity with us in assuming our fallen humanity, Christ sanctified it in himself so that he was sinless *unlike* us. Since our fallen human nature Christ which assumed was sanctified in and through the hypostatic union, Christ was not only sinless but lived out a perfectly and vicariously obedient life before God.[59] In this regard, it is obvious that for Torrance, as Ho points out, "the sanctification process of the assumed sinful human nature" of Christ occurs through his "self-sanctification" in the incarnation in which Christ sanctifies himself.[60] Through the incarnation where the hypostatic union was actualized, our fallen human nature was sanctified by the divine nature of Christ. As Torrance puts it:

> The Son is wholly like us, in that he became what we are, but also wholly unlike us, in that he resisted our sin, and lived in entire and perfect obedience to the Father. . . . Here Jesus was wholly unlike us in his actual human nature, for in his human nature he overcame the opposition and enmity of our fallen

union). On the other hand, since the doctrine of *enhypostasia* explicitly affirms and presents the full and real humanity of Christ in perfect oneness with the complete divinity of Christ *within* the hypostatic union, Docetic, Apollinarian, and monothelist Christologies are also ruled out. For Torrance the two doctrines must be inseparable, for *anhypostasia* and *enhypostasia* work together, emphasizing the "indivisible union of the divine and human natures in their undiminished reality in the one Person of Jesus Christ" (Torrance, *Karl Barth*, 125, 199, 200; "Singularity of Christ," 230). For further understanding of how the terms were at work in the discussion between Cyril and proponents of christological heresies, see also King, "Introduction," 10–14.

57. Torrance, *Doctrine of Jesus Christ*, 121.

58. This theological argument of Torrance—that is, Christ assumed the fallen adamic humanity from the Virgin Mary which is our corrupted and diseased human nature estranged from God—derives partly from Barth. But this is not an original idea of Barth or Torrance, but of the patristic fathers (Torrance, "Justification," 231).

59. In this regard, the conception has conceptual and theological continuity with the conception of the vicarious humanity. Here we can also find Torrance's unitary perspective in which who Christ is and what Christ did, his being and work, are interrelated without being separated.

60. Ho, *Critical Study on T. F. Torrance*, 72.

human nature to God, and restored it to peace with God first in glad and willing submission to God's judgement, and then in the resurrection from the dead.[61]

In this respect, the concept of the fallen humanity of Christ offers the identity and reality of a Christ who is both *like* us and *unlike* us in a soteriological sense, which opposes any kind of external sanctification of the fallen human nature taken by Christ. As to the internality of the atonement, it must be said that sanctification is internally worked out in Christ himself. Thus, for Torrance it would be difficult, and in fact impossible and theologically misguided, to embrace theological attempts to make the humanity of Christ sinless through such conceptual sanctification as the Roman Catholic teaching on the immaculate conception and the assumption of Jesus Christ.[62]

Furthermore, the fact that Christ assumed our fallen humanity, sanctifying it in the incarnation draws our attention to what Torrance calls, "the inner logic of grace." As elucidated, the theological couplet *anhypostasia/enhypostasia* unfolds the relationship between divine and human agency in the incarnation of Jesus Christ. The incarnation, as Torrance argues, was embodied through "the grace of God alone, without any human cooperation, yet in such a way that through the sheer act of divine grace the human nature of Christ, the incarnate Son, was given complete authentic reality as human nature in inseparable union with his divine nature."[63] Thus, it can be said the fallen humanity Christ assumed in the incarnation fully discloses the important theological point that "all of grace involves all of man."[64] This is also evident in Christ's vicarious life and death for our sake which will be clearly unfolded in the following section.

---

61. Torrance, Incarnation, 205.

62. Torrance, *Conflict and Agreement in the Church I*, 149–51. Torrance also opposes Irving, the Scottish preacher arguing that "the sinlessness of Jesus Christ was not due to his own nature but to the indwelling of the Holy Spirit." On this view, the fallen humanity of Christ is sanctified in virtue of the Spirit, so that sanctification of our fallen human nature is regarded as being external (Torrance, *Doctrine of Jesus Christ*, 121). Interestingly, we can find what appears to be a similar argument in Calvin. In his *Institutes* Calvin asserts that since the Holy Spirit sanctified Christ's human nature in conception, his humanity in generation was as that of Adam's before the Fall (Calvin, *Institutes of the Christian Religion*, 481).

63. Torrance, "Singularity of Christ," 230.

64. Torrance, "Singularity of Christ," 230.

The Vicarious Humanity

The term "vicarious humanity" signifies that Christ, who assumed our fallen human nature, exists and acts as a man "in our place, in our stead, on our behalf."[65] Since for Torrance Christ's life and work from incarnation to ascension are interpreted in "a vicarious as well as redemptive way," in our place for our behalf, Christ's whole human life is one of vicarious humanity with soteriological significance.

As Torrance says, in Christ's life and work we find a twofold movement "from God to humanity" and "from humanity to God."[66] The humanward ministry of Christ is emphasized in the fallen humanity of Christ in particular, which is evident in the hypostatic union, the atoning union. The Godward ministry of Christ as man is emphasized in the vicarious humanity of Christ. Christ takes our place and represents us before God, giving the perfect response of faith and obedience towards God "on behalf of all humankind for our sake."[67] In other words, in offering up the perfect faith and response of man to God, the vicarious humanity of Christ "fulfils a representative and substitutionary role in relations with God, including every aspect of human response to Him: such as trusting and obeying, understanding and knowing and worshipping" which we cannot fully offer in our place for our sake.[68] In this respect for Torrance, as Colyer points out, what Christ has done for us before God "*within* our *actual* humanity from birth, through life, death and resurrection" becomes "*all* of *our* basic responses to God."[69]

In the concept of the vicarious humanity of Christ, we find two points of extreme theological significance for Torrance: (1) human faith is grounded in the vicarious faith of Christ which underlies the doctrine of justification and (2) the vicarious humanity of Christ does not undermine individual and personal faith and response to God, but rather undergirds and intensifies them.

In terms of the nature of faith, Torrance argues that faith is not to be construed as "an autonomous, independent act which we do from a base in ourselves."[70] The biblical conception of faith has to do with the

---

65. Torrance, *Mediation of Christ*, 80–81.
66. Torrance, *Incarnation*, 205.
67. Torrance, *Incarnation*, 113–14.
68. Torrance, *God and Rationality*, 145.
69. Colyer, *How to Read T. F. Torrance*, 113.
70. Torrance, *Mediation of Christ*, 82.

reciprocity between God and man, that is, "with the polarity between the faithfulness of God and the answering faithfulness of man."[71] In the Old Testament, this is evident in the community of reciprocity between God and Israel. In spite of the rebellion and disobedience of Israel, God does not let his people go but holds on to them in "the undergirding and utterly invariant faithfulness of God."[72] This means that the faithfulness of God towards Israel revealed in his steadfast and unconditional love for them becomes the ultimate basis and motive of Israel's faithfulness towards God, upon which Israel's redemption rested. The New Testament conception of faith is not different, although it has an intensely personalized character in the incarnate Son. Jesus Christ, as the incarnate faithfulness of God to us, actualized the truth of God in our midst, and he as the embodiment and actualization of human faith also vicariously offered the perfect faith and obedience to God in our place on our behalf.[73]

In this sense, the perfect reciprocity between God's faithfulness and humanity's corresponding faithfulness has achieved its end in Jesus Christ, so that our human faith rests upon Christ's vicarious faith and response.[74] As Torrance puts it:

> Jesus steps into the actual situation where we are summoned to have faith in God, to believe and trust in him, and he acts in our place and in our stead from within the depths of our unfaithfulness and provides us freely with a faithfulness in which we may share.... That is to say, if we think of belief, trust or faith as forms of human activity before God, then we must think of Jesus Christ as believing, trusting and having faith in God the Father on our behalf and in our place.[75]

As regards the vicarious faith of Christ and its relation to justification, Torrance understands that the vicarious faith of Christ is the real locus of justification, for we are justified not by our faith but by "the faith of Christ."[76] Since Jesus Christ vicariously offered to God the perfect faith and response which we are not able to do, he as the obedient one was himself justified before God. Through union with Christ by the Holy

---

71. Torrance, *Mediation of Christ*, 82.
72. Torrance, *Mediation of Christ*, 82.
73. Torrance, *God and Rationality*, 154.
74. Torrance, "One Aspect of the Biblical Conception of Faith," 113.
75. Torrance, *Mediation of Christ*, 82.
76. Torrance, "Justification," 236.

Spirit, we share in his very faith, perfect obedience, and trust to God, and thereby are "justified in *him* in whom we believe."[77] Thus it is argued that for Torrance, to be justified is to participate in the righteousness or "the actualised holiness of Jesus Christ" in our place for our sake, which repudiates all our own acts, such as repentance, confession, trust, and response to be justified before God.[78]

However, it is important to recognize the fact that Torrance has been criticized for his emphasis on the vicarious humanity of Christ and its relation to human faith, response, and justification. Put simply and briefly, since in the conception of the vicarious humanity of Christ, it is Jesus Christ alone who offers the perfect faith and response to God, it is argued there is no room for individual and personal faith and response. As a result, the importance of the individual believer's faith and response are attenuated and even invalidated. Such critique of Torrance is evident in John Webster's argument: "In Torrance's account of the matter [the vicarious character of Jesus' being and act in relation to humanity], Jesus' humanity threatens to absorb that of others."[79] In this sense, for Webster human faith and response is in danger of being dissolved within a theology of Christ's vicarious humanity overemphasizing "the incarnational grace."[80]

Webster's critique poses such questions as, how can the vicarious humanity of Christ validate and undergird the need for individual faith and response? Even though intellectually Webster articulates his critical view with regard to the role of human agency in the vicarious humanity of Christ, it seems to be a misunderstanding of "the nature of grace" or "the inner logic of grace" embodied in Christ's vicarious humanity.

As elucidated, his fallen humanity taken from us was healed and sanctified by Christ in the incarnation and hypostatic union. Jesus Christ lived and acted in our place on our behalf, providing the perfect human

77. Torrance, *Theology in Reconciliation*, 141.
78. Torrance, *Theology in Reconciliation*, 141.
79. Webster, *Barth's Ethics of Reconciliation*, 171.
80. Webster, "Editorial," 371. Webster's critique is closely related to his primacy of moral theology in which "to talk of justification is to talk of the way in which our being lies beyond us in the true man Jesus" (Webster, *Eberhard Jüngel*, 102). For Webster, Torrance's view of the vicarious of humanity of Christ causes an invalidation of our faith and response to the gospel or Christian moral life, so that it offers an excuse for human inaction with regard to morality. We shall see the point in more detail as this chapter proceeds, particularly in "Critical Appreciation of the Soteriological Suspension of Ethics."

faith and obedience which we could not offer to God. In the soteriological way that Christ has done this for us, we must understand that he now summons us to share and participate in "his vicarious response of faithfulness toward God."[81] This means that there is no room for human inactivity, for God's grace revealed in Jesus Christ does not emasculate our response of faith to his vicarious faith for us, but rather "Christ's faithfulness undergirds our feeble faith and faltering faith and enfolds it in His own."[82] Thus it is argued that for Torrance, as Walker rightly points out, Christ's vicarious humanity is "radical substitution and far from ruling out the need for individual and personal faith on our part it actually intensifies it."[83]

The New Humanity

It has been noted that Christ entered into our fallen existence in assumption of our fallen human nature. But in his incarnational atonement, Christ transmuted our fallen humanity into "a new humanity," healing and sanctifying it in himself. In his vicarious response of faith and obedience Christ not only broke through "the continuity of adamic existence," but also opened up "a new continuity in a new Adam, in a new humanity" in himself.[84] In this respect for Torrance, the new humanity of Christ is the soteriological reason and purpose behind the vicarious and fallen humanity of Christ.[85]

It is noteworthy that Torrance relates his understanding of Christ's new humanity to both soteriology and anthropology/ethics. Here it is important to spell out first what the new humanity of Christ is and how it plays a pivotal role in our redemption, for these which are conceptual

---

81. Torrance, *God and Rationality*, 154.
82. Torrance, *God and Rationality*, 154.
83. Walker, "Editor's Introduction," lxxv.
84. Torrance, *Incarnation*, 94.
85. According to Kettler, the vicarious humanity of Christ becomes the basis and source of a new humanity, for "Christ not only takes our place, and becomes our representative, thereby creating a new humanity, but also incorporates us into his new humanity" (Kettler, *Vicarious Humanity of Christ*, 128). Even though Torrance puts Christ's humanity forward under two different aspects (fallen and new), it must be emphasized that the fallen/vicarious humanity and the new humanity of Christ are in ontological continuity and interrelation in a soteriological sense. They work together in theological and conceptual correlation, making up together Christology and soteriology.

grounds for the second issue, the new humanity of Christ in its soteriological relation to anthropology and ethics.

In terms of the nature of the new humanity of Christ, for Torrance there are two focal points from which we can best understand it: the incarnation and resurrection. The incarnation reveals the ways in which "the saving grace of God takes with our fallen humanity" and how God brings out of "fallen and sinful existence a new humanity that is holy and perfect" in Jesus Christ.[86] In the incarnation, since Christ opened up "a new way" in which our old humanity was transmuted into a new humanity by virtue of the atoning nature of incarnation, the fallen and hypocritical humanity finds its "true being and true human nature" in Jesus Christ.[87] In this sense, it must be said that Jesus Christ was the new and true humanity, living out his new humanity in the perfect response of faithfulness and obedience to God throughout his whole life on our behalf for our sake.

It is the resurrection that reveals that Jesus Christ *was* the new man, the firstborn of the new creation, and the head of the new race,[88] and that draws our attention to "the actual existence of the new and glorified humanity of Christ" in the resurrection and ascension which together present the fact that Jesus Christ *is* the new man, new creation in our on-going space and time.[89] In the resurrection from the dead and ascension into heaven, it is Jesus Christ who lives now as a new man before the Father, enabling us to share, participate, and live in his new humanity through the Holy Spirit.[90] This for Torrance is of critical soteriological significance. As he puts it:

> In the Resurrection and Ascension we have the affirmation of man by God, and his exaltation to be a partaker of a new

---

86. Torrance, *Incarnation*, 98; *Theology in Reconciliation*, 97. In this regard, it is said that for Torrance in the incarnation Christ is both "in continuity and in discontinuity with our fallen humanity" (Torrance, *Incarnation*, 94).

87. Torrance, *Incarnation*, 94.

88. Torrance, *Incarnation*, 94. Here Torrance cites Colossians 1:18 and Romans 8:29 in order to emphasize Christ's new continuity in his new humanity.

89. Torrance, *Space, Time and Resurrection*, 84–85.

90. According to Torrance, participation in the new humanity of Christ signifies that "the human nature of the participant is not deified but reaffirmed and recreated in its essence as human nature, yet one in which the participant is really united to the Incarnate Son of God partaking in him in his own appropriate mode of the oneness of the Son and the Father and the Father and the Son, through the Holy Spirit" (Torrance, *Theology in Reconstruction*, 186).

humanity, a new righteousness, and a new freedom as a child of God, as a brother of Christ, as a joint-heir with him, as one who together with him has the same Father.[91]

In this regard, for Torrance the new humanity of Christ is justification and reconciliation *per se*. In his new humanity, Jesus Christ offered the perfect faith and obedience through the whole course of his vicarious life, death, resurrection, and ascension, so that we are justified by and reconciled to God as we freely participate in and live out his new humanity. Furthermore, it is with regard to the conception of the new humanity of Christ that Torrance addresses his anthropological/ethical thought and sacramental action in the church. This will be addressed in the following section and the next chapter.

The Human Person and Personhood in the New Humanity of Christ

For Torrance the new humanity of Christ offers implications not only of soteriological, but also of anthropological and ethical significance. All of humanity, in union with the new humanity of Christ, is reconciled with God and fellow humans through his atoning reconciliation and justification. Anthropologically, the depths of our self-centered and hypocritical humanity are ontologically healed, restored, and transformed, and thus we are personalized or humanized as persons in true relation with others. Such restoration and transformation in human person and personhood not only has a profound effect on human social relations, but also opens up a new moral life and order.

Transformation of Humanity in the New Humanity of Christ

For Torrance the restoration and transformation of the human person arise through participation in the new humanity of Christ. The Son of God, as he argues, became man among us so as to gather up our corrupt humanity into his humanity, thereby healing and renewing all humanity within his person "through the perfection and holiness of his own human nature and life," that is, in his "new humanity."[92] In his perfect and vicarious truth and obedience to the Father, Christ breaks through "the

---

91. Torrance, *Theology in Reconstruction*, 151.
92. Torrance, *Trinitarian Faith*, 267.

continuity of adamic existence" and begins "a new continuity in a new Adam, in a new humanity" in which reconciliation between God and us and between us and our fellow humans is actualized.[93]

We can derive three anthropological and ethical implications of significance from the fact of the onto-relational healing and restoration of our humanity in and through the Christ's new humanity. First, his new humanity presents the horizontal dimension of redemption. Second, in his new humanity, Christ transmutes the fallen humanity into the new humanity necessary for inter-personal human relations. Third, the human person or humanity personalized by Christ, the personalizing person, becomes fully and truly responsible for moral obligations in human society and community.

As elucidated in previous sections, the incarnate Word of God assumed our full human form, our very bone, skin, heart, and mind in the humanity of Christ. As man Jesus forged a new humanity for all human existence in his person. In the humanity of Christ God fully joined himself to our fallen, sinful, adamic humanity and creatively and truly transformed it to "a new humanity" by his perfectly vicarious and obedient life and death, resurrection and ascension to the Father in our flesh and place for our sake.[94] In death on the cross and resurrection from death, Christ in our flesh was transformed in glory as *new* man, *new* humanity, and is through the Spirit involving us in his death and resurrection in order for us to participate in his new life and humanity.[95] Christ's new humanity is now with the eternal triune life of God, yet he still remains in our human form that is essentially what we are.[96]

On the basis of all he has done vicariously for our new humanity, Christ unites us to his new humanity through the action of the Holy Spirit by which our humanity is united with the Godhead and the onto-relational reconciliation between God and us is realized.[97] Here, Torrance states that there is a mutual correspondence between God and us which

---

93. Torrance, *Incarnation*, 31; *Atonement*, 375.

94. In this sense, the concept of the vicarious humanity of Christ is conceptually and theologically inseparable and indivisible from the concept of the new humanity of Christ, for Christ became new man (humanity) and last Adam *vicariously* in our place for our sake.

95. Walker, "Editor's Introduction," lxvii.

96. Torrance, *Conflict and Agreement in the Church II*, 188.

97. Torrance, *Conflict and Agreement in the Church II*, 188; *Theology in Reconstruction*, 152.

has its reality in the twofold movement—the movement of God toward us in the incarnation and the movement of us toward God by participating in the new humanity of Christ.[98] To put it another way, knowing God is attained only by God's self-communication to us in the incarnation and the onto-relational reconciliation of God and human is actualized in us only by means of participation in the new humanity of Christ.

It does not mean that the reconciliation is confined only to the reconciliation in the God-human relation, that is, the vertical relation and dimension. Rather, the vertical reconciliation in its soteriological purpose between God and us inevitably engenders the reconciliation of person with fellow person in "the horizontal relation and dimension."[99] As Torrance puts it:

> For humanity, the redemption of the cross involves at the same time reconciliation of man with fellow man, of all men and women with each other, and particularly of Jew and Gentile, for the middle wall of partition has been broken down and God has made of them one *new man* in Christ Jesus. . . . It entails a judgement upon the old humanity of Babel and the proclamation of the new humanity in Christ Jesus.[100]

In this sense, for Torrance reconciliation entails not only the vertical relation but the horizontal relation also, for "participation in Christ carries with it participation in one another, and our common reconciliation with Christ carries with it reconciliation with one another."[101] As Speidell rightly points out, in Torrance's soteriological understanding of reconciliation "the vertical invades and redeems the horizontal."[102]

Importantly, for Torrance the human reconciliation is not beyond "the bounds of divine reconciliation."[103] This is the reason why he derives the horizontal dimension of reconciliation not from an anthropocentric

---

98. Torrance, *Theology in Reconstruction*, 100–102.

99. Torrance, *Atonement*, 197–200. For Torrance, "redemption affects all humanity and relates us to the whole of creation." This perspective reflects St. Paul's understanding of reconciliation.

100. Torrance, *Atonement*, 199. Here, the term "the old humanity of Babel" signifies the disobedient and arrogant nature of human beings found in the story of the tower of Babel (Gen 11:1–9). For Torrance, it is the new humanity of Christ that breaks up our old humanity and creates new humanity in the human person.

101. Torrance, *Atonement*, 375.

102. Speidell, *Fully Human in Christ*, 14.

103. Torrance, *Mediation of Christ*, 71.

ground but from the reconciling work of Christ, particularly the doctrine of the hypostatic union and the atonement. In the hypostatic union, as he states, "the human nature of Jesus Christ is taken up, established, secured and anchored forever in its undiminished integrity in the Son of God."[104] This hypostatic union is not separated and divided from the atoning union, for our fallen humanity is redeemed, healed, and renewed in Christ's new humanity.[105]

On that basis Torrance asserts that the restoration and renewal of our humanity in the new humanity of Christ enable us not only to have *true and inter-personal relations with fellow humans*, but also to be fully responsible for *moral deeds and social ethics*.[106] Torrance elucidates first the reason why the restoration and sanctification of our humanity is so necessary and important for the reconciliation in inter-human relations. The problem, as Torrance puts it, that is inherent and embedded in our humanity or personality is "a deeply set schizoid condition which regularly, and indeed inevitably, gives rise to insincerity and hypocrisy in us. Through estrangement from the personalising source of our being, the image we present, and wish to present, to others has become detached from what we actually are, so that it becomes a deceptive mask."[107] Hence the state of our human person is placed in "a self-centred individualism" in which genuine relations with others are cut off, so that "the very personal relations in which persons subsist as persons are damaged and twisted" by virtue of the Fall.[108]

---

104. Torrance, *Mediation of Christ*, 70.

105. Torrance, *Mediation of Christ*, 70.

106. Torrance, *Mediation of Christ*, 70. For Torrance, the redemptive work of Christ involves the universal level. The universal range of reconciliation takes in not only all humanity but the whole created world. This universal perspective of the redeeming love of God in Christ displays "the catholicising of the person of Christ" in a cosmic significance where God's reconciling work in Christ is universalized and includes all things visible and invisible, earthly and heavenly alike. Here Torrance reflects St. Paul's understanding that the divine reconciliation has such a universal dimension. This could open the door to how Christian soteriology contributes to our environmental and ecological problems in the reconciliation of all things in Christ (Torrance, "Singularity of Christ," 249; *Atonement*, 200).

107. Torrance, *Mediation of Christ*, 68.

108. Torrance, *Mediation of Christ*, 68–69. It is important to take note of the term "individualism" with regard to personal relations. Within individualism (or pathological freedom), as Gunton puts it, "humanity to those unable to stand on their own feet" is denied. By contrast, within collectivism (or abstract equality), the differentiation or distinctive characteristic in a person which is essential for human

An important point is the fact that Torrance recognizes that the necessity of moral obligations arises in and out of the very condition of the human personality in its schizoid nature. Moral relations and the patterns and structures of moral behavior required of us reflect the fundamental gap between "what we are" and "what we ought to be," for the very fact of moral obligations means that "we are not the human beings we ought to be."[109] Although we seek to justify ourselves before God and our fellow humans by "a formal, impersonal fulfilment of the divine law," our humanity falls a prey to the very process of dehumanization operating in the self-deceptive condition of our being and humanity.[110]

Here it becomes apparent that in order to have the fully personal relations among humankind, and be truly responsible for moral life and order, our insincere and hypocritical humanity must first be healed and restored. For Torrance, it is the work of the new humanity of Christ. Since the Fall of Adam, as Torrance states, all humanity has been dehumanized on account of sin.[111] Yet Christ's new humanity cuts the continuity of our fallen humanity and transforms it into a new humanity in the midst

---

community is denied. An important point here is that both individualism and collectivism as "mirror images of one another" engender the loss of the human person (Gunton, *Promise of Trinitarian Theology*, 88–92, 99, 117, 133, 171). Macmurray also critiques both individualism and collectivism, for "the Self is constituted by its relation to the Other." In other words, "self" and "other" only exist as persons in their interrelations to others. Thus, for Macmurray "our human Being is our relations to other human beings . . . our relation to God is itself real only as it shows itself in our relation to our neighbours" which reflects his epistemological emphasis on theology and anthropology. In this light, an important and fundamental theological question, for Macmurray, is "is what exists personal?" not "does God exist?" (Macmurray, *Persons in Relation*, 86, 215; *Search for Reality in Religion*, 72).

Interestingly, Macmurray's epistemological emphasis seems to underlie Torrance's onto-relational understanding of the word "person." As Torrance puts it, "while God is three Persons, Father, Son, and Holy Spirit, they are not separated from one another like human persons. They are *Three in One*." In other words, the three divine persons in one Godhead are to be understood in relations in which they are not static and impersonal, but dynamic, relational, and personal (Torrance, "Sermon on the Trinity," 40–44). As Fergusson maintains, the epistemological influence of Macmurray on Torrance's realist theology is also linked to "an anthropology that insists upon the embodiedness and sociality of human life, themes that are strongly Hebraic and that also find support in Macmurray's writings" (Fergusson, "Influence of Macmurray on Scottish Theology," 146–47).

109. Torrance, "Singularity of Christ," 251; *Mediation of Christ*, 70.
110. Torrance, *Mediation of Christ*, 70–71.
111. Torrance, *Incarnation*, 94.

of our "inhumanity."[112] In and through the new humanity of Christ, the humanity which is dehumanized finds its "true being and true human nature in union with God."[113] Thus for Torrance, in his new humanity Christ is "the personalising person" and "the humanising man" healing and restoring our "dehumanisation" in the depths of our being and person.[114] As Torrance puts it:

> The personalising Person of the Son of God became incarnate, but, instead of becoming insincere and hypocritical himself, he healed the ontological split in human being through the hypostatic and atoning union which he embodied within it, thereby reintegrating image and reality in and through a human life of perfect sincerity, honesty and integrity in the undivided oneness of his Person as Mediator.[115]

In his new humanity, Christ as the personalizing person humanizes and personalizes the human person, and thereby healing and renewing our humanity. Through the personalizing and humanizing work of Christ, the loss of human personal relations in individualism (and collectivism) is overcome and restored. Because, as Molnar rightly points out, for Torrance the new humanity of Christ overcomes "all that is "depersonalising" in humanity and establishes us as persons in relation to him and through

---

112. Torrance, *Incarnation*, 94.

113. Torrance, *Incarnation*, 94.

114. Torrance, *Mediation of Christ*, 69–71. In relation to the term "personalising person," Torrance insists that all human persons are dependent and contingent (or created), that is, "personalised persons." By contrary, "God alone is personalising Person, *persona personans*," the "fullness of person being." Thus, God as the personalizing person is "the creative Source and Author of all other personal reality." Here Torrance puts forward two significant insights. First, since the eternal Son of God became man in Jesus without overwhelming or displacing the rationality and human person of man but rather establishing it, "no human being has such as full and rich personal human nature as Jesus." Second and in this light, it makes sure that our humanity or personal existence is not damaged but renewed, healed, restored, and deepened through the saving and renewing activity of God in the incarnation of Christ and the outpouring of the Holy Spirit. That is to say, our humanity is renewed and personalized through union with the new humanity of Christ in baptism. We will see in chapter 4 how our humanity is healed in baptism (and the Eucharist) in the outworking of the new humanity of Christ in the church as the body of Christ (Torrance, *Trinitarian Perspectives*, 97–98). See also Torrance, *Trinitarian Faith*, 230; *Mediation of Christ*, 68–69.

115. Torrance, *Mediation of Christ*, 69.

that relation as those who are free to relate with our fellow humans in ways that are no longer self-centered and hypocritical."[116]

From this perspective, Torrance relates the work of the new humanity of Christ personalizing or humanizing human persons to "transforming human social relations."[117] Inter-personal relations between human beings are healed and restored in union with the new humanity of Christ in which the interrelations are "constantly renewed and sustained through the humanising activity of Christ Jesus" within "the ontological and social structures" to which human beings belong.[118] In this regard, for Torrance "the promise of transformation and renewal of all human social structures is held out in the Gospel, when society may at last be transmuted into a community of love centring in and sustained by the personalising and humanising presence of the Mediator."[119]

Furthermore, for Torrance the new humanity of Christ opens up "a new moral life and order" by humanizing or personalizing our humanity. As elucidated, the very patterns and structures of moral obligation reveal the fact that in the ontological depths of our twisted humanity we are trapped within "the unbridgeable rift between what we *are* and what we *ought* to be" before God and our fellow humans.[120] But Christ sets "the whole moral order upon a new basis," his new humanity.[121] Christ as new man, and new humanity in his person, embodies a new moral life and order which derives from "grace in which external legal relation is replaced by inner filial relation to God the Father."[122] In his atoning life and death, Christ *was* and *is* "the one man who is who he *ought* to be" in moral relations with God without any insincerity and hypocrisy in his perfect and vicarious obedience.[123] In union with Christ in his new humanity, the insincere and hypocritical image and reality

---

116. Molnar, *Thomas F. Torrance*, 144. See also Torrance, *Mediation of Christ*, 69. For Torrance the personalizing person of Christ, as Walker argues, also enables us to have "personal knowledge of God in faith." As God is personal or personalizing person, he can only be known *personally* to us in faith and worship as the proper and personal way (Walker, "Editor's Introduction," xxix).

117. Torrance, *Mediation of Christ*, 72.

118. Torrance, *Mediation of Christ*, 72.

119. Torrance, *Mediation of Christ*, 72.

120. Torrance, "Singularity of Christ," 251; *Trinitarian Faith*, 160.

121. Torrance, *Mediation of Christ*, 71.

122. Torrance, "Singularity of Christ," 252.

123. Torrance, *Mediation of Christ*, 71.

of our humanity are personalized and turned into "filial union with the father."[124] Thus in our brother Jesus Christ, we as sons and daughters of the Father live out a new moral life and order where we human beings are no longer trapped in the unbridgeable rift in moral life and structure. As a result, our morality is no more "externally governed by the imperatives of the law" but rather "inwardly ruled by the indicatives of God's love."[125]

In the light of the work of Christ's new humanity personalizing and humanizing our humanity, it is obvious that for Torrance reconciliation between God and us—in the life and work of Christ's new humanity—fundamentally entails anthropological and ethical and not only doxological dimensions. Thus, for Torrance the anthropological and ethical implications are *inherently* embedded in the work of the new humanity of Christ.

Second, this fact explicitly expounds the reason why Torrance does not directly deal with and develop anthropology and ethics in an autonomous moral philosophy, but deals with them on christological grounds where Christ's atoning work is regarded as a *foundational* and *structural starting point* for "the fundamental moral frame work of thought."[126] As Torrance insists:

> [The new moral order] is the utterly radical nature of atoning mediation perfected in Christ, for it involves what might well be called "soteriological suspension of ethics" in the establishing of a new moral life. . . . This radical change is to be grasped, as far as it may, not in the light of abstract moral or legal principle, nor in terms of the works of the law, but only in the light of what Christ has actually done in penetrating into the dark depths of our twisted human existence where moral obligations and duties conflict with one another, in doing away with the unbridgeable rift with which the moral nature of human being has been bound up since the fall.[127]

Torrance's whole theological ethics with its anthropological significance and implications, as Speidell points out, is informed by what Torrance calls a "soteriological suspension of ethics."[128] For Torrance, therefore,

124. Torrance, "Singularity of Christ," 238.
125. Torrance, "Singularity of Christ," 253.
126. Torrance, "Singularity of Christ," 254.
127. Torrance, "Singularity of Christ," 253. See also Torrance, *Trinitarian Faith*, 160.
128. Speidell, *Fully Human in Christ*, 8.

any kind of Christian anthropology and ethics cannot have autonomy but only a heteronomy in which human personal relations and morality are formed by the personalizing work of the new humanity of Christ.

Third, Torrance's soteriological priority in dealing with humanity, relationality, and morality seems to focus more on "where" Christian anthropology and ethics occur and derive their motive force from (which for him is definitely the new humanity of Christ) rather than on "how" Christian theology serves them. As elucidated in chapter 2, social trinitarians have used the relational understanding of divine persons, e.g., the concept of *perichoresis*, to support human societies that are egalitarian, diverse, mutual, and inclusive. Yet unlike Torrance they show a shared tendency to pay little attention to the significance of Christ's mediatorial ministry. In this light Torrance's soteriological emphasis on Christian anthropology and ethics draws our attention to the significant role of Christology, particularly the new humanity of Christ, as a foundational source for personal relationality and morality with regard to God and others.

Critical Appreciation of the "Soteriological Suspension of Ethics"

As we have seen, Torrance does focus on Christ's reconciling and personalizing work as the ground of soteriology and ethics. This theological focus in Torrance is understood as *a rejection of self-justification* or *self-justifying ethics* in which Christ, as Torrance argues, is "thrust into a corner where he could hardly be noticed, while the ethical and indeed the casuistical concern dominated the whole picture."[129]

Christopher Holmes argues that this christological focus in Torrance focuses on "the acting subject whose agency is never exhausted but continues to have its way by working what he is, by the power of the Spirit, into us," in which ethics is viewed as a function of the presence and ministry of Christ, "continually operative in his reconciling intervention."[130] This view, as Holmes asserts, rejects "exemplarism" in Christian ethics, which is insensitive to what God *is doing* in this world in and through Christ "to make and to keep human life human, to achieve

---

129. Torrance, *God and Rationality*, 60.
130. Holmes, *Ethics in the Presence of Christ*, 23–24; cf. Torrance, *Atonement*, 170.

the maturity of men, that is, the new humanity," enabling our conformity to God's command that we do as he does.[131]

However, this does not mean that it is only such a view which can contribute to Christian anthropology and ethics, for it is important to *also* investigate and suggest the way in which biblical moral principles are interpreted and applied to human society so as to propagate and establish Christian moral values. In particular, as far as our religiously plural society (where Christians live in company with non-Christians) is concerned, it is clear that building Christian anthropology and ethics requires not only understanding "where'" their impetus arises from, but also understanding "how" Christian moral principles (e.g., love of neighbor and enemy, forgiveness, loving kindness, justice, mercy for the weak and defenceless) can be acceptable and accessible to human societies for seeking inter-personal relationality, community, and morality among us in religiously plural human communities. In this light, focusing on and developing such Christian moral principles is not a theological attempt to achieve a self-justifying ethic but a theological approach or response to the question of how Christianity can serve a world rampant with economic-socio-political injustice, immorality, and dehumanization.

Christian moral principles found in the Bible could all be referred to "the love command of God." The love command, as Rudman elucidates it, has traditionally been examined and summarized as "Christian ethical teaching" which explicitly presents God's personal concern for

---

131. Holmes, *Ethics in the Presence of Christ*, 24–25. See also Lehmann, *Ethics in a Christian Context*, 177. Holmes asserts that in the idea of "exemplarism" in Christian ethics, Jesus is read as an example or an instantiation of something that lies beyond himself, so that he becomes "the paradigm for talking about social justice or for what personal piety in the religious life might look like." What matters in this thought is not so much "who he is" and "what he has done and continues to do for us," but "what he can point us" towards. In this regard, Holmes rejects "exemplarism" that excludes Jesus Christ *himself* and his ongoing reconciling and transforming ministry in our midst (Holmes, *Ethics in the Presence of Christ*, 24–25).

Importantly, in order to support his argument, Holmes cites Torrance, Paul Lehmann and Kathryn Tanner, who have regarded Christ himself and God's continual reconciling and humanizing activity in and through Christ as key to our understanding of "ethics." By contrast, Holmes refers to William Schweiker, Bernd Wannenwetsch, Samuel Wells, and David Cunningham as contemporary thinkers who have paid little attention to the presence and ongoing ministry of Christ in their discussions of ethics, to the degree that ethics is understood as being "where individuals or the church begin and, concomitantly, where Jesus leaves off." This, for Holmes, refers to "the displacement of Christology" in Christian ethics (Holmes, *Ethics in the Presence of Christ*, 1–17).

loving treatment of human beings and the creaturely world.[132] Here it is to be recognized that Christian ethical teaching, as Manson rightly points out, clearly derives from the very life and teaching of Jesus himself in the New Testament.[133] By the practice of certain rules and ways of Christian ethical life on the one hand, and the possession of certain theological beliefs based on who Jesus Christ is and what he does on the other hand, Christianity has its own particular ethic.[134] It is the understanding and interpretation of the life and teaching of Jesus Christ in Scripture which constitutes the content and role of biblical moral principles and which is still relevant to Christian ethics today and applicable to Christians/non-Christians at the intellectual level.

It is obvious that there cannot be the ethical practice of Christianity by itself apart from epistemological and ontological conversion of human mind and thought in union with Christ and *vice versa*. In other words, the practice of Christian ethical life is a natural corollary of the transformed and renewed humanity, and it is living union with Christ which engenders the practice of biblical moral principles and values before God and our neighbors. Thus in terms of the content and context of Christian anthropology and ethics, it can be said that it is just as significant and necessary on the one hand to spell out where Christian anthropology and ethics occur and derive their motive force from, as on the other hand how biblical moral principles and values are interpreted and applied to our religiously plural society. This is what Torrance could accommodate and deal with much more without any undue revision to his overarching anthropological and ethical concerns.

In reference to this, Webster's critique and Fergusson's critical evaluation of Torrance help us to develop a more holistic view of what Torrance

---

132. Rudman, *Concepts of Person and Christian Ethics*, 225.

133. Manson, *Jesus and the Christian*, 95, Manson was one of the influential teachers of Torrance at New College and Torrance wrote a very appreciative introduction for Manson's book *Jesus and the Christian*. Manson expounds the ontological relation between Christology and the Christian life. For Manson Christian ethics is the ethics resulting from union with Christ and its primary feature is Christ himself "as the vital source both of Christian doctrine and of the Christian impulse to moral living" based on his own life and teaching (Manson, *Jesus and the Christian*, 91–159). This same theological direction is found in Torrance's concern about the relationship between Christology and Christian anthropology and ethics. Yet, as already expounded, it cannot be denied that Torrance focuses more on Christ's atoning and personalizing work as the soteriological and ethical ground and grammar, rather than on "how" the life and teaching of Jesus underlies and encourages a Christian moral life.

134. Manson, *Jesus and the Christian*, 92–93.

calls a "soteriological suspension of ethics." They suggest that Torrance's theology undermines certain questions: (1) whether Torrance's emphasis on the priority of the christological-soteriological in terms of ethics discourages people from reflecting Christian ethical teachings in their moral activities and (2) whether the Christocentric view of humanity and morality in Torrance develops ethical deliberation in wider realms.

In Webster's criticism, we find the accusation of human inaction arising from Torrance's soteriological priority with regard to personal and moral activities.[135] Webster poses the question as follows: "If Christians are *what they are* by virtue of their participation in the benefits of God's saving acts in Christ, then what room is left for *human ethical activity* in our account of what makes a person into the person he or she is?"[136] It is argued, in Webster's view that "the subject as agent" in the ethical dimension is negated or displaced by "the *sole* agency of Christ" because the vicarious character of Jesus's being and action in his new humanity becomes regarded as something assimilating our humanity.[137] For Webster here, Torrance's christological and soteriological emphasis on our humanity and morality, particularly the concept of the vicarious humanity of Christ, invalidates our humanity and then engenders "excuses for inaction," that is, passive human ethical activity.[138]

The view of Webster seems to be a clear theological emphasis on "the primacy of Christian ethics." For Webster, Torrance's soteriological suspension of ethics can only attenuate not only the moral responsibility of human agents but the universal practice of Christian ethics. In other words, if Christian ethics has its dynamic and proper function *only within* a christological-soteriological boundary (of atonement and justification), then for Webster the human agent becomes inactive and

---

135. This criticism of Webster is closely related to his critique to the concept of the vicarious humanity of Christ. See the previous section "the vicarious humanity of Christ."

136. Webster, "Imitation of Christ," 95–96.

137. Webster, "Imitation of Christ," 105; *Barth's Ethics of Reconciliation*, 171.

138. Webster, "Christian in Revolt," 126. In this respect, even though there are many similar points between Barth and Torrance, Webster argues in favor of Barth that Barth's real divergence from Torrance features "the covenantal character of the relation between God and humanity, which Barth sees as ethically fundamental. . . . In Barth's account, Jesus' humanity graciously evokes corresponding patterns of being and doing on the part of those whom it constitutes" (Webster, *Barth's Ethics of Reconciliation*, 171). See also Molnar's viewpoint on this matter for better understanding (Molnar, *Incarnation and Resurrection*, 150).

Christian ethics does not have its universal characteristic but rather one based on a unique soteriological basis with "insufficient emphasis on the primacy of moral action."[139] In this sense, Webster asserts that "the imitation motif," the imitation of Jesus Christ in the New Testament, "may help us hold together the derivative character of human morality and its character as a human project involving choice, conscious allegiance and deliberation."[140] Thus, for Webster "Christ's action is more than vicarious: it is evocative, it constitutes a summons to a properly derivative mimesis."[141]

Although his core argument is different, Fergusson, following up Webster's criticisms, points out "the relative absence of the ethical and political significance" in Torrance, particularly in relation to the significance of the ascension in his thought.[142] For Fergusson, despite occasional hints about ethical and political significance, Torrance's theology as a whole does not give *sufficient scope* to issues of ethical and socio-political significance such as social justice, human equality, and world peace. In this respect, it is argued, the most significant movements and relations found in Torrance are vertical and doxological, not horizontal and ethical, and thus the wider socio-political implications of the gospel cannot but help be confined to the individual and ecclesial areas, rather than to the social dimension.[143]

Fergusson then suggests the royal Psalms, Jesus's teaching of the kingdom, and recent ethical and political theologies provide an important complement to the relative absence of horizontal and ethical significance in Torrance.[144] This suggestion of Fergusson, alluded to but not expanded on, appears to be an attempt to integrate the doxological significance and the ethical-socio-political significance in theology for further development in Torrance's relatively doxological theology. It is clear that for Fergusson, as for Webster in his critique, the christological-soteriological

---

139. Webster, *Eberhard Jüngel*, 92. Here Webster puts his criticism of Jüngel to Torrance.

140. Webster, "Imitation of Christ," 95–96.

141. Webster, "Christology, Imitability and Ethics," 321.

142. Fergusson, "Ascension of Christ," 101.

143. Fergusson, "Ascension of Christ," 101.

144. Fergusson, "Ascension of Christ," 101. Here Fergusson suggests Nicholas Wolterstorff and Oliver O'Donovan who have dealt with the ethical and political dimensions in theology.

emphasis of Torrance lacks sufficient recognition and discussion of its ethical and social-political dimensions.

The criticisms and critical evaluations above have some significant implications. Webster's critique of Torrance's focus on the centrality of soteriology in Christian ethics highlights the question of moral responsibility and action from the human side. The primacy of the moral found in the imitation motif seems to help Christian ethics be applicable to Christians/non-Christians in our religiously plural society. It might be an effective and acceptable approach and methodology to use the imitation motif as a way in which biblical ethical teachings and values can be shared with all humanity as a universal ethics in our society.

Moreover, Fergusson's critical evaluation of Torrance's emphasis on vertical movements and relations spells out the significance of doxological and ethical integration in Christian theology. This view of Fergusson highlights the important fact that dogmatics, particularly atonement and justification, cannot be divided from its practical significance and implications. In this respect, Fergusson would argue that theology properly functions and contributes to human society only when it is understood in integration with practical anthropological, ethical, and socio-political concerns. While Torrance's theology has the capacity to do this, this tends to be a latent capacity in need of further development.

In response to Webster's critique and his apparent misreading of Torrance's intention in dogmatics, the main point can be put simply and briefly: *Torrance does not neglect ethics*. As expounded above, it is evident in Torrance's understanding of Christ's atoning and reconciling work. The vicarious character of the new humanity of Christ does not undermine human action but rather heals and establishes our fallen humanity for human personal response to God and others. Christ's new humanity *personalizes* and *validates* our dehumanized humanity as and when we *live* and *act* in union with Christ by the Holy Spirit. Through participating in the new humanity of Christ, "our moral selves and relations" before God and others are healed, and "our actions and motives as disciples of Christ" begin to function properly as the work of the personalizing person, the new humanity of Christ.[145]

Second, in terms of the imitation motif in Webster, it can be questioned how the imitation of Jesus can be achieved. For Torrance this is to be understood as part of a new life from reconciliation with God. As

---

145. Speidell, *Fully Human in Christ*, 8.

already elucidated, our moral actions and motives as disciples of Christ are actualized in union with Christ's new humanity, illustrating the fact that reconciliation with God inevitably transforms our morality and personal relations with God and our fellow humans. In this sense, for Torrance Christology and soteriology *do not neglect* or *ignore* the significance and implications of Christian anthropology and ethics but rather *uphold* and *undergird* the two, not in an autonomous moral philosophy but in the new humanity of Christ.

Third, in relation to Fergusson's argument that there is insufficient scope given to the wider social and political dimension of Christian ethics entailing social justice, human equality, and world peace in Torrance, it is clear that Torrance's articulation of and emphasis on the reconciling and personalizing work of Christ in his new humanity and its resultant ethics does not develop sufficiently ethical and social issues in wider realms as much as one might expect. Given that Torrance's Christology involves inherent anthropological and ethical concerns, this can be regarded as an area that he could develop from his theology. Nevertheless, what is not overlooked is that, as already expounded, Torrance focuses not on Christian ethics *itself*, but on Christ's reconciling and personalizing existence and work as the *foundational* and *structural* basis for Christian anthropology and ethics. This is a focus on *priority* in relation to our thinking about ethics.[146] Further, while his work is under-developed in some areas where it is not at its strongest (e.g., in Christian ethics), there are ways of improving upon this within the christological framework that he mapped out.[147]

---

146. In terms of the difference between Barth and Torrance in dealing with Christian ethics, Speidell cites McGrath's comment on Webster's two books *Barth's Ethics of Reconciliation* and *Barth's Moral Theology*, and McGrath's statement that "Barth addressed some issues on which Torrance has not chosen to focus in depth, such as the foundations and structure of Christian ethics." But Speidell uses McGrath's comment on Barth not as a proof of Webster's position but for the opposite, arguing that although Torrance unlike Barth has not directly addressed Christian ethics with specialized discussions in depth on ethics and dogmatics, Torrance's theology concerns itself with this exact foundational and structural issues: "Christian ethics are grounded in Christ's reconciling work, not in our own human morality." Thus for Speidell, Torrance's evangelical ethic is regarded as deeply grounded in God's grace in fundamental agreement with Barth which is contrary to Webster's overstated contrast between Torrance and Barth (Speidell, *Fully Human in Christ*, 4).

147. There are several theological ways to address this inadequacy. However, inasmuch as Calvin and Barth, who *like* Torrance regard the reconciling being and work of Christ as the key to Christian moral thought and life, but *unlike* Torrance address the

Despite the relative absence of wider ethical and social issues, alluded to but not fully expanded on, in Torrance, it is important to note that there are some ethical issues that Torrance explicitly spells out in his theology, that is, in relation to women in ministry, man-woman relations in marriage/divorce, abortion, and the priestly role of humanity in ecology. This reveals that his christological theology does recognize and provide significant practical and horizontal implications in which *Christocentrism* constitutes and engages with the content and structure of individual and social issues. This will be addressed in the following section in more detail.

New Humanity and Anthropological and Ethical Issues

As we have seen, for Torrance the new humanity of Christ is the ground for Christian anthropology and ethics. His new humanity transmutes our old humanity into new humanity. This ontological and inter-personal change in our humanity derives only from Christ himself, who alone enables us, as an integral part of his redemptive saving, to live out an ethical and moral life before God and among our fellow humans. This is the basis on which "when we encounter Jesus Christ, we have to do with the eternal and unchangeable Will of God embodied in him, and therefore with an enduring and permanent ethic."[148] In this sense, all kinds of Christian ethics are regarded as *resultant ethics* arising from the process realized by soteriological union with Christ.

Importantly, for Torrance, in our new humanity, healed, restored, and transformed by union with the new humanity of Christ, our thinking about ethics based on such rational, psychological, sociological, biological, and ecological understanding is also transformed. In this light, ethics is to be regarded as understood and treated on the basis of the reconciling and atoning work of Christ and its relevance to the creative work

---

wider ethical and socio-political dimension of Christian ethics and develop financial ethics and social ethics, that is, the issues of usury (Calvin) and social justice (Barth) *in their views of church/culture relations and church/state relations*; Calvin and Barth can thus be read as important examples of what Torrance could have paid attention to and developed for churches in the face of wide-ranging practical issues. We will consider this matter in more detail in the following chapter dealing with Torrance's expanded discussion of anthropology and ethics in his ecclesiology.

148. Torrance, *Christian Doctrine of Marriage*, 9.

of God and its purpose, that is, *redemption* and *creation*.¹⁴⁹ This view of ethics deeply engages with the following issues: women in ministry (gender egalitarianism), man-woman relations in marriage/divorce (sexual ethics), abortion (medical ethics), and the priestly role of humanity in creation and ecology (environmental ethics).

Gender Egalitarianism: Women in Ministry

Torrance addresses the issue of women in ministry on the twofold biblical and doctrinal basis: the creation of God and the redemptive and healing work of Christ. The two grounds underlie the evangelical understanding of gender egalitarianism particularly for women in the holy ministry. In the beginning God made woman and man as an image of God (Gen 1:27) and God made them in such a way that "what he has joined together may not be put asunder (Matt 19:4f; Mark 10:6f)."¹⁵⁰ This biblical statement for Torrance offers a theological and doctrinal reason why woman can be ordained and consecrated for the holy ministry. In creation, woman and man are put in full gender equality by virtue not only of their being the image of God but of the equal and mutual relationship between them. As woman as well as man was made in the image of God and they are in an equal partnership, for Torrance it is to be understood in such a way that both woman and man can be ordained to "the Holy Ministry of Word and Sacrament."¹⁵¹ Hence, any rejection or exclusion of the call and ordination of women to participate in the holy ministry of the gospel is regarded as involving "a quite offensive notion of womankind," which

---

149. The two doctrinal grounds of creation and redemption underlie not only all notions of man-woman or male-female relations and all the ethics they involve, but also the understanding of the unborn child in relation to medical ethics. See Torrance, *Christian Doctrine of Marriage*, 3–9; *Ministry of Women*, 4–8; *Soul and Person of the Unborn Child*, 8–19; *Being and Nature of the Unborn Child*, 4–10.

150. Torrance, *Ministry of Women*, 4–5.

151. Torrance, *Ministry of Women*, 12. According to Torrance, "in modern times it has been argued that only a man can represent Christ in the celebration of the Eucharist, for it is only a man who can be an *ikon* of Christ at the altar." In order to support this argument, some have used the Pauline statement that "man is the image and glory of God, but woman is the glory of man, for man was not made from woman but woman from man (1 Cor 11:7–8)." Yet Torrance rejects this argument, for it is in direct conflict with another Pauline statement that "in Christ Jesus there is neither male nor female (Gal 3:28)." For further detail on Torrance's rejection (arising from his interpretation of some biblical passages and church tradition) of any prominent position of man over woman, see also Torrance, *Ministry of Women*, 1–4.

is in conflict with the evangelical gender egalitarianism found in the creation of God.[152]

Furthermore, the redemptive and healing work of Christ also underlies gender egalitarianism. As Speidell points out, for Torrance the call and ordination of women for the holy ministry, are thoroughly rooted in "an evangelical egalitarianism that presupposes the radical change effected in Christ."[153] What then is the radical change in Christ and how does it engender the evangelical egalitarianism? It is obvious that for Torrance the radical change arises from the redemptive work of Christ. In Christ all divisive relations and gradations in human relationships are healed and overcome by his reconciling and healing work, and thus it is argued that "a radical change had come about with Christ."[154] In other words, in this radical change brought about from the redemptive work of Christ, all divisive and polarizing relations are healed and reconciled, so that our relationality is set upon the new and radical footing, that is, evangelical egalitarianism. As such, Torrance deals with the issue of women in ministry on this christological-soteriological basis of egalitarianism. As he puts it:

> In Christ there is no intrinsic reason or *theological* ground for the exclusion of women, any more than of Greeks or Gentiles, from the holy ministry, for the old divisions in the fallen world have been overcome in Christ and in his Body the Church. That applies to the division between male and female just as much as it does to the division between Jew and Gentile, or between slave and free.[155]

Here, Torrance derives the theological justification for gender equality in the ministry of the gospel from Gal 3:28. However, for him this is not confined only to the ecclesial dimension. The gender egalitarianism arising from the christological-soteriological perspective is expanded and applied to the wider ethical dimension also. Even though the theological

---

152. Torrance, *Ministry of Women*, 4. Interestingly, according to Jock Stein, this view of Torrance is not consistent with his early position in which he understood that "women have a diaconal, not a presbyterial, ministry in the Church." However, Torrance later realized that this approach was not going to be fruitful, and he supported the ordination of women to the ministry of word and sacrament (Stein, "Editor's Introduction," 14).

153. Speidell, *Fully Human in Christ*, 30.

154. Torrance, *Ministry of Women*, 4, 13.

155. Torrance, *Ministry of Women*, 4.

focus of Torrance at this point is about women in ministry, we should note that he rejects all sinful separation and gradation occurring in human relations. This view of Torrance seems to indicate much wider anthropological and ethical implications of significance in which any discriminative human relations would be rejected.[156]

It is necessary to expound the reason why there have been divisions between man and woman (not just over ordination). Torrance asserts that any divisive and distorted relations between man and woman derive from "the curse imposed upon them at the fall (Gen 3:16)."[157] Although woman as well as man made in the image of God, the result of the Fall is that there have been divisive relations between them. But the incarnation of Christ for Torrance means "the saving assumption of the whole human being, male and female" and "the healing of our complete human nature."[158] Through the incarnation, thus, the domination of man over woman that resulted from the Fall was overcome and rejected. As Torrance elucidates it:

> Thus any preeminence of the male sex or any vaunted superiority of man over woman was decisively set aside at the very inauguration of the new creation brought about by the incarnation. In Jesus Christ *the order of redemption* has intersected the order of creation and set it upon a new basis altogether. Henceforth *the full equality of man and woman* is a divine ordinance that applies to all the behaviour and activity of the new man [the new humanity] in Christ, and so to the entire life and mission of the Church as the Body of Christ in the world.[159]

In light of Christ's redemptive work, the gender egalitarianism (which was established in the beginning but broken and distorted due to the Fall) is set upon a new basis, the new humanity of Christ. In his

---

156. Torrance, *Ministry of Women*, 4.

157. Torrance, *Ministry of Women*, 5.

158. Torrance, *Ministry of Women*, 5. Here Torrance cited Barth in order to focus on "a judgment upon man" in the virgin birth of Jesus. In the virgin birth of Jesus, we find no "previous sexual union between man and woman." This explicitly implies "a judgment upon the sinful, not the natural, element in sexual life, but it is also to be understood as a judgement upon any claim that human nature has an innate capacity for God; human nature has no property in virtue of which man may act in the place of God." In this respect, for Torrance the incarnation is to be regarded as the saving assumption for all humanity by grace alone in which there is human action but no male or female domination.

159. Torrance, *Ministry of Women*, 5 (italics added).

new humanity all impersonal, divisive, and estranged human relations are healed and reconciled, so that the full equality of man and woman in this soteriological egalitarianism becomes a divine ordinance.

In this regard, for Torrance "there are no intrinsic theological reasons why women should not be ordained to the Holy Ministry of Word and Sacrament [in the church]; rather, there are genuine theological reasons why they may be ordained and consecrated in the service of the Gospel."[160] Thus it is argued that Torrance does reject any kinds of notion in which man has ontological superiority over woman, which is evident in his understanding of the ordination of women for the holy ministry based on evangelical egalitarianism.

Man-Woman Relations in Christian Marriage (Sexual Ethics)

For Torrance Christian marriage is grounded first on God's creative activity. Torrance understands the truth of marriage to be set forth in "the context of creation."[161] On this basis, Christian marriage has a far deeper foundation than a social contract, a human convention and a sex-relation. In Genesis God joins a man and a woman together to make them one flesh. It is God himself who leads the bride to the bridegroom, so that God gives them each other. Torrance argues that "that feature has been preserved through the centuries in Jewish marriages, where the family-friend has the duty of seeking out the bride for the bridegroom" which symbolizes "the act of God as we read of it in Genesis."[162]

This feature, Torrance goes on to say, is even found in today's Christian marriage ceremony where "the bride is given away by her father or guardian."[163] This also signifies the fact that it is God himself who brings the two together. Thus, for Torrance marriage is regarded as not just "a social contract or a human convention" but as "an act of God himself" inasmuch as "God is at work in it completing his creative act in making man and woman one flesh, and through them creating new life."[164]

160. Torrance, *Ministry of Women*, 5, 12.
161. Torrance, *Christian Doctrine of Marriage*, 3.
162. Torrance, *Christian Doctrine of Marriage*, 4.
163. Torrance, *Christian Doctrine of Marriage*, 4.
164. Torrance, *Christian Doctrine of Marriage*, 4. In this sense, for Torrance Christian marriage is regarded as "a divinely ordained partnership" in which woman is of equal humanity and dignity with man and *vice versa*. As already expounded, this view of Torrance is grounded in the gender egalitarianism arising from the evangelical understanding of man-woman relations.

Torrance states that the creative act of God joining a man and a woman together reflects "divine love and society" which mirrors "the image of divine Life in the human family."[165] In this understanding, Christian marriage is not simply the unity of the individual human being, man or woman, but the unity of their inter-personal being as man and woman. In marriage man and woman share in "their innermost being" and their union unfolds "the active will of their Creator," that is, inter-personal relationality, "not only with one another but with the Creator and Sustainer of their personal being."[166] Hence, the man-woman relation in marriage is far deeper and wider than the sex-relation, for the marriage-relation not only covers more than sex, but also entails the inter-personal structure of human being.[167]

Torrance also understands that Christian marriage occurs within "the context of reconciling and atoning work of God in Jesus Christ."[168] The basic unity between man and woman in marriage has been damaged and twisted since the Fall, but the unity is now re-established on the basis of its "new birth or recreation in Christ Jesus."[169] Union with Christ gives rise to the ontological restoration and reconciliation of separated and divided churches, homes, and man-woman relations. For Torrance it is particularly important and urgent today in the field of Christian marriage, for *without union with Christ* it is impossible for man and woman in marriage to enter inter-personal relationship to God and with one another.[170] The inter-personal relationship to God and with husband and wife in Christian marriage is God's original intention in the creation of man and woman and is reconstructed on the basis of the healing and reconciling work of Christ. This is the work of the new humanity of Christ healing and personalizing the self-centered and impersonal self in us. Through union with Christ, man and woman in Christian marriage

---

165. Torrance, *Christian Doctrine of Marriage*, 4.

166. Torrance, *Christian Doctrine of Marriage*, 5. Inter-personal relationality is not confined to the marriage-relation, for it does not derive simply as a natural corollary of marriage, but from the wider creative will and love of God. Thus, for Torrance unmarried people should not be understood as in any sense "second-class citizens," for "they too have a positive inter-personal role to play within the man-woman complementarity of human society" (Torrance, *Christian Doctrine of Marriage*, 5).

167. Torrance, *Christian Doctrine of Marriage*, 5.

168. Torrance, *Christian Doctrine of Marriage*, 9.

169. Torrance, *Christian Doctrine of Marriage*, 10.

170. Torrance, *Christian Doctrine of Marriage*, 5, 11, 15.

participate ontologically and dynamically in the Christian life, in which their unity is resorted to "its original ground and truth in the Creation" and then mirrors "the reality of the Love of God."[171]

In this respect for Torrance, the doctrinal grounds, the creative and redemptive work of God, are regarded as grounds of an *enduring* and *permanent* ethics in relation to man-woman relations.[172] On this basis, Torrance rejects a "situation ethics" in which Christian ethics is not "what you ought to do" regardless of "change in human culture and fashion," but "the attitude in which you do it that is held to be important."[173] Thus it has to be said that for Torrance the creative and redemptive work of God in Christ is not a just dogmatic exposition, but the unchangeable grammar and ground not simply for the issues above but for Christian ethics in general. As Torrance puts it:

> Take away this doctrinal basis, and at once all notions of marriage, of man-woman relations, all our ideas of sex, and all the ethics they involve, become merely relative. They are then only aspects of human evolution and change, only matters of social custom or psychological convenience; the pattern of life they involve is of man's own devising and can have only pragmatic justification. On this view we are not concerned in morality with relating human behaviour to permanent truth, for then "ethic" is only the expression of how society happens to function and order its life at the time.[174]

On this understanding, Torrance deals with issues such as monogamy, adultery, pre-marital sexual union, and divorce. Although there might be some reasonable opposition to polygamy, adultery, pre-marital sexual union, and divorce based on socio-psychological and biological grounds, for Torrance it is the creative and redemptive work of God which is the unchangeable and evangelical ground for all the ethics that man-woman relations involve.[175] Inasmuch as the deep inter-personal relation and

---

171. Torrance, *Christian Doctrine of Marriage*, 10, 15.

172. Torrance, *Christian Doctrine of Marriage*, 9.

173. Torrance, *Christian Doctrine of Marriage*, 8.

174. Torrance, *Christian Doctrine of Marriage*, 8.

175. In terms of the reason for monogamy, Torrance points out that monogamy belongs to "the inner form of human nature given it by God when he created man for fellowship with himself." In the beginning, God made man as God's child and human beings so as to have inter-personal relationship with God. The marriage of one man with only one woman reflects "the constitutive relation between God and man" which is inseparably associated with "the personal and social structure of human life" arising

communion with God and each other found in Christian marriage are found deeply damaged and destroyed in the above behaviors, they have to be rejected. In this regard, we can say that for Torrance recognition of the importance and value of the inter-personal relationship and fellowship rooted in the creative and redemptive work of God becomes pivotal to understanding all ethics involving man-woman relations.

Abortion (Medical Ethics)

In terms of abortion, Torrance begins with the understanding of the unborn child as a human being with body and soul and personal being. This is deeply rooted in the creative and personalizing work of God. In creating human being, as Torrance elucidates it, "God did not give being and life to the body by itself, or to the soul by itself, but to man/woman in whom body and soul form a living unity."[176] In this sense, the human being is an integrated existence, that is, "an embodied soul and a besouled body."[177] The human being as an integrated whole, as elucidated in chapter 1, is personal being, for human beings live together in personal

---

from and mirroring "the Life of God." For Torrance, this view is regarded as being enduring and permanent regardless of how our human reason and society make sense of and treat matter (Torrance, *Christian Doctrine of Marriage*, 5). It also sheds light on the reason why Torrance rejects adultery and pre-marital sexual union. In marriage, God joins man and woman together as one flesh where "God is at work fulfilling his creative purpose of love." This is a "divinely ordained unity" in inter-personal relationship with God and with each other. In this respect, for Torrance any sexual acts before and after marriage are sin rejecting and violating the unity of inter-personal being in marriage (6–7).

When it comes to divorce, Torrance applies the teaching of Jesus and elsewhere in the New Testament. But he disagrees that "when a marriage is arranged and takes place God is automatically and necessarily at work joining a man and a woman together." In this sense, Torrance insists that if a marriage is against the creative and redemptive will of God, this must fall under the judgement of God. In such a case, for Torrance "divorce becomes not only a possibility but an option." Here, Torrance emphasizes the role of the church in taking the greatest care for the possibility of divorce among church families, for Christian marriage and family play an essential role in "the Church's witness to Christ and in its proclamation of the Gospel to the world" (Torrance, *Christian Doctrine of Marriage*, 14–15).

176. Torrance, *Soul and Person of the Unborn Child*, 7–8.

177. Torrance, *Soul and Person of the Unborn Child*, 8. The expression, "an embodied soul and a besouled body," is one used by Barth in his *Church Dogmatics* (see, e.g., *CD* III/2:325, 327, 344, 350). It is cited by Torrance to expound his understanding of the unborn child as a unitary whole, not as soul *and* body and shows that Torrance shares the same anthropological understanding as Barth here.

life and inter-personal relations which reflect the inter-personal communion of the three divine persons.[178]

For Torrance this understanding of human being or the concept of person can be applied to the nature of the human embryo or foetus. Following St Gregory of Nyssa's argument, Torrance asserts that the human soul and body are created by God and grow together from *the moment of conception*.[179] This for him is regarded as being similar to modern scientific finding that "the human being is genetically complete in the embryo from the moment of conception."[180] In this sense, in spite of its incomplete state in itself, the human embryo has to be regarded as a human being, as already a physical or biological organism with "its consciousness, feeling, hearing, recognition and learning which makes abortion and foeticide as morally and utterly abhorrent as infanticide."[181]

Furthermore, for Torrance it is clear that human personal life and inter-personal relations begin with conception and are nourished through "inter-personal relations with the mother."[182] As he puts it:

> Certainly it is God himself who is the Creative Source of all personal being and inter-personal relations—he is the personalising Person, who brings us into personal life and being through the inter-personal activity of a father and mother, which begins with our conception, and blossoms within the inter-personal life and love of a human family.[183]

It draws our attention to the fact that the human person and even personhood begin with conception in inter-personal resonance with the mother. This is why Torrance rejects not only abortion but medical attempts to develop "artificial wombs" mechanizing the process of human birth, eliminating "the all-important inter-personal relation between the foetus and the mother" and "growth in the personal being of the unborn child."[184] Thus, for Torrance the creative and personalizing work of God penetrates medical ethics helping to inform what understanding of the human embryo should really involve.

---

178. See chapter 1, dealing with the concept of person.
179. Torrance, *Soul and Person of the Unborn Child*, 9.
180. Torrance, *Soul and Person of the Unborn Child*, 9.
181. Torrance, *Soul and Person of the Unborn Child*, 9.
182. Torrance, *Soul and Person of the Unborn Child*, 18.
183. Torrance, *Soul and Person of the Unborn Child*, 15.
184. Torrance, *Soul and Person of the Unborn Child*, 16.

Torrance also deals with the issue of abortion on a christological basis. In particular, the doctrine of the virgin birth of Jesus, as Torrance points out, plays a pivotal role in understanding not only "the redemptive life and mission of Christ," but also "the nature and status of the unborn child."[185] In the womb of the Virgin Mary, as Christ became a human being for our redemption, he also became an embryo for the sake of all embryos. In this soteriological sense, Torrance relates the importance of the holy embryo of Christ to the understanding of all our human embryos. Thus, for Torrance it is a Christian way of thinking that every unborn child has been brothered by the Lord Jesus, which provides us with a "Christian understanding of the being, nature and status in God's eyes of the unborn child in his/her body and soul."[186]

The understanding of the unborn child above provides two implications, not only of theological but also of medical significance. On the one hand, it enables us to have a deeper and more complete understanding of the human foetus as an embryonic human being and personal being; on the other hand, it enables us to take into account the fact that the embryo is "rather more than the sum of its constituent genetically analysable parts, an all-important factor in its wholeness."[187] This is fully grounded in the understanding of the creative, personalizing, and redemptive work of God, which for Torrance becomes not only the reason why he does reject abortion, but also a richer and deeper theological and medical pole of understanding "when we learn from our medical scientists, gynaecologists and physicians about what they tell us of the life and experience of the human foetus."[188]

The Priestly Role of Man in Creation and Ecology (Environmental Ethics)

Although Torrance in his theology does not directly address the theme of environmental ethics with any wide-ranging ecological issues and discussion, we do find a clue to a theological ecology indicated by him in his understanding that humanity has "a special place in the creation" by virtue of a "priestly role" to reveal the intrinsic intelligibility of the

---

185. Torrance, *Being and Nature of the Unborn Child*, 6.
186. Torrance, *Being and Nature of the Unborn Child*, 6.
187. Torrance, *Soul and Person of the Unborn Child*, 10.
188. Torrance, *Being and Nature of the Unborn Child*, 7.

universe and transmute disorder in the creation into the God-given order in which the cosmos came into being.[189]

In Torrance's thought there are two reasons why human beings have a unique place in the creation. First, it is only human beings who enable the natural world to unfold its rational order and intelligibility in their orderly articulation of it.[190] This role of human beings is particularly achieved through their scientific investigations into and interaction with the universe, through which human beings can articulate more fully the contingent beauty, order, and rationality in the universe.[191] The contingency and orderliness in the world enable us to understand the universe as the universe which God "freely created out of nothing, yet not without reason" and sustains in its created rationality and order which is dependent on "his uncreated transcendent reality."[192] In this God-world relation, the world finds its proper end of unfolding the glory of God, the Creator. In this regard, human scientific interaction with the universe becomes a "religious duty" in order to perceive and recognize the order in the universe as a consequence of God's creative act.[193]

Moreover, only human beings who lie on the boundary of visible and invisible reality can mediate divine order to the contingent order, thereby restoring the damaged order or the disorder which arises in the

---

189. Torrance, *Divine and Contingent Order*, 128–41.

190. Torrance, *Ground and Grammar of Theology*, 5–6.

191. Torrance, "Divine and Contingent Order," 84–85. Torrance argues that although nature's order and beauty are articulated through human scientific interaction with the natural world, human beings can act rationally *only under* "the compulsion of reality and its intrinsic order" (Torrance, *Reality and Evangelical Theology*, 26). As elucidated in chapter 3 of this book, this view is rooted in his understanding of critical realism where reality that is beyond our cognition discloses *itself* to us. In terms of a critical realist ontology/epistemology, see "Ontological and Epistemological Significance of the Humanity of Christ for Knowledge of God" in chapter 3. Further, for Torrance the order and intelligibility of the world is not immanent which is evident in ancient Greek and Roman natural law and Newtonian universe, but contingent which is found in the doctrine of creation (*ex nihilo*) and the a posteriori characteristic of theological and scientific knowledge. In the light of this, we need to understand that in Torrance's thought the pursuit of natural science is one of the ways in which human beings function as not creators but "bearers" or "interpreters" of the contingent order of the universe, leading the created world into its praise and glorification of God (Torrance, *Ground and Grammar of Theology*, 5; *Reality and Evangelical Theology*, 26).

192. Torrance, "Divine and Contingent Order," 84.

193. Torrance, *Ground and Grammar of Theology*, 5–6.

natural world.[194] The first role of human beings is achieved through human scientific activities, while this second role is actualized when human beings are healed of their own inward schizoid condition and disorder in relation to God and with nature, thereby exercising "a truly integrative and re-ordering role in the world" around them.[195] This is the human "redemptive role" of restoring the natural world in such a way that ecological chaos and the disorderly state of affairs in nature (which have been caused by human disrespectful and greedy exploitation of nature) are remedied by redeemed humanity.[196] In this light, the incarnation and its re-ordering power play a decisive role in our understanding of how the disorder and disharmony in humanity and the created world are healed and renewed, bringing about a new or redemptive order in God/ourselves/world relations.[197] Thus, for Torrance it is clear that the salvific ministry of Christ is not confined to individual redemption alone but extended to the cosmic dimension, in which redeemed persons effect a redemptive order in the natural world.

For Torrance, the uniqueness of humanity is rooted in their human priestly and redemptive role in the creation which is a participation in God's own redeeming ministry in the world. Although Torrance deals with ecological concerns under "the theme of order" in the creation, he offers theological principles and approaches which are relevant to environmental ethics.

In the understanding of human beings as priests of creation, it becomes a human vocation to respect and serve the natural world. In this light, the world is not regarded as a world for human beings to govern and

194. Torrance, *Christian Frame of Mind*, 62.

195. Torrance, *Divine and Contingent Order*, 138.

196. Torrance, *Divine and Contingent Order*, 130–33. Torrance points out that "when man himself is seized of evil, and his interaction with the Creator is damaged and disordered, his interaction with nature becomes damaged and disordered as well," an understanding which is evident in "the field of biology" and the so-called "technological society" where human beings have not respected but imposed upon nature, converting order and harmony into disorder and disharmony (Torrance, *Divine and Contingent Order*, 130–31). See also Torrance, *Ground and Grammar of Theology*, 9. But as elucidated it is as human beings themselves are redeemed that the reconciled or renewed order in humanity can flow into the world which has been so infected by the disorder of humanity. As a result, human scientific actions would then no longer abuse the natural order for human sake, but rather help to articulate "the forms of order and beauty of which it [the world] would not be capable otherwise" (Torrance, *Divine and Contingent Order*, 130).

197. Torrance, *Christian Frame of Mind*, 62–63.

control for their own sake, but rather as a world for them to lead into its purpose of expressing the glory of God. The election of humanity, thus, requires a responsible stewardship which rejects the exploitative and authoritative characteristics of the human position in relation to the rest of creation.[198] This militates against any notion that the Christian dogma of creation is the direct cause of ecological crisis in virtue of any intrinsic anthropocentrism that legitimizes human exploitation of nature.[199]

Moreover, inasmuch as in the cosmic dimension of redemption, human beings and the natural world are both placed under the soteriological category, it is clearly shown that God's redemptive purpose lies in both humanity and the world. In this regard, the world is to be conceived not mechanistically but soteriologically and as a contingent world, an understanding which sheds light on the fact that humanity and the created world are in a community in which the world is recognized as being under God's salvific grace and in intimate relation with God and humanity.[200]

However, when Torrance focuses on the election of humanity as priests in the creation, he has a tendency to pay little attention to other lifeforms' own role and purpose without regard to larger ecological sensibilities. The tendency might suggest an inherent *anthropocentrism* that results in ecological anxiety. It would then be of little surprise if in Torrance's thought deep consideration of non-human organisms and their

---

198. Here we need to understand the fact that human dominion over the rest of creation is indeed depicted in Genesis 1, but that for Torrance the human dominion is not linked to human exploitation of the natural world for their sake but rather to be understood in the light of stewardship. In somewhat similar vein, Bauckham argues that Genesis 1 does not offer a biblical ground for the human scientific-technological project of unlimited dominion of the world, for in Genesis 1 human use of the earth is limited to its vegetation and human dominion over other creatures refers to human responsibility of care for them (Bauckham, *Bible in the Contemporary World*, 89–90).

199. It is evident, in White's argument, that by interpreting human beings as beings who have dominion over the rest of creation, the Christian dogma of creation has justified human exploitation of nature and created a dualism of humanity and nature in which the human monopoly on the rest of creation is reinforced and confirmed (White, "Historical Roots of Our Ecological Crisis," 1205–7). See also Nash, *Rights of Nature*, 88–97.

200. Similarly, Sittler argues that Christianity speaks of a continuity of the relationship between God, nature, and human beings which is understood within the proclamation of cosmic redemption. According to Sittler therefore, it is difficult to find a dualistic relation between humankind and nature in Christian tradition (Sittler, "Theology for Earth," 367–74).

symbiotic relations with us in nature was not highlighted, which might undermine ecological practice.

The reason for the tendency could be traced to Torrance's theological ontology in which, as elucidated, humanity has a unique place both in the divine-human relation and the human-nature relation. It is clear that by addressing, unlike Barth, the contingent order in the world in a theological and scientific manner, Torrance was able to speak much of the world itself in any God/ourselves/world interrelations and bring the world to a central place in theology. Nevertheless, it is true that in his soteriological understanding of the relations, humanity has autonomy in an active and dynamic role, while the natural world has heteronomy in a passive and static role. In this, discussions of other lifeforms' own role/purpose, relation to God, and dignity around us tend to be downplayed.[201]

In this respect, some might advocate Fox's argument for a *creation-centered spirituality* should have primacy over a fall/redemption theology, for the former enables us to view the world not as a world of original sin, but a world of original blessing.[202] The shift focuses our attention on the original goodness of creation and "one divine energy" and "word" flowing through the natural world, which generates a theological focus on the sacredness of nature or a sacramental cosmology, that is, a recognition of the world that is good, active, dynamic, and full of the divine presence.[203]

The panentheistic view of the world is also found in process thought and feminist theology where we are required to see the natural world through a panentheistic lens that emphasizes the world's sanctity and its interrelatedness with the divine in virtue of the divine immanence and

---

201. Torrance laments Barth's limited account of the created order about human beings, without sufficient focus on the cosmos itself (Torrance, *Karl Barth*, 132). Although Torrance deals with the theme of order both in humanity and the world, it cannot be denied that he, like Barth, seems to show an inadequate theological focus on non-human organisms. For an understanding of Barth's anthropocentrism in his doctrine of creation and its ecological deficit, see Fergusson, "Karl Barth's Doctrine of Creation," 414–31. Here Fergusson points out that when the election of the human is emphasized in Barth's theology of creation, "a double location of our humanity both in the life of God and in the created world" is generated and thus the natural world might be regarded as "an instrumental function in the human-focused drama of the covenant history." In this regard according to Fergusson, "Barth's theological ontology suffers at times from an inherent anthropocentric leaning with its attendant ecological deficit" (Fergusson, "Karl Barth's Doctrine of Creation," 430).

202. Fox, *Original Blessing*, 44–56, 69.

203. Fox, *Original Blessing*, 38–39.

indwelling in all creation.²⁰⁴ In this view it is understood that all lifeforms are in, and of, and have their distinct relation with, the divine presence, an understanding which creates a shift from an anthropocentrism to an *ecocentrism* that unpacks the intrinsic value and purpose of *all lifeforms* in the cosmos, thereby stressing a mutual web of horizontal relations between human and other organisms in nature.²⁰⁵

However, as Barth argues, panentheism and pantheism do not distinguish God and the world so definitely that God's freedom or absoluteness is threatened.²⁰⁶ In a similar vein, but with ecological concerns, Gunton critiques the undetachable character of God from the world in panentheism in which, on the one hand, the autonomy of God's action is not preserved, and, on the other hand, the creaturely world is endangered because "it is too easily swallowed up into the being of God, and so deprived of its own proper existence."²⁰⁷ The emphasis on God's otherness and transcendence is therefore crucial to the integrity and freedom of creation and in this regard the distinction between creator and creation should be reaffirmed and not belittled.²⁰⁸

204. According to Cobb who derives his process theology from Whitehead's process philosophy, God must be understood as a God who is interrelated to all creation on account of his indwelling the natural world (something on which theism does not adequately focus) without becoming the sum of all parts of the cosmos (a point which pantheism fails to make clear) (Cobb, *God and the World*, 19–41). Although the panentheistic view in process thought has several directions, e.g., the relation between God and the world and the problem of evil, one of the directions is towards ecology. This might help us to have wider ecological sensibilities because of the emphasis on the divine presence and immanence in the natural world in which a God is interrelated not only to humanity but to non-human materials and organisms. For the wide-ranging directions of process theology, see Cobb and Griffin, *Process Theology*, vii–xvii, 1–158.

205. As a feminist theologian McFague insists that the fact that the natural world as "the body of God" is in, and of God, shows an *organic* system of God-nature relations and brings about a harmony between human and non-human lifeforms in nature (McFague, *New Climate for Theology*, 112–15).

206. Barth, *CD* 2/1:312. Despite a panentheistic focus on the togetherness of God's transcendence and immanence in relation to the world, panentheism fails to ensure divine transcendence and thus it cannot be distinguished from pantheism (Gunton, *Triune Creator*, 142). In this respect, for Barth, as Molnar expounds, pantheism and panentheism mix God with something else, either idealistically or materialistically, and lead either to materialism or to spiritualism (Molnar, *Divine Freedom and the Doctrine*, 282).

207. Gunton, *Triune Creator*, 66. See also Gunton, *Christ and Creation*, 91.

208. Macmurray's personalist thought can be useful in understanding this matter in greater depth. According to Macmurray, the nexus of relations that unites us in society is not *organic* or mechanical, but *personal*, in such a way that "the person

Importantly, in Torrance's thought, God's otherness and transcendence are entirely consistent with God's dynamic and personal involvement and presence in all creation, which is evident in the concept of incarnation. For Torrance, as Purves states, "God, the creator of space, stands in a non-spatial relation to creation, yet God has entered into space in such a way that all his relations with us occur within spatial (and temporal) reality."[209] At this point divine transcendence refers to God's historicity and humanness, that is, the ontological possibility of an interrelationship between God, humanity, and the world. As such, Torrance's incarnational theology fully unfolds divine transcendence and togetherness in personal interaction with all creation.

Nevertheless, it is clear that Torrance's theological principles of the natural world could benefit from a deeper set of ecological perceptions in a broader and more nuanced ecotheology. Despite Torrance's holistic and relational anthropology, this implication was not developed into a wider ecological dialogue; it needs to be complemented in order to create a profounder theological ecology. This draws our attention to Habets's critique that by elucidating the human priestly role simply in connection with natural science, Torrance confines human vocation in creation to human scientific activities without engaging adequately in wider realms.[210] Habets's critique alleges a limited direction and undeveloped theological perception in Torrance of other realms with respect to the discussion about the priestly role of humanity, e.g., in ecology.

But given that the ecological implications which Torrance's theology unpacks are discussed under "the theme of order," we can understand that his interest resides primarily not in ecology but in the contingency and orderliness in the world and the human priestly or reordering role in creation. In this regard, McGrath states that, although Torrance did not develop some ideas to the extent that one might like to show their ethical and ecological implications, his exposition of the priestly role of human beings is "sufficient to indicate the theological importance of the theme

---

interacts with other persons in relations that ought to be marked by freedom, love and friendship." In such a personalist category of thought, it can be understood that divine transcendence and its significance for the integrity and freedom of creation become prerequisite for the *personal* relationship between God and the world and therefore an organic or pantheist unity of God and the world that precludes the ascription of personal terms to that relation must be rejected. See Macmurray, *Persons in Relation*, 46–47; Fergusson, "Persons in Relation," 291–92, 304.

209. Purves, "Christology of Thomas F. Torrance," 56.

210. Habets, *Theosis in the Theology of Thomas Torrance*, 46.

of order, which can be seen to link together creation and redemption, incarnation and atonement."[211] Thus Torrance's ecological deficit, particularly the tendency to show an indifference to other lifeforms, should not be regarded as his personal or theological indifference as such to ecology itself but as the fact that his intention was to develop the theme of order.

Furthermore, although Torrance's anthropocentrism with respect to the human-world relation in his soteriology does not directly address the themes of other lifeforms' own purpose, dignity, and relation to God, the focus on responsible human stewardship and their mediatorial role in creation can serve the natural world by leading us to protect and care for all creation.[212] Hence it cannot be said that Torrance does not in principle provide us with proper theological insights for ecological praxis.

Conclusion

This chapter has explored Torrance's concept of the humanity of Christ and its attendant practicality and anthropological/ethical implications. We have found that the epistemic, ontological, and soteriological significance of the humanity of Christ is not confined to the divine-human vertical relation but extended to the horizontal relations. In terms of its practical significance in particular, Torrance presents the concept of vicarious and new humanity of Christ as the ontological foundation for the transformation of the human person necessary for personal human relations and ethical practice. This can be regarded as a Christocentric view of anthropology and ethics, focusing on the locus from which the Christian anthropological and ethical category of thought has to arise.

We have also addressed the following criticisms: (1) Torrance's theology does not fully address and develop the ways in which biblical moral principles and values are interpreted and applied to our religiously plural society, (2) the undue emphasis on the all-important role of Christ's

---

211. McGrath, *Thomas F. Torrance*, 227-28. Inasmuch as for Torrance human priestly ministry may be confined to, but involves both unfolding the contingent order in creation and bringing a new and redemptive order into the world, human scientific interaction with the natural world does become a proper example of how human beings as priests of creation can help both to express and to redemptively reshape the world's contingent order.

212. In terms of the human responsibility for ecological practice and its protective effect on nature, Ruether's remark is notable that "like it or not, if the diverse biota of earth are to be protected and preserved, it will only be by the human community asserting an enlightened guardianship over it" (Ruether, *Gaia and God*, 222).

vicarious humanity for us fosters the inactivity of human response, and (3) in a similar vein to the first critique, Torrance's doxologically focused theology leads to insufficient participation in the wider ethical, social, and political issues of Christian ethics, so that the practical and horizontal significance is downplayed.

Yet in response to such critiques, the personalizing character of the vicarious and new humanity of Christ clearly shows that the vicarious character of his new humanity does not undermine human action but rather upholds and undergirds it in relation to God and others. In addition, despite the relative absence of wider issues relating to social justice, human equality, and world peace, the inherent anthropological and ethical implications in Torrance's Christology and some of the ethical issues that he spells out reveal that Torrance does recognize and offer not only work of vertical and doxological significance, but also that of practical and horizontal significance.

Nevertheless, although Torrance provides the foundational and structural basis for our thinking about ethics and practical implications, his theological approach to anthropology and ethics requires greater ethical dialogue and engagement in wider social and political realms. We need to show how a Christocentric anthropology and ethics can generate wide-ranging practical implications for human social, cultural, and political existence. In this respect, as elucidated, Fergusson's suggestion of the royal Psalms, Jesus's teaching of the kingdom, and recent ethical and political theologies can be useful for expanding the scope and depth of ethical applications in Torrance. Further, as we will see in the following chapter, Calvin on usury and Barth on social justice can be read as providing an important complement to the inadequacy noted above. This theological task, continued in Torrancian mode, can in turn prevent a naïve independent ethicism and help to maintain an appropriate balance between theology and ethics.

It is important that the anthropological and ethical implications of Torrance's theology are not found only in Christology, for Torrance also develops his practical and ethical interests in the sphere of ecclesiology. Further, for Torrance it is the sacramental and diaconal action of the church which has a key place in the personal and relational outworking of Christ's new humanity. This shows how the ongoing life-transforming ministry of Christ and its resultant Christian moral, ethical, and social life are realized in and through the church, a topic which will be addressed in the following chapter.

4

The Sacramental and Diaconal Action of the Church

The Personal and Relational Outworking of Christ's New Humanity

Introduction

THROUGH THE PREVIOUS CHAPTERS we have seen that for Torrance Christology is the precise point from which Christian anthropology and ethics occur and derive their impetus.[1] Importantly, for Torrance it is not only Christology, but also ecclesiology where union with the new humanity of Christ and its resulting practical significance are unpacked. In the Word and the sacraments, the *participatio Christi* through the Spirit enables the church to share in his new humanity and become the new creation.[2] As a christological reality or the body *of* Christ, the church then lives out its reconciled and diaconal life on earth, thereby unfolding its practicality in and for the world.

---

1. In particular, the concepts of the vicarious and new humanity of Christ have revealed that the reconciliation between God and humanity embodied in the vicarious life of Christ created a new humanity for us, and in union with his new humanity through the Spirit the dehumanization in the depth of human being is restored and transformed, by which "a new moral life and order" is set up, along with "a transformation of social relations" (Torrance, "Singularity of Christ," 251–52; *Mediation of Christ*, 72). As already elucidated, this kind of view offers not only a corrective to the social model of the Trinity, but also the theological foundation for ethical praxis in Torrance's theology.

2. Torrance, *School of Faith*, cxxi.

Such a focus on the church's *participatio Christi* sheds light on "where" its being and life derive from and "what" determines its practicality. As such, for Torrance the new humanity of Christ and union with him are the ontological foundation and dynamic for ecclesial life and praxis. Accordingly, for him the church is regarded as the personal and relational outworking of the new humanity of Christ.[3]

However, with regard to the christological emphasis in Torrance's ecclesiology, it can be questioned whether or not (1) the church's ontological encounter with Christ creates its life and praxis in the specific social context and (2) his ecclesiology, heavily conditioned by Christology, can offer a properly theological understanding of the church's identity and practical life to contemporary churches.

The former reflects Habets's critique that when Torrance's main focus lies on *theosis* (deification or adoption) in the incarnate Son and how this may be so in the life of the church, he ultimately fails to develop horizontal applications.[4] This kind of critique requires us to test and assess in detail whether Torrance's focus on the inward relationship between the church and Christ precludes developing outward considerations. The latter is related to the differentiated approach to the church and its practicality between Torrance's ecclesiology and the trinitarian ecclesiology of social trinitarianism. While for Torrance Christ's vicarious and new humanity and the church's participation in him are the determining factors of the being, life, and mission of the church, for social trinitarians it is the Trinity *per se*, or the trinitarian relations and attributes in the economy, which underlie ecclesial being, life, and practices.[5] This difference draws

---

3. Torrance, *School of Faith*, cxx–cxxi. See also Torrance, *Atonement*, 354–55. As Walker argues, the doctrines of the incarnation and atonement in Torrance's theology are seen to have "far reaching implications in its outworking and shaping of the life and worship, doctrine and mission of the church" (Walker, "Editor's Introduction," lx). Thus, for Torrance ecclesiology is not independent but *constituted by Christology*, in which the nature, life and mission of the church are deeply rooted.

4. Habets, *Theosis in the Theology of Thomas Torrance*, 186–89, 196.

5. Although there are different focuses on the church's role and function among social trinitarians, for them the church is generally regarded as an earthly anticipation or image of the Trinity, reflecting the trinitarian life in its non-hierarchical and inclusive structure, order, and relationship, shedding light on what human life and society should be. For instance, Zizioulas understands the church as "the image of the Triune God," reflected in the world God being as communion or *koinonia* (Zizioulas, *Being as Communion*, 15, 19, 134–35). Moltmann derives the church's social and political life and practice from the trinitarian love and relationship exemplified in the life and death of Jesus and, in this light, for him the church is regarded as a messianic fellowship

our attention to the ways in which Torrance can provide a clearer and better theological understanding and methodology of the church and its praxis in comparison to the ecclesiology envisioned by social trinitarians.

With the above questions in mind, this chapter will first address Torrance's view of the church as the personal and relational outworking of Christ's new humanity. It will then deal with the sacramental and diaconal action of the church, through which the church participates in his new humanity and works as a reconciling community. This elucidation will indicate how the church's *participatio Christi* engenders its evangelical, ethical, and social life. Lastly, Torrance's Christocentric ecclesiology and its practical significance will be suggested as a corrective to the ecclesiology of social trinitarianism.

Through this ecclesial exploration, it will be argued that for Torrance it is the new humanity of Christ and the church's *participatio Christi* that plays a determining role in the being and life of the church. With regard to the practicality of the church, this means that the church's ethical life and practice result from its ontological encounter with Christ, whose ongoing humanizing activity and the transforming impact of this on our being, relations, and social structure continue in and through his body. This is excluded in social trinitarianism in terms of the creative and directive source of the church's practical life; thus, Torrance's ecclesiology can be an important corrective to these recent trends. Nevertheless, when Torrance does not develop clear theological principles for the social life of the church in a specific context, more detailed language, expression, and direction are required for the horizontal applications.

The Church as the Outworking of the New Humanity of Christ

In Torrance's thought, the church is not merely a human community formed by the voluntary association of like-minded people and existing

---

(Moltmann, *Church in the Power of the Spirit*, 64–65). However, when "the trinitarian *koinonia* and *perichoresis*" and "the fellowship and self-giving love of the Trinity exemplified in Jesus's life and death" are used in social trinitarianism for ecclesial vision, the same problem, that is, "Christological deficiency," which was discussed in chapter 2, occurs again in social trinitarians' ecclesiology. In this context, some previous and new critiques (particularly those posed by Tanner) of the insufficient Christological reasoning in social trinitarianism will be presented to support Torrance's Christocentric ecclesiology that offers a more properly theological understanding of the church's being, life, and practice.

by and for itself.⁶ The church is fundamentally rooted in God's trinitarian being and life where God has not willed his living alone, and has created others for intimate fellowship with himself, pouring out his Spirit and sharing his life and glory with them as the triune God.⁷

As a divine creation the church came into being in the divine economy. Torrance argues that the church did not take shape automatically with creation, nor all at once in the course of human history, but rather it emerged in space and time "as God called and entered into communion with his people and in and through them embodied and worked out by mighty acts of grace his purpose of love which he brought at last to its fulfilment in Jesus Christ."⁸ As such, the church is of divine origin and exists as the supreme object of divine grace, which is the mystery and destiny of the church hidden from the foundation of the world.⁹

Despite the oneness of the church throughout all ages, Torrance sees three stages or phases of the life of the church in its ontological relation to Christ: a preparatory form before the incarnation, a new form in Jesus Christ, and a final and eternal form when Christ returns at the end of time.[10]

The *preparatory* form of the church refers to "the divine election of Israel" as the chosen people of God under the economy of the old

6. Torrance, *Trinitarian Faith*, 277.
7. Torrance, *Theology in Reconstruction*, 192.
8. Torrance, *Theology in Reconstruction*, 192–93.
9. Torrance, *Theology in Reconstruction*, 192–93.

10. Torrance, *Atonement*, 342. Torrance states that the oneness of the church means that the church, which entails an infinite multitude of people in history and comprises diversity, is essentially one in Jesus Christ, the only one mediator between humanity and God, who reconciles and gathers together all things in himself. This oneness, together with holiness, catholicity, and apostolicity, is one of the marks of the church, which, together with the word of God purely preached, the sacraments of the gospel rightly administered, and godly discipline, indicates where the true church is to be found (Torrance, *Atonement*, 380–81). Although Torrance unfolds significant implications in terms of the marks of the church, e.g., Christological understanding of the unity of the divided church, the sanctification of the church in the world, and the universal mission of redemption reaching out to incorporate humankind, this chapter will not address the marks themselves, i.e., the meanings of the marks. Since the key focus of the chapter is to examine Torrance's understanding of the nature of the church as the outworking of the new humanity of Christ and its practicality in relation to the world, we will concentrate on such themes as the incarnation, the atonement, the Holy Spirit, and the sacramental and diaconal action of the church, in which he unpacks his own ecclesiology more in death. For further understanding of the marks of the church in Torrance's thought, see Torrance, *Trinitarian Faith*, 279–288; *Atonement*, 380–400.

covenant. The revelation, interaction, and reconciliation of God were given to the existence and life of Israel in order to fashion the chosen people as "the bearer of the Messiah," the mediation of God's final self-revelation, communication, and reconciliation to all people in the midst of humanity.[11]

The church was given a *new* form in Jesus Christ. This means that in Christ, who gathered up, fulfilled, and transformed the one people of God in himself, and poured out his Spirit upon broken and divided humanity through his atoning birth, life, death, resurrection, and ascension, all humanity might be reconciled to God and to one another, participating in the trinitarian life and love as "the new undivided race."[12] However, the

11. Torrance, *Theology in Reconstruction*, 195–97. Torrance traces the church back to Adam, where we can see communion between God and that which was formed by him. Although in Adam the church fell through disobedience and its immediate relationship with God was broken by sin and guilt, "it fell not as a divine institution but in its constituent members, and therefore the Church upheld by the eternal will of God took on at once a new form under his saving acts in history." It is when God called Abraham that the church began to be brought into definite form as the appointed sphere of God's redemptive activity, through which all people and all creatures would be blessed (Torrance, *Theology in Reconstruction*, 193–94). In this sense, for Torrance "election" is not an exclusive term presupposing the few who are chosen and the many that are lost, which is evident in conservative Calvinism, but an inclusive one, because God called Israel for the fulfilment of his redemption, including the whole race, which was finally fulfilled in the gospel with the actual coming of the Son of God in the flesh and the physical reality of Christ's saving passion of the cross (Torrance, *Divine Meaning*, 85–87). Thus, in Torrance's soteriological concept of election, Israel is understood to be related to the church in view of Christology, an understanding that unpacks soteriological, christological, and ecclesiological aspects of the election of Israel. For further understanding of the election of Israel and a discussion about universalism, see Torrance, "Universalism or Election?" 310–18; Habets, "Doctrine of Election in Evangelical Calvinism," 334–54.

12. Torrance, *Atonement*, 342. In order to properly understand the above reference, it is necessary to provide more detail. From the start of his ministry, Jesus proclaimed the Kingdom of God, exhorted people to repent and believe in the gospel and called them to himself "in his mission to gather and redeem the people of God." With his advent and presence, the Kingdom of God had arrived and was active among people for their salvation, which was the entire historical-redemptive act of God in Israel, but also his universal fulfilment that transcended the boundaries of Israel. In this regard, Torrance sees the Kingdom of God and the people of God as inter-related concepts in the matrix of Israel. Through Christ the Christian church is grafted onto the trunk of Israel so that the members of the church are of the race of Abraham. We cannot therefore imagine that God has cast off his chosen people or that the promises made to Israel as a people of divine election and institution have only a spiritualized fulfilment. In the resurrected body of Christ, together with the Gentiles, Israel shares its riches and forms the one people of God (Torrance, *Atonement*, 348–49).

church will only take on its *final* and *eternal* form when Christ returns to judge and renew his creation. Then, the church that now lives in a condition of humiliation and in the ambiguity of history will be manifested as a new creation, eternally sharing in the trinitarian life.[13]

What is crucial here is that the church is a divine creation in the historical drama of revelation and reconciliation: "(1) stretching back in history to the calling of Abraham and the covenant relation with Israel; (2) continuing through the incarnation, vicarious life, death and resurrection of Christ, to the outpouring of the Spirit of the Father and the Son at Pentecost; and (3) pressing forward to Christ's return and the consummation of all things in Christ."[14] As such, for Torrance Christology plays a decisive role in the being, life, and mission of the church.

On this grounds, Torrance insists that despite the important names and images that refer to the church in the scriptures, the term "the body of Christ" is the most significant, for it is "the most deeply Christological of them all."[15] Thus, "the body *of* Christ" can best describe the relationship between the church and Christ and it focuses not on the body, but on Christ *himself* who is the essence of the church.[16] As the church is called the body of Christ, it is not regarded as a sociological or anthropological magnitude, nor as an institution or a process, but as "the immediate

---

This is the context in which Jesus Christ and his messianic community come into view in the scriptures. Jesus called his disciples and formed the messianic community so as to restore the people of God and build God's kingdom in their midst. This messianic office was fulfilled in the historical ministry of Jesus, such as his preaching that the kingdom was summoning everyone to repentance, his seeking and saving the lost, healing the sick, and forgiving sins, which are regarded by Torrance as an integral part of the atoning reconciliation of Jesus Christ through his vicarious humanity. Jesus chose the twelve disciples as the inner nucleus of the new Israel to participate in his ministry, and at the Last Supper Jesus inaugurated the new covenant in his body and blood and they were incorporated into a royal priesthood. Then came the crucifixion, the scattering of the disciples, the fulfilment of the old covenant, and the rebirth of the church in union with the risen Jesus through the Spirit (Torrance, *Atonement*, 350).

13. Torrance, *Theology in Reconstruction*, 193.
14. Colyer, *How to Read T. F. Torrance*, 250.
15. Torrance, "What Is the Church?" 6.
16. Torrance states that the definition of the church as the body of Christ is evident in Pauline, Irenaeusian, and Athanasian lines of thought. Although the church's self-understanding in the early centuries was not grounded in a definite ecclesiology, the church recognized itself as the body of Christ, feeling itself to be entirely subordinate to "the living Word and Truth of the Lord Jesus Christ who with his Spirit dwells in the Church thereby making it a servant of his mission and kingdom" (Torrance, *Trinitarian Faith*, 252–68).

property of Christ which he made his very own and gathered into the most intimate relation with himself."[17] Therefore, the church as the body *of* Christ is not a figurative but an onto-relational reality participating in Christ, which is one of grace and adoption embodied in and through the incarnation and his vicarious life.[18]

In this regard, for Torrance it is the *incarnation, atonement,* and *the Holy Spirit* in which we can best understand the constitution of the church as the body *of* Christ and its life and mission. The incarnation is the place where the union and communion between God and humanity were realized in Jesus Christ who "embodied himself in our humanity and as such gathers our humanity in himself into oneness with God."[19] This affects our adoption as children of God and participation in the trinitarian communion and life.[20] Hence, the incarnation becomes the *starting point* where we must recognize that the church or the rebirth of the church began in and with the incarnate Son, the Word made flesh. As Torrance describes it:

> He [the incarnate son of God] identified Himself with us, made Himself one with us, and on that ground claims us as His own, lays hold of us, and assumes us into union and communion with Him, so that as Church we find our essential being and life not in ourselves but in Him alone.[21]

While the incarnation is the starting point for the internal and ontological relationship between the church and Christ, for Torrance atonement is the *precise point* where "the union between God and humanity in Christ in which the church is rooted could only be consummated through the expiation of sin and the removal of enmity."[22]

This does not mean that as an external element atonement should be added to the union in order to complete it, for atonement is "the culmination of God's incarnational penetration into the alienated roots of

---

17. Torrance, "What Is the Church?" 7.
18. Torrance, *Trinitarian Faith*, 10–11, 264–65.
19. Torrance, *Atonement*, 362.
20. Torrance, *Trinitarian Faith*, 264.
21. Torrance, "What Is the Church?" 9. For Torrance, Christ is the church, that is, the predicate of its being and existence, a proposition that cannot be reversed. This, for him, is partly why it is theologically defective to say that the church has to be regarded as an extension of the incarnation, a prolongation of Christ himself, which is evident in Roman Catholic teaching. Torrance, "What Is the Church?" 9.
22. Torrance, *Atonement*, 366.

humanity."[23] As Torrance argues, "Christ in us" and "Christ for us" are completely interlocked in the oneness that lies at "the core of the church as the body of Christ."[24] Christ became one body with us so as to "gather up our corrupt humanity into bodily existence in himself, healing and renewing it within himself through the perfection and holiness of his own human nature and life" and thus he became "the beginning of the new humanity."[25] Therefore, when he argues that atonement consummates the union between us and God in Christ, it does not divide the incarnation from atonement and *vice versa*, but rather sheds light on the reconciling work of Christ *for* us, which took place *in* and *through* his incarnate person and vicarious life.

In this respect, atonement draws our attention to the new concrete and life-giving substance of the church: the new humanity of Christ.[26] Through the atoning reconciliation and justification of Christ realized in his vicarious birth, life, death, resurrection and ascension we are given a "new life," his new humanity takes our old and sinful humanity, healing, sanctifying and transforming it into the new one in Christ.

At this point Torrance asserts that it is *the Holy Spirit* who enables the church to participate in Christ's new humanity in order that "the

---

23. Torrance, *Divine Interpretation*, 59. For reference to Torrance's view on the internality of incarnational atonement, see "Soteriological Significance of the Humanity of Christ for Reconciliation" in chapter 3 of this book.

24. Torrance, *Trinitarian Faith*, 266. Torrance derives his understanding of the oneness of "Christ in us" and "Christ for us" from Athanasius, who pointed out that "the apostle spoke of the incarnation of Christ and his high-priesthood as having functioned together" (Torrance, *Trinitarian Faith*, 266). In this sense, it is impossible to move directly from the incarnation to the church, for "the cross comes in between" (Torrance, *Atonement*, 366). Thus, Christ's atoning life and death articulate why Christ became one of us in such a way that "the death of Jesus is part of Christ's assumption of all human experience that needs to be redeemed"; this is clear in Torrance's holistic view of the incarnation, which entails the life, death, resurrection, and ascension of Christ as a whole gospel story (Eugenio, *Communion with the Triune God*, 61). See also Torrance, *Theology in Reconciliation*, 117.

25. Torrance, *Trinitarian Faith*, 267.

26. Torrance, *Trinitarian Faith*, 267. For Torrance, as expounded in chapter 3, the incarnation and resurrection are two focal points from which we can best understand this. On the one hand, the incarnation reveals how God took our sinful humanity and, out of the fallen humanity, created "a new humanity" in Christ and, on the other hand, the resurrection leads us to "the actual existence of the new and glorified humanity of Christ" in the resurrection and ascension, which together present the fact that Jesus Christ who *was* new man *is* new man, new creation in our ongoing space and time. See "The New Humanity" in chapter 3 of this book.

church draws its life and nature from Him, sharing in all He has done for it and sharing in His very Life as the Son of the Father in the communion with the Holy Spirit."[27] Thus, participation in him through the Spirit is "the ontological basis or *esse* of the church," through which the church finds not only its being, but also its nature as a *community of reconciliation* sharing in his new humanity on earth.[28] As Torrance puts it:

> It is only through participating and sharing in Christ that the Church is to be regarded as His Body, as His image and likeness among men, as the expression of His love and truth, as the reflection of His humility and glory, as the instrument of His Gospel, as the earthen vessel that holds His heavenly treasure and holds it forth for all men to share freely. Only on the ground of this participation in Christ Himself is the Church a community of believers, a communion of love, a fellowship of reconciliation on earth.[29]

This is what Torrance calls "the special work of the Holy Spirit," through which "mankind as a whole may share in the New Humanity of Christ and therefore in the new creation."[30] What is fulfilled in the church, that is, the real reception of and participation in the trinitarian life and love in Christ through the Spirit, directs the church to universal fulness in all creation, moving "from the particular to the universal, from the nucleus to the fulness, from the one hundred and twenty at Pentecost to all mankind."[31] This is the movement of the body (*soma*) to fulfilment

---

27. Torrance, "What Is the Church?" 9.
28. Torrance, *Atonement*, 373.
29. Torrance, "What Is the Church?" 9.
30. Torrance, *School of Faith*, cxxi.
31. Torrance, *School of Faith*, cxxi–cxxii. Torrance expounds a three-fold dimension that we have to understand in terms of the operation of the Spirit. The first is a universal dimension in which all humanity is included in the atoning reconciliation and the church is universalized or catholicized, reaching out to the fullness of Christ who fills all in all. The second is a corporate dimension, that is, "a Communion of mutual participation through the Spirit in Christ and His grace." The third is a personal dimension, in which the individual believers have union with Christ within the corporate communion (Torrance, *School of Faith*, cxxiii–cxxiv). As such, in Torrance's ecclesiology pneumatology is bound up with Christology and *vice versa*, which is also evident in his trinitarian theology as a whole. As Torrance argues, "Jesus Christ was born of the Virgin Mary into our human nature through the power of the Spirit; at his Baptism the Holy Spirit descended upon him and anointed him as the Christ. He was never without the Spirit for as the eternal Son he ever remained in the unity of the Spirit and of the Father, but as the Incarnate Son on earth he was given

(*pleroma*). The Spirit leads the church to fulfilment in a movement in which, by the Spirit, the church becomes the body of the risen Christ, growing up into "the fulness of Christ (Eph 3:17; 4:13, etc.)," and then it reaches out both to "the ends of the earth and to the ends of the ages (Eph 1:23; 4:10, etc.)."[32]

To sum up, for Torrance, the church, the body *of* Christ, is the christological reality with "a teleological and an eschatological movement of fulfilment."[33] Its *telos* refers to the church's ontological union with Christ and its eschatology points to the mission of the church that will continue until his second advent. Inasmuch as the new humanity of Christ becomes the creative source of the church's being, life, and mission, for Torrance the church is the personal and relational outworking of Christ's new humanity, the life-giving substance for the church.[34]

---

the Spirit without measure and consecrated in his human nature for his mission as the vicarious Servant" (Torrance, *Theology in Reconstruction*, 246).

The above reference rejects Habets's critique that "Torrance did not incorporate the Spirit nearly enough in his overemphasis on the eternal Word as the direct divine activity on the assumed human nature" (Habets, *Theology in Transposition*, 194). This draws our attention to Walker's critique of Habets: that in proposing Torrance's lack of an adequate pneumatology, Habets fails to recognize that, for Torrance, it is impossible to speak of the radical reconstruction of Christology, that is, integration of patristic and Reformation Christology, and of Christology with pneumatology and the doctrine of the Trinity "without a far deeper and more exacting pneumatology" (Walker, Review of *Theology in Transposition*, 114).

32. Torrance, *Royal Priesthood*, 24.

33. Torrance, *Royal Priesthood*, 24.

34. Given that, for Barth, the church's relation to Christ is created by the Word that gathers together (*congregatio*) and by the free response of humanity, the "perfect freedom of obedience" to that Word, Torrance's ecclesiology can be read as a more ontological one than that of Barth because, for Torrance, the church's relation to Christ is determined only by its participation in, or incorporation into, his new humanity (Barth, "Church—The Living Congregation," 68). However, the expression "the church's incorporation into Christ" is still found in Barth's language. Barth uses the term "incorporation" to expound the church's relation to Christ, but his actual preference is for "gathering together" and its attendant free human response (68–69, 72). This is why Torrance laments Barth's insufficient focus on "incorporation" in his ecclesiology, in which the church's participation in Christ for its being and life is not fully emphasized (Torrance, "Concerning Amsterdam," 256). This difference between Torrance and Barth in terms of the relation between the church and Christ is also evident in their views on the sacraments. As Hunsinger argues, although they regard the sacraments as actions or events that are bound up with the Word itself, in the sacraments Torrance's focus is on our union with and eucharistic participation in Christ, while Barth's focus is on a "response to grace" (Hunsinger, "Dimension of Depth," 139–56).

However, Habets argues that when Torrance's main focus is on making only general statements about *theosis* (deification or adoption) in Christ and how this may be so in the life of the church, he ultimately fails to develop its *horizontal applications* for churches today.[35] In a similar vein, Chung insists that although Torrance articulates the horizontal dimension of the church as the locus of revelation and reconciliation on earth, he is rather silent on "how the church ought to live and do in the world of pluralism and secularism."[36]

This does not imply, however, that Torrance's ecclesiology (or his theology in general) is "impractical" because (1) although Torrance has not addressed the issue of ecclesial praxis in the wider social dimension as sufficiently as might be expected, he indicates a practical vision of the church by depicting the horizontal characteristic of the church sent out into the world for the ministry of Christ himself; and (2) given that Torrance offers good theological resources for practical development, it is clear that his theology lends itself to practical and applied theology.[37] Nonetheless, in the inadequacy of practical points on the church's social life, Torrance can be read as paying little attention to the church's social and cultural life in the face of ethical, social, and political issues and the need for theological principles and applications for churches in specific contexts.

This will be investigated further in the following section, but it is important to mention here that when Torrance argues that the teleological and eschatological movement of the church takes place through the Word (*kerygma*) and the sacraments, and by its nature engenders the church's distinctive social ethics in its task of reconciliation and *diakonia* in human social and cultural existence, this does not simply expound how *theosis* in Christ still occurs in the life of the church, but also unpacks the fact that the *participatio Christi* shapes the church's praxis in its social life.[38] This shows the horizontal movement of the church, in which ecclesial life and praxis in society are not ignored or excluded, but instead formed and upheld by sacramental participation in Christ that creates the specific manners of living and acting, that is, the reconciliation and *diakonia* that

---

35. Habets, *Theosis in the Theology of Thomas Torrance*, 186–89, 196.

36. Chung, *Thomas Torrance's Mediations and Revelation*, 155–56.

37. Habets, *Theosis in the Theology of Thomas Torrance*, 152, 187, 191; Chung, *Thomas Torrance's Mediations and Revelation*, 157. See also Anderson, "Reading T. F. Torrance," 161–83.

38. Torrance, "What Is the Church?" 13–20; *Gospel, Church, and Ministry*, 151.

the church must pursue in this world. However, an important question to consider in this discussion is whether Torrance develops theological principles applicable to the life of the church in the specific ethical, social, and political context, so that horizontal applications for the church are clearly suggested. This will be addressed in more detail in the following section.

The Sacramental and Diaconal Action of the Church

For Torrance it is the Word (*kerygma*) and the sacraments in which the church's *telos* (its ontological union with Christ) and eschatology (the movement of *soma* to *pleroma* in its task of reconciliation) take place.[39] Put another way, the church's sacramental action creates its life and praxis in a way that it is drawn into the reception of, participation in, and communion with Christ, and it is thereby renewed as a fellowship of reconciliation, living out its reconciled and diaconal life on earth.[40] This reflects Torrance's theological logic of the church's practicality, in which the *participatio Christi* is regarded as the creative source of ecclesial life and praxis and as the transforming power of human society.

In this section, we will see, on the one hand, how the sacramental action underlies the church's reconciled and diaconal life and how the ecclesial life engenders relational and social transformation, and, on the

---

39. As Torrance expounds, *kerygma* refers to "both the thing preached and the preaching of it in one" and thus it is "the proclamation of the Christ-event" actualized through the Spirit among us (Torrance, *Conflict and Agreement in the Church II*, 158). Through *kerygma* the self-proclamation and self-communication of Christ is embodied under the creative impact of the risen Lord and his Spirit, which has assumed the form in the apostolic witness and tradition (Torrance, *Divine Meaning*, 59). Despite the significance of *kerygma* itself, in this section, however, *kerygma* is not addressed independently, for in Torrance's thought baptism and the Eucharist by their nature entail *kerygma*. This is the reason why baptism and the Eucharist must be bound to the proclaimed Word, which makes them effective and prevents them from being "an empty sign that is nothing but ceremony" (Torrance, "Eschatology and the Eucharist," 313). In this sense, it can be said that for Torrance *kerygma* works together with baptism and the Eucharist, pointing to the whole saving life and act of Jesus Christ in their distinctive forms—an epistemologically-focused sacramental form (*kerygma*) and ontologically-focused sacramental forms (baptism and the Eucharist). For further understanding of the interrelation between *kerygma* and the sacraments in Torrance's epistemology, see Ziegler, *Trinitarian Grace and Participation*, 210–15.

40. Torrance, *Theology in Reconciliation*, 82; *Gospel, Church, and Ministry*, 151.

other hand, whether Torrance develops clear horizontal applications for the church in this discussion.

According to Torrance, there are two basic sacraments of the gospel: baptism and the Eucharist.[41] With their respective meanings and foci, they are both deeply rooted in the incarnation and Christ's vicarious humanity. Thus, the sacraments have to do with one ultimate ground, the entire historical and redemptive reality of Jesus Christ, and therefore their content, reality, and power are derived not from themselves, but from the saving act of God for us in Christ and the reconciling and sanctifying act of God in his vicarious humanity.[42] In the sacraments the church receives what he has done for us in his vicarious humanity (*reception*), it participates and shares in his new humanity (*participation*) and it has communion with him and thus is drawn into the trinitarian life and love (*communion*).[43] In light of this, for Torrance "the primary *mysterium* or *sacramentum* is Jesus Christ himself," who "has incorporated himself into our humanity and assimilated the people of God into himself as his own Body" in his vicarious and new humanity.[44]

---

41. Torrance, *Mediation of Christ*, 90.
42. Torrance, *Theology in Reconciliation*, 82.
43. Torrance, *Theology in Reconciliation*, 82.
44. Torrance, *Theology in Reconciliation*, 82. The above reference is what Torrance refers to as "a third dimension" in the doctrine of the sacraments, which focuses on the vicarious and new humanity of Christ alongside his divinity. In the sacraments we are not only concerned with "the two dimensions," with the act of God and the act of our response, but rather we are concerned above all with "the third dimension," with the vicarious and new humanity of Christ, the essence of the sacraments. It is evident that, for Torrance, the significance of the saving humanity of Christ, along with his deity, is derived from the teaching of Irenaeus and Athanasius. This then has a fuller and deeper account in the doctrines of atonement and the sacraments of Calvin who worked out in detail the place of Christ's human obedience in his doctrine of atonement and focused on the new humanity in Christ with divinity and humanity as "the *substance* or the *matter* of the sacraments," in which we are by grace allowed to participate and our salvation and new life consist. For Torrance, the adequate account of the humanity of Christ in soteriological terms and the focus on our union with his new humanity in the sacraments give a theological correction to (1) the two camps in the early church—"the Alexandrian school," which stressed the eternal nature of Christ as divine Logos, and "the Antiochian school," which stressed the historical humanity of Jesus; and (2) "the forensic conception of salvation" in which the whole focus of attention is not directed towards the constitution of the person of Christ, but the work of Christ in his actual death and "the liberal conception of the Jesus of history" under the influence of Schleiermacher and Ritschl, which seeks to recover the humanity of Christ by eliminating the divine elements, such as judgment and transcendence, from the gospel (Torrance, *Gospel, Church, and Ministry*, 85–92).

On the basis of this, Torrance regards the sacraments as enshrining two essential moments of our participation in Christ. On the one hand, baptism is the sacrament of our *once and for all participation* in Christ on the grounds of his finished work, and, on the other hand, the Eucharist is the sacrament of "our *continuous participation* in Christ and all he has done and continues to do for us by his grace."[45]

Baptism

Torrance regards baptism as "the sacrament of justification," for what we are given in baptism is what God has already done for us in the whole vicarious life of Christ.[46] It is therefore baptism in which we receive Christ's vicarious baptism and through the Spirit we share in his atoning reconciliation and justification embodied in all his vicarious acts and his life. In order to understand in depth the relationship between baptism and justification, here we need to take note of the significance of his vicarious humanity with regard to this relationship. As Torrance puts it:

> The incarnate Son of God received the Spirit upon the humanity he had taken from us, not for his own sake, but for our sake. That is to say, it was our humanity that was baptised, anointed, sanctified and sealed in him. Thus when he was baptised *for us* we were baptised in him. Our baptism in the name of the Holy Trinity, therefore, is to be understood as a partaking through the Spirit in the *one unrepeatable baptism of Christ* which he underwent, not just in the Jordan river, but *throughout his life and in his death resurrection*, on our behalf.[47]

---

45. Torrance, *Mediation of Christ*, 90–91 (italics added). According to Alexandra Radcliff, for Torrance the sacraments are tangible expressions of human participation in Christ, in which we practically and ontologically participate in Christ's vicarious response. In Torrance's thought on the sacraments, it is the Spirit who enables us to participate in Christ's vicarious response and ongoing ministry for us, an understanding that, as Radcliff argues, is in sharp contrast to that of Thomas Smail, who asserts that it is the Spirit who enables us to develop our own response to Christ. In this context, Radcliff points out that Smail is at risk of stressing the autonomous human response, leading to the salvific efficacy that our human response has, while Torrance emphasizes and reveals Christ's entirely sufficient response in which we are given to participate through the Spirit, which therefore excludes "any subtly synergistic notion of co-redemption" (Radcliff, *Claim of Humanity in Christ*, 94–98).

46. Torrance, *Space, Time and Resurrection*, 150.

47. Torrance, *Trinitarian Faith*, 292–93 (italics added).

What is crucial at this point is that as Jesus's baptism at the Jordan River is undoubtedly of soteriological significance, for it is bound up with his whole vicarious life. As the event belonging to the substitutionary aspect of atonement, his baptism was the proclamation of divine Sonship as servant and savior and thus it was not a mere rite, but a redemptive event pointing back to the incarnation, the starting point of his vicarious life, and forward to his sacrificial life and death on the cross, the consummation of his vicarious humanity.[48]

In this regard, baptism must be interpreted in a "dimension of depth" reflecting back on God's saving work in Christ so that its content, reality and power are ultimately grounded in his vicarious birth, life, death, and resurrection.[49] Hence, when we are baptized in the trinitarian name in the church, it is Christ himself who is present "baptising with his Spirit, acknowledging and blessing the action of the Church as his own, fulfilling in the baptised what he has already done for them and making them share in the fruit of his finished work," that is, his *righteousness*.[50] This is the one baptism common to Christ and the church based on his finished work for us in his whole vicarious humanity, which also elucidates why our baptism is an *unrepeatable participation* in Christ as the sacrament of justification.

The Eucharist

Torrance regards the Eucharist as "the sacrament of sanctification," for, through it, regularly repeated, our continuous participation in Christ and all he has done and continues to do for us is embodied, whereby "we live unceasingly not from a centre in our selves or our own doing but from a centre in Christ and his doing."[51] This highlights the fact that

---

48. Torrance, *Theology in Reconciliation*, 85, 87. It is important to recognize Jesus's baptism as the point of proclamation of his divine Sonship. When we see that Jesus was consecrated as the servant and savior for sinners in his baptism, this draws our attention back to his incarnate birth as the saviour of the world and forward to his death on the cross, the fulfilment of his atoning redemption. For Torrance this is the reason why the early church regarded Jesus's baptism, "not as Jesus' adoption to be the Son of God, but as the public proclamation of his divine Sonship" (Torrance, *Theology in Reconciliation*, 85).

49. Torrance, *Theology in Reconciliation*, 83.

50. Torrance, *Theology in Reconciliation*, 87.

51. Torrance, *Mediation of Christ*, 91. See also Torrance, *Space, Time and Resurrection*, 150.

as the church we are forgiven and wholly justified in Christ (baptism), *yet* we need daily cleansing to partake of the divine forgiveness that is freely granted to sinners through our continuous participation in his self-sanctification on our behalf (Eucharist).[52]

For Torrance, "just as justification is not something that is to be repeated for it has taken place once and for all, so the sanctification of the church is already complete in Christ and is the enduring reality into which it is unrepeatably initiated in baptism and in which it is *continually participant* in holy communion."[53] This presupposes that although the church has already been forgiven, justified, and sanctified in him, so long as it lives in the world and engages in its sinful patterns and forms, the church is involved in error and wrong and thus it needs constant cleansing and forgiveness in Christ.[54]

There is a twofold movement in the Eucharist in which we do this anamnesis of Christ, which is essential for the continuous sanctification of the church. Firstly, it is the *God-humanward* movement or "Christ's self-giving" in which the focus is on the incorporation of Christ himself into our humanity in his incarnation so as to make what is ours his own and therefore heal, purify, and renew it in himself. However, given that Christ did not simply come to act and live *in* man but *as* man in order to restore human beings to proper Sonship in the *imago Dei*, the *human-Godward* movement or "Christ's self-offering" becomes a natural corollary. In his self-offering, Christ shared in human existence and life from his incarnate birth to death, he offered himself in holy obedience and atoning sacrifice to God for us in our place as our own act toward God and he lives forever to intercede for us.[55]

The eucharistic anamnesis, however, is not merely something that we do by way of remembrance of Christ's self-giving and self-offering; it

---

52. Torrance, "What Is the Church?" 12–13.

53. Torrance, *Atonement*, 387 (italics added).

54. Torrance, *Atonement*, 388. The fact that the church in the sinful world shares in its guilt illustrates "the earthly characteristic of the church" in which although the church is given to share in the new creation embodied in Christ, and it therefore becomes the body of Christ, it is also a body of sinners in its corporate earthly life. The church on earth is not only still the pilgrim people, composed of sinners, saved by grace and forgiven and cleansed, as their baptism testifies and as the Eucharist reaffirms, but it also still waits for the redemption of the body and resurrection of the dead. In this light, for Torrance, the church is a christological reality with eschatological hope in the earthly condition (Torrance, "What Is the Church?" 12).

55. Torrance, *Theology in Reconciliation*, 117.

is something that we do in our participation through the Spirit in his real presence, the eucharistic *parousia*.[56] This is the real presence of the whole Christ, the incarnate, crucified, risen, and ascended Son of God, which is not just the presence of his body and blood, nor the presence of his Spirit or Mind, but his actual presence.[57] The objective movement of the redemptive descent and ascent of Christ, that is, *katabasis* and *anabasis*, is mediated through the Spirit to us so that "we participate in the self-giving of God in the incarnate Son which is consummated in his passion and resurrection, and participate in the self-offering of the ascended Son which is grounded in his passion and resurrection."[58]

In this sense, despite the centrality of the finished work of Christ in both baptism and the Eucharist, the Eucharist has *a dimension of depth* that is slightly different from that of baptism, for its focus relies on his real presence, the eternal and perpetual validity for our continuous renewal.[59] As often as the church partakes of the eucharistic *parousia*, it

---

56. Torrance does not expound "how" Christ is present in the Eucharist, for his real presence that is given to us in the Eucharist is objectively grounded in "the presence of God to himself" (Torrance, *Theology in Reconciliation*, 121). Thus, as Colyer rightly points out, "Christ's real presence is explicable only in terms of God's creative activity which transcends any explanation we can construct, and is bound up with Torrance's interactionist God-world relation in which God *acts* directly in the world and is *himself* the content of his action in Jesus Christ and the Holy Spirit, and therefore in the Eucharist" (Colyer, *How to Read T. F. Torrance*, 270). Thus, for Torrance, the real presence of Christ in the sacrament is not something that we can explain through any analogy, causality or spatial relation, but with the eucharistic *parousia* through the Spirit. With regard to problematic attempts to explain how Christ is present in the Eucharist, e.g., the doctrine of transubstantiation, see Torrance, *Theology in Reconciliation*, 122–31.

57. Torrance, *Theology in Reconciliation*, 119.

58. Torrance, *Theology in Reconciliation*, 118.

59. According to Hunsinger, for Torrance the focus of baptism is the *perfect tense* of Christ's finished work for our justification, while the focus of the Eucharist is the fact that the perfect tense is *present*, in which, through the Spirit, we participate in the new humanity of the risen Christ who lives eternally and perpetually in his one vicarious, perfect, and finished work. This is "a brilliant new synthesis" of Calvin and Barth because, on the one hand, like Calvin (but unlike Barth) Torrance sees the sacraments as "forms of God's Word, establishing and renewing the Church in its union and communion with Christ" (the focus of the *present tense*), and, on the other hand, like Barth (but unlike Calvin), Torrance has "an unambiguous grasp on how salvation must be spoken of essentially in the perfect tense" (the focus of the *perfect tense*). In this regard, Hunsinger states that Torrance's view of the sacraments is "the immense contribution to an understanding of the sacraments in the Reformed tradition" (Hunsinger, "Dimension of Depth," 142–43, 149).

shares in the "self-consecration of Jesus Christ who sanctified himself for our sakes" so that "we might be sanctified in reality and be presented to the Father as those whom he has redeemed and perfected (or consecrated) together with himself in one."[60] In the anamnesis of Christ,

---

Importantly, Torrance's focus on the perfect and present tense in the sacraments refuses to view the sacraments in the flat as an event in itself, either as a ritual act that has its meaning in and with its performance, or as an ethical act that has its meaning in the human response to what God has already done in Christ (Torrance, *Theology in Reconciliation*, 83). It is notable that, as Torrance elucidates it, the early church avoided the term *baptismos*, which denotes a rite of religious ablution, and it employed instead the term *baptisma*, which refers to the *reality* behind the ritual act itself. He states that the church may have coined the term *baptisma* so as to present Christian baptism in this objective sense, in which it is evident that "the interest of the Church did not lie in the ritual act itself, indispensable as it is, but in the event that stands behind it and that impinges upon us through it" (Torrance, *Theology in Reconciliation*, 83; *Trinitarian Faith*, 293). On that ground he argues that although baptism is properly understood not only as an objective event in Christ (Athanasius's focus), but also as a subjective event in our experience of Christ through the Spirit (Cyril's focus), so we must think of our adoption in Christ as children of God in baptism not as viewed in ourselves, but as viewed in what God has already done for us in Christ's vicarious humanity (Torrance, *Trinitarian Faith*, 292–93). In this sense, we can say that Torrance follows the Athanasian focus on the reality *signified* in the sacraments, that is, the vicarious and new humanity of Christ, a focus that points to *what should be the priority* in terms of the sacraments and their attendant practical implications.

This can offer a theological corrective to the theological efforts to relate the church's sacramental practices *directly* to its ethical engagement with the world. For example, White argues that baptism has a wide impact on issues of social justice because, through baptism, where we are made as sisters and brothers in Christ and thus "no rich or poor, no communists or capitalists," "a sense of absolute equality" is conveyed to the world, so that deeds of love and charity for our fellow members of the church, including the homeless and poor, are required as "a form of living out our baptism" (White, *Sacraments in Protestant Practice and Faith*, 71). Yoder insists along similar lines that the sacramental acts of the church shape Christian ethics in which the practice of breaking bread and drinking wine in the Eucharist itself is regarded as "an economic act of sharing" and baptism shaping one common and equal community of people, regardless of their different social, political, and economic status, is a "social act of egalitarianism" (Yoder, *Body Politics*, 21, 33, 40). Continuing this line of thought, although Christ underlies the sacramental practices of the church and its attendant ethical implications, the main focus is *not* on *Christ himself*, but on the *ethical and sociopolitical meanings* that the sacraments offer in themselves. Although such theological efforts might facilitate an effective ecclesial practice, the undue ethical focus on the sacraments distracts our attention from the primary focus, that is, Christ himself and our participation in him, which can run the risk of prioritizing the ethicality that the sacramental practices can reflect (the *signifier*) over the life and work of Christ (the content, power, and reality *signified*) in the sacraments. For further understanding of this matter, see Moore-Keish, "Sacraments in General," 396–409.

60. Torrance, *Space, Time and Resurrection*, 158.

therefore, the church consistently participates through the Spirit in him, the sanctifying content and agency, which explains why the Eucharist is the sacrament of sanctification.

The Sacraments and Their Practical Implication

In this part we turn our attention to the ways in which sacramental participation of the church leads to its praxis in Torrance's ecclesiology. Firstly, in the sacraments the church is renewed as a community of reconciliation and this engenders its reconciled life. The church's sacramental participation in what Christ has done (justification) and what he continues to do (sanctification) creates not only its own essential form, that is, the body *of* Christ or a community of the reconciled, but also its own unique life, that is, the reconciled life on earth.[61] In particular, for Torrance the reconciled life of the church is of evangelical as well as social significance because when the church lives out its reconciled life in the actualities of humanity, it brings healing and reconciliation to those who are alienated from God and divided from one another in estrangement and conflict.[62]

For Torrance this refers to a *task of reconciliation* that must be driven deeply into human existence and thought in this world where the divisive forces of sin and error are embedded.[63] It is when the church is renewed as a community of reconciliation that people are drawn into the fellowship of those who are reconciled with God and one another and into union with Christ. This has a reconciling impact, not only on their relationship with God and others, but also on social relations and structures, for through reconciliation and renewal in Christ human hostilities and divisions caused by sin in our social and cultural existence are continually reconstructed and restored.[64]

---

61. Torrance, "What Is the Church?" 13–18.

62. As such, Torrance regards reconciliation as belonging to "the essential nature and mission of the church" (Torrance, *Theology in Reconciliation*, 7; "What Is the Church?" 17).

63. Torrance, *Theology in Reconciliation*, 72.

64. Torrance, *Theology in Reconciliation*, 21–24. What is emphasized here is not the church's social and political actions to overcome the divisions of humanity in the world, but instead Christ's ongoing reconciling and transforming ministry in and through his body. This kind of approach to social transformation that the church effects reminds us of how Torrance relates the personalizing work of Christ to the transformation of human social relations and structures. As elucidated in chapter

Torrance states that this kind of relational and social transformation was evident in the life of the early church, where every barrier and all enmity between Jew and Gentile was broken down and removed, creating out of them "one new race" in Christ.[65] As elucidated, this is the universality of the church that refers not to "an exclusive coterie of the few but to an ever-widening communion in which the Body (*soma*) presses out in expansion toward a fulness (*pleroma*) in the love of God" and thus all people are gathered up into the body regardless of their racial, social, and political status.[66] As such, the church's universality draws people into its own fellowship of peace with God in Christ and with all humanity, overcoming divisive forms in human social and cultural existence. It is when the church is incorporated into Christ that, as the body *of* Christ, its universality takes place and begins to work, so that the divine reconciliation in Christ is unfolded horizontally within the divisions of the world into which the church is sent.[67]

The church that is incorporated into Christ also develops "a way of organised corporate and public life" in deep divisions of the world, which is in agreement with the gospel it proclaims.[68] For Torrance this is an ecclesial life to express, realize, and preserve the intrinsic universality of the church. In this sense, the ecumenical activity and movement become a reflection of the universal existence and life of the church.[69] When the church partakes of Holy Communion, therefore, it "must live out in its own bodily existence the union and communion in which it participates

---

three, in our union with the new humanity of Christ, who is the personalizing person healing the dehumanization in the depths of the human person, (1) our self-centered and hypocritical humanity is healed and restored, which establishes us as "persons" in relation to God and, through that relation, as those who are free to relate to our fellow humans so that human inter-personal relations are healed and restored, (2) the inter-personal relations are constantly renewed and sustained through the humanizing activity of Christ within the social structures to which human beings belong, and (3) human social structures in conflict and disharmony may at last be transmuted into a community of love and reconciliation constituted by the personalizing and humanizing presence of Christ. See "Transformation of Humanity in the New Humanity of Christ" in chapter 3 of this book. In this sense, it is clear that, for Torrance, the ecclesial life that transforms human relations and society in its reconciled existence is a natural corollary of its ontological union with the new humanity of Christ.

65. Torrance, *Theology in Reconciliation*, 22–23.
66. Torrance, "What Is the Church?" 17.
67. Torrance, *Theology in Reconciliation*, 21–22.
68. Torrance, *Theology in Reconciliation*, 24.
69. Torrance, *Theology in Reconciliation*, 23.

in Christ."⁷⁰ Through this, the church addresses the divisions of the world in its unity and seeks the renewal of humanity in the reconciling and recreating work of Christ who gathers and unites all things in himself.⁷¹

Secondly, the church's sacramental participation in Christ determines ecclesial praxis in the service of mercy to others, that is, *diakonia*.⁷² Through the sacraments, the church has union with Christ, thereby participating in the justification and sanctification that he has undertaken for the church. For Torrance this union refers to union with Christ *clothed with his gospel*, which also means union with Christ *clothed with the need and misery of humanity*. As Torrance elucidates, Christ identified himself with us in our hopeless misery and abject need, making the whole human plight his very own in his vicarious life and thus he became himself the *diakonos par excellence*, "the perfect model or example of compassionate service to the needy and distressed."⁷³ In the sacramental action of the church, Christ incorporates the church into his diaconal being and life and thus the church is transformed into "the bodily instrument which Christ uses in the proclamation of the divine mercy to mankind and in prompting their responses to that mercy."⁷⁴

70. Torrance, "What Is the Church?" 18.

71. Torrance, *Theology in Reconciliation*, 23.

72. According to Stein, despite its theological importance with regard to the integrated relation between systematic theology and practical theology in Torrance's thought, the theme of *diakonia* is regarded as a neglected part of his thought (Stein, "Editor's Introduction," 14).

73. Torrance, *Gospel, Church, and Ministry*, 145.

74. Torrance, *Gospel, Church, and Ministry*, 151. Torrance insists that "the ministry of Christ clothed with his gospel has been kept apart from the ministry of Christ clothed with the need and plight of men, with the result that the ministry of the gospel has often lost *its relevance to men in the concrete actualities of their existence*, and the ministry of the divine mercy has lacked *its penetrating power to strike into the deepest root of human need in men's guilty estrangement from God*—thus grave disorder has appeared in the life of the Church and its mission is often fraught with a deep sense of futility" (Torrance, *Gospel, Church, and Ministry*, 158 [italics added]). Therefore, for Torrance, the holistic understanding of the vicarious humanity of Christ clothed with his gospel and with the need and plight of humanity becomes what the church must have for its being, life, and mission. On that basis, he critiques both fundamental and liberal theologies in which the significance of the saving humanity of Christ is undermined by virtue of their unfortunate concentration on the saving work of Christ on the cross, where his incarnate birth and life in human actualities is not regarded as internally related to atonement, but as merely instrumental (fundamental theology), and on the historical Jesus or what he symbolizes, where what is important is not Jesus Christ himself (liberal theology) (Torrance, *Gospel, Church, and Ministry*, 91; *Mediation of Christ*, 81).

For Torrance, it is the vicarious humanity of Christ that reveals the very property of the divine mercy in which the nature of human need and misery are viewed above all in light of *soteriology*. As Torrance puts it:

> What distresses God so deeply as he looks upon man in his fearful condition is not simply his sickness and pain, nor even the torment of anxiety that gnaws at his inner being, but the fact that in his hostility to God man has become possessed of sin in his very mind and is caught in the toils of a vast evil that extends far beyond him, and what vexes God also is that man's existence breaks up under the pressure of guilt in it all and under the threat of the divine judgement upon him. In view of this tragic state the mercy of God takes on a dynamic and creative form in which he allies himself with man.... That is why there took place in Jesus such a struggle with evil, a struggle that was waged between God and evil power not only in the heart and mind of man but in his bodily and historical existence, and a struggle to reclaim the existence of man as human being from its subjection to futility and negation.[75]

Here Jesus's entire diaconal life and ministry on earth are interpreted not simply as "the service of kindness for kindness' sake, but a far profounder service of mercy that dealt with the real sting of evil by penetrating its sinful motion and undoing its guilt in atonement."[76] This is the characteristic of *diakonia* fulfilled through Christ's vicarious life and "a service *commanded* by him and laid by him as a *task* upon every baptized member of his body."[77] Therefore, the church that is united with Christ and clothed with the need and misery of humanity gives its *diakonia* to the hungry, thirsty, naked, sick, and imprisoned, which the ongoing diaconal ministry of Christ continues to do in the concrete actualities of humanity through his body.[78]

Inasmuch as the church's *diakonia* cannot be isolated from the organized services of the state for welfare and become an ecclesial deed that assumes the corporate responsibility between the church and state to provide for the needs of humanity, for Torrance the church's diaconal

---

75. Torrance, *Gospel, Church, and Ministry*, 146.

76. Torrance, *Gospel, Church, and Ministry*, 152.

77. Torrance, *Gospel, Church, and Ministry*, 140. Torrance states that inasmuch as *diakonia* is the spontaneous expression of all members of the body of Christ, the church's diaconal life is not an imposed necessity upon the baptized, but the *free movement* of their love (Torrance, *Gospel, Church, and Ministry*, 140).

78. Torrance, *Gospel, Church, and Ministry*, 156–57.

life is not only of evangelical but also social significance.[79] In this sense, for him the church's diaconal life is a way that the Christian community reveals its distinctive social ethics, which is initiated only through the *participatio Christi*, the supreme *diakonos* in his vicarious humanity.

In sum, for Torrance it is the sacraments where the church is drawn into the reception of, participation in, and communion with Christ, and it is thereby renewed as the community of reconciliation, living out its reconciled and diaconal life in the divisions of the world. Therefore, for him the *participatio Christi* through the sacraments is the creative source of ecclesial life and its attendant social transformation. This displays Torrance's theological logic of the church's practicality. What we can find in this understanding is that, for him, the church's life and praxis result from its ontological participation in Christ and thus what makes them most distinctive and effective is not the use of social and political instruments, nor religious concerns, but "the life and work of Christ" for the church.[80]

As we saw in chapter 3, this christological focus of Torrance stresses "the acting subject whose agency is never exhausted but continues to have its way by working what he is, by the power of the Spirit, into us."[81] This rejects "exemplarism" in Christian ethics that is insensitive to what God *is doing* in this world in and through Christ "to make and to keep human life human, to achieve the maturity of men, that is, the new humanity," which enables our conformity to what God commands us to do.[82]

As such, the centrality of Christ in Torrance's ecclesiology precisely points out "where" the church's being, life, and praxis arise and "what" determines its practicality or ethics, that is, the vicarious and new humanity of Christ and the church's sacramental participation in Christ, a living person who grounds and creates "ethics" in his ongoing reconciling and diaconal life and work. In this, Christ is profoundly revealed as the

---

79. Torrance, *Gospel, Church, and Ministry*, 154.
80. Torrance, *Gospel, Church, and Ministry*, 153–55.
81. Holmes, *Ethics in the Presence of Christ*, 23–24; cf. Torrance, *Atonement*, 170.
82. Lehmann, *Ethics in a Christian Context*, 177. Here it is important to recall what Holmes refers to as the idea of "exemplarism" in Christian ethics. Exemplarism interprets Jesus as an example or an instantiation of something that lies beyond himself, so that he becomes "the paradigm for talking about social justice or for what personal piety in the religious life might look like." What is significant in this understanding is not so much "who he is," but "what he can point out to us." In this sense, Holmes rejects exemplarism that excludes Jesus Christ *himself* and his ongoing reconciling and transforming ministry in our midst (Holmes, *Ethics in the Presence of Christ*, 24–25).

creative source of the church's ethical life and praxis and as the transforming power to address the divisions of the world.

It is important to note, however, that although Torrance rightly articulates the horizontal dimension of the church constituted by its ontological participation in Christ, in which he expands on the concrete manners of living, that is, the task of reconciliation and *diakonia* that the church lives out on earth, and their relational and social impact, in this discussion he does not develop the ways in which ecclesial life should be in the specific ethical, social, and political context. In this inadequacy, Torrance's ecclesiology can be read as excluding clear horizontal applications for ecclesial life and, in this regard, as Chung argues, without addressing practical issues in the church's social life his ecclesiology can run the risk of losing a "prophetic voice of speaking authoritatively and relevantly to the life of the church in specific context."[83]

In this respect, Calvin on usury and Barth on social justice are examples that Torrance could have reflected and developed in his ecclesiology. Calvin and Barth, like Torrance, put the life and work of Christ at the center of their ecclesiology, particularly in their thoughts about ecclesial life and praxis, although they, unlike Torrance, address how the church of Christ should act in a specific context so that the church's financial ethics and social/political ethics are developed in their views on church/culture and church/state relations.

In particular, Calvin develops financial ethics in his discussion of usury, which derives from his "conversionist" view of church/culture

---

83. Chung, *Thomas Torrance's Mediations and Revelation*, 156. Here citing Schwöbel's argument, Chung goes on to say that the inadequacy in Torrance's ecclesiology creates a "gap between the factual existence of the Church in society and the theological formulae in which its nature is expressed," and reflection of ecclesiology as an academic operation that excludes the social context of the church is "unable to relate to the practical questions which face the Church in its struggle for survival in a society more and more shaped by a plurality of religious and quasi-religious world views" (cf. Schwöbel, "Creature of the Word," 117).

Of course, as seen in chapter 3, Torrance deals with some ethical issues, i.e., the issues of women in ministry, marriage/divorce, abortion, and the priestly role of humanity in creation. Although Torrance's thoughts on these issues can be used in his theology as horizontal applications for ecclesial life in specific contexts, it is evident that when theological discussions about the issues do not take place in view of church/culture or church/society relations, but in view of creation and redemption, more detailed ecclesial thinking and acting necessary in a wider social dimension is obscured. In terms of Torrance's Christocentric approach to the issues, see "New Humanity and Anthropological and Ethical Issues" in chapter 3 of this book.

relations.[84] As Jones states, for Calvin, God's renewal of humanity in and through Christ results in the restoration of order in the social and cultural life of humanity, because humanity restored by Christ restructures and reorders the human relationships in a *loving manner*.[85] This manner is "a display of authentic love" between brethren or people as a manifestation of equity or divine justice.[86] Importantly, Calvin employs the term "equity" as "the interpretive rule of love to effect justice in human life" and the goal of equity is to bring about justice defined as rendering to each what is his/her due.[87] This is "an authentic life pursued with consideration for God's nature, for fellow human beings, and with social solidarity."[88]

On this basis, Calvin understands that the church is called upon to impact culture through "the conversion of individuals" and to mirror God's desire for the restoration of harmony and order in society by using God-given reason and governing ability in the secular order to organize society so that it reflects God's order, love, and justice.[89] In his view of church/culture relations, Calvin develops what the life of the humanity restored by Christ means in human life, particularly in the economic dimension, in which the issue of the practice of usury is thoroughly addressed and his financial ethics of usury for the church is established.[90]

84. The standard analysis of Calvin's view on the relation between the church and culture appears in H. Richard Niebuhr's classic text *Christ and Culture* (1951). In this book, Niebuhr finds Calvin to be an early advocate of the "conversionist" view of church/culture relations, in which Christ is seen as "the converter of humanity" and the transformation of humanity by Christ influences not only human nature, but also human society and culture where the perversion of humanity appears so that the world may be transformed into a kingdom of God. However, according to Jones, what is not expounded fully in Niebuhr's assessment is that Calvin's view of church/culture relations includes a concept of the restoration of God's order in the social and cultural actualities of humanity, from which Calvin develops his finical ethics for the church, particularly the ethics of usury (Jones, *Reforming the Morality of Usury*, 73).

85. Jones, *Reforming the Morality of Usury*, 77.

86. Jones, *Reforming the Morality of Usury*, 77.

87. Haas, *Concept of Equity in Calvin's Ethics*, 63.

88. Sauer, *Faithful Ethics According to John Calvin*, 182.

89. Jones, *Reforming the Morality of Usury*, 78.

90. According to Douglass, with regard to the issue of usury Calvin analyzed the contemporary economic situation of Europe, and especially Geneva, and studied the Bible from a scholarly viewpoint, concluding that "there is a difference between loans to be consumed because of immediate need and loans for production." For Calvin the Old Testament prohibitions against usury are clearly related to the former, and Luke 6:35 does not address the question of loans with interest. Thus, Calvin understands that loans without interest to a neighbor in need should continue to be regarded "as

Barth derives the church's social and political ethics from his view of church/state relations. For Barth, the divine reconciliation and justification embodied in Christ create human participation in his loving relationship with the Father, a participation that renders human freedom to love fellow humans with a concrete orientation.[91] The church, as a witness of the divine reconciliation and justification, that is, of "the act in which God in Jesus Christ established and confirmed His original claim to man and hence man's claim against sin and death," is primarily interested in human beings, which for Barth underlies the church's particular call for human justice in the civil community.[92] The call for justice in society, therefore, arises from the election of humanity in and through Christ, which creates human correspondence to the divine justification in this world.

In this regard, Barth asserts that the church is called to "raise its voice and with its proclamation of the Gospel summon the world to reflect on social injustice and its consequences and to alter the conditions and relationships in question."[93] In the political sphere, hence, as Barth notes:

> [The church distinguishes] between the just and the unjust State, that is, between the better and the worse political form and reality; between order and caprice; between government and tyranny.... And it will judge all matters concerned with the establishment, preservation and enforcement of political order in accordance with these necessary distinctions and according

---

an act of love and mutual responsibility" and that "the loan or money for investment and production, however, can legitimately return interest to the lender without the taint of "usury," provided that the "rule of equity" is respected" (Douglass, "Calvin's Relation," 130–31).

Based on this understanding, Calvin suggests seven rules for the church's financial ethics of usury: "No interest should be taken from those in need. Lenders must not put all their resources at interest since some should be available to share with those in need without interest. The Golden Rule should be respected in setting conditions for loans. Interest cannot be demanded if the money does not earn more than was borrowed. The public interest must be taken into account, not just private considerations, since interest rates affect the public good. Finally, twice elaborated, rates should not exceed what is legally permitted locally; but even what is licit in a sinful world is not necessarily licit for a Christian. What is just and fair should be measured by the Word of God, not merely human custom" (Douglass, "Calvin's Relation," 131).

91. Brettmann, *Theories of Justice*, 162.
92. Barth, "Christian Community and the Civil Community," 34–35.
93. Barth, *CD* 4/3:893.

to the merits of the particular case and situation to which they refer. On the basis of the judgement which it has formed it will choose and desire whichever seems to be the better political system in any particular situation, and in accordance with this choice and desire it will offer *its support* here and *its resistance* there.[94]

In the making of such distinctions, judgements, and decisions, the church "reminds the world of God's Kingdom, God's commandment and righteousness and thereby of the responsibility of governments and the governed (Barmen Thesis No. 5)," which for Barth is the way that the church stands for social justice corresponding to the divine justification given to it in and through Christ.[95]

Thus, it can be argued that, as Calvin and Barth did, Torrance could have developed horizontal applications from his Christocentric ecclesiology so that "what the reconciled and diaconal existence and life of the church mean *in the specific social and cultural context*" could be explained. Hence, on the basis of Christ's ongoing reconciling and humanizing work more detailed practical language, expression, and direction for ecclesial life and praxis can be used for further development of Torrance's ecclesiology.[96]

---

94. Barth, "Christian Community and the Civil Community," 27 (italics added).

95. Barth, "Christian Community and the Civil Community," 26. For further understanding of Barth's view of church/state relations and how he conceives of the church's thinking and acting with regard to the themes "resistance to tyranny," "democratic socialism," and "international peace," see Hunsinger, *Conversational Theology*, 181–204.

96. For instance, Torrance's ecclesiology can also provide a useful theological insight based on Wolterstorff's focus on the relationship between liturgy and justice. Taking several passages from the Old and the New Testament as examples, Wolterstorff argues that "the authenticity of the liturgy is conditioned by the quality of the ethical life of those who participate: no authentic liturgy without justice," and that "the point of the liturgy is to give symbolic expression to the commitment of our lives to God" (Wolterstorff, *Hearing the Call*, 38–58). In this understanding what Torrance can accommodate and develop is that the reconciled existence of the church constituted by Christ affects and develops the ethical life in the public, social, economic, and political spheres of those who participate in the worship, that is, worship acceptable to God.

Torrance's Christocentric Ecclesiology and Its Corrective to the Ecclesiology of Social Trinitarianism

We have seen the attributes of Torrance's ecclesiology in which (1) the church, the body *of* Christ, is a christological reality that he made his own and gathered into the most intimate relationship with himself, (2) the church and its internal relation with Christ are best understood in the incarnation, atonement, and pneumatology, (3) the church's participation through the Spirit in Christ is its *esse*, or the basis through which the church finds its nature as a community of reconciliation sharing the new humanity of Christ, and (4) in the sacraments, the church is united with Christ who is clothed with his gospel and clothed with the misery and plight of humanity and it then lives out this reconciled life as a reconciling community and the diaconal life in service of mercy to others. Despite the inadequacy of horizontal applications of the church's life and praxis in any specific context, Torrance does articulate the derivative characteristic of the church from the life and work of Christ in which the church's ethical life and praxis are understood as resulting from its participation in he who creates ethics in his ongoing reconciling and humanizing ministry.[97]

Interestingly, Torrance's ecclesiology does create a different understanding of and approach to the church and its practicality from the ecclesiology of social trinitarians who, as Kilby argues, have demonstrated how the social analogy of the Trinity can positively inform the church's being, life, and practice, thereby shaping its social vision.[98] Importantly, inasmuch as their ecclesiology based on social trinitarianism does not show adequate christological reasoning in soteriological terms, Torrance, who profoundly shows "where" the being and life of the church are derived from and "what" determines its practicality, that is, Christ's vicarious and new humanity and the *participatio Christi*, can offer a corrective to that ecclesiology.[99]

---

97. As we have seen, in any kind of theological attempt to derive ethical meanings *directly* from the sacramental actions and "exemplarism" in Christian ethics, this recalls what must be the priority, that is, the thing *signified* or the life and work of Christ *himself* continually operative in his reconciling and recreating work. Given that there is little attention to who Christ is and what he is doing for the church in the ecclesiology of social trinitarianism, this kind of reminder can be applied, which will be addressed in more detail as this section proceeds.

98. Kilby, "Perichoresis and Projection," 432.

99. Tanner argues that in the ecclesiology of social trinitarianism, where the focus is not on the person of Christ, but on imitation of the trinitarian identity and relations

In this section, therefore, we will see the ways in which Torrance provides a christological corrective in critical dialogue with the ecclesiology envisioned by the social trinitarians, a dialogue that will reveal in greater depth the theological validity and effectiveness of his ecclesiology and its practical significance in and for the world.

As seen in chapter 2, social trinitarians shared four insights: "three personal God," "relational ontology," "historical re-orientation," and "practical relevance."[100] With regard to practical relevance in particular, they regard the Trinity as a *practical doctrine of the church* that guides and informs the thinking and acting of the proper individual and all social relations. According to Moltmann, the social doctrine of the Trinity reveals that God is a community of the divine persons—Father, Son and Spirit—"whose unity is constituted by mutual indwelling and reciprocal interpenetration."[101] The divine sociality for him helps us to find its earthly reflection, "not in the autocracy of a single ruler but in the democratic community of free people, not in lordship of the man over the woman but in their equal mutuality, not in ecclesiastical hierarchy but in a fellowship church."[102] In this sense, the church is viewed as an earthly reality that reflects *koinonia* and interrelationships in the perichoretic life of the divine persons in itself and in the world and thus it is as an *image of the Trinity*.[103]

It is in the sacraments that the church is drawn into the trinitarian communion and life and therefore it becomes the image of the triune God. Zizioulas, for instance, argues that in baptism a person *in* the Spirit is a participant *in* Christ and the person is converted from "the *hypostasis* of *biological existence*" to "the *hypostasis* of *ecclesial existence*," which refers

---

embodied in Christ, the significance of Christ's soteriological life for the church's identity and life and the church's union with him are excluded (Tanner, "Trinity, Christology, and Community," 69–73; *Christ the Key*, 222). See also Holmes, "Three Versus One?" 88–89.

100. Brink, "Social Trinitarianism," 336. See also "Critical Appreciation of Torrance's Christocentric Approach to Trinitarian Personhood in Relation to Social Trinitarianism" in chapter 3 of this book.

101. Moltmann, *Trinity and the Kingdom*, viii.

102. Moltmann, *Trinity and the Kingdom*, viii.

103. This is also evident in Zizioulas's thought in which the church is "not simply an institution, but a mode of existence, a way of being" reflecting God's being as communion or *koinonia* in the world and therefore "an image of the triune God" (Zizioulas, *Being as Communion*, 15, 19, 134–35). See also Volf, *After Our Likeness*, 2, 200.

to his/her acceptance into the communion of the divine persons taking place in Christ.[104] It is in the Eucharist that Christ makes the many "*a single body, his body*," taking them up into himself[105] so that the church is given to "taste in the very life of the Holy Trinity" in which "communion and otherness are realized *par excellence*."[106]

The church that is transformed according to "God's way of being" needs to be reshaped and hence "a non-hierarchical but truly communal ecclesiology based on a non-hierarchical doctrine of the Trinity" is formed and developed.[107] Despite differentiated arguments about the ecclesial structure and order among social trinitarians, their shared trinitarian vision produces "a vision of the church that is more communion than hierarchy, more service than power, more circular than pyramidal, more loving embrace than bending the knee before authority."[108] In this

---

104. Zizioulas, *Being as Communion*, 50–62, 113; Volf, *After Our Likeness*, 89.

105. Volf, *After Our Likeness*, 98.

106. Zizioulas, *Being as Communion*, 21; *Communion and Otherness*, 7.

107. Volf, *After Our Likeness*, 4. The theme "hierarchy vs. non-hierarchy or equality" is a pivotal issue for social trinitarians. They believe that hierarchically-ordered thinking, structure, and relationships in human societies and churches are derived from a monotheistic conception of God prevailing in western trinitarian theology based on the Augustinian priority of substance over person (Moltmann, *Trinity and the Kingdom*, 191–200; Boff, *Trinity and Society*, 20). As elucidated in chapter 2, social trinitarians use the social doctrine of the Trinity as a replacement for monotheism in order to provide a theological corrective to that situation, so that the trinitarian communion and equality penetrate all hierarchical ecclesial, social, and political structures and orders. However, exemplifying Puritan parliamentarians' denial of any analogy between a divine sovereign and the civil power and Barthians' objection to the totalitarian claims of Hitler, Nicholls argues that a monolithic God does not necessarily lead to autocracy or absolutism in politics (Nicholls, *Deity and Domination*, 232–34).

108. Boff, *Trinity and Society*, 154. See also LaCugna, "Practical Trinity," 683; Grenz, *Theology for the Community of God*, 76. Inasmuch as there are different ecclesial traditions and theologies that have deeply influenced social trinitarians, their different focuses on the ecclesial structures and orders could be understandable. For instance, while Moltmann and Volf's standing on the Reformed tradition rejects the hierarchical structures of clergy and laity in Roman Catholicism and other similar monarchical episcopates, advocating a free church with its emphasis on prioritizing the local congregation, Boff in the Roman Catholic tradition and Zizioulas in the Orthodox tradition do not reject the non-hierarchical and dominant role of clergies. Despite their different positions on the issue, it is evident that the trinitarian inner life underlies the ecclesiology that they envision. For the understanding of different arguments among social trinitarians with regard to the ecclesial structure and order, see Brink, "Trinitarian Ecclesiology and the Search for Unity," 215–35.

ecclesial vision, all hierarchical structures and relations in the church are rejected, e.g., the Roman Catholic Church's structure and order in which the exercise of sacred power is centralized in the clergies and the pope; an authoritarian leadership precludes the participation of the laity and decision-making structures reflect a monarchical understanding of power.[109]

This does not simply refer to a rejection of hierarchical ecclesial structures and relations, but to a rejection of all earthly forms of hierarchies. The divine sociality and relationality that are reflected in the life of the church shed light on what social structures and relations should be pursued in human society in general and Christian community in particular.[110] Thus, the church that corresponds to the trinitarian life in which the Trinity forms an open communion for one another and the world cannot be a self-enclosed community of believers, but an "open community" bearing the image of the triune God in and for the world, which is its ecclesial identity.[111] This also becomes an *ethical obligation* of the church as the image of the Trinity.[112]

It is notable that some social trinitarians recognize that there are limitations to how the trinitarian *perichoresis* can be directly applied to the ecclesial and social dimension. Volf, for example, argues that in a strict sense there cannot be correspondence between the trinitarian communion and human community. While the divine persons are internal in their *perichoresis*, human persons by definition are external to one another and the actualities of human existence are marred by sin, evil, and transitoriness, so the perfect creaturely images of the Trinity in

---

109. Hunt, "The Trinity and the Church," 218. Inasmuch as hierarchically-ordered ecclesial structures have been bound up with "patriarchy," social trinitarians have endorsed feminist theologies, particularly in terms of such issues as women's ordination, position, and ministry in the church. LaCugna, for instance, argues that our understanding of "the divine community of three coequal Persons" informs the shaping of family and church authority forms and contents in which all androcentric and complementarian categories of thought in the home, the church, and society are excluded. On this basis, she rejects the opposition to women's ordination (LaCugna, *God for Us*, 266–78). See also Volf, *After Our Likeness*, 2; Moltmann, *God for a Secular Society*, 56–57, 65–66.

110. Cunningham, *These Three Are One*, 89–119.

111. Boff, *Trinity and Society*, 149. See also Volf, "Trinity Is Our Social Program," 410.

112. Grenz, *Social God and the Relational Self*, 251.

human community are eschatologically destined.¹¹³ Hence, in order that the ecclesial and social community is modelled on the trinitarian life, it should be understood that human beings can only correspond to the triune God in *creaturely* and *historically* appropriate ways.¹¹⁴

Here the focus is shifted from the immanent Trinity to the economic Trinity—how the Trinity rescues in human history. In the economic Trinity we can find the Trinity brought closer to what human beings are capable of so that it is not necessary to bring "an account of the Trinity together with what one knows about the limits of human life to figure out how human relationships could come to approximate trinitarian ones."¹¹⁵ In the economy the divine identity and relations of the Trinity are revealed in Jesus Christ through whom we historically understand: (1) the perfectly mutual indwelling of the divine persons in "a dialogical fellowship of love and mutual service" between Jesus and the Father (and the Spirit);¹¹⁶ and (2) the nature of the triune God as involving self-giving love or self-donation to others through the cross of Christ.¹¹⁷

---

113. Volf, *After Our Likeness*, 207; "Trinity Is Our Social Program," 406. In this regard, quoting an article written by LaCugna and McDonnell, Volf states that "a certain doctrine of the Trinity is a model acquired from salvation history and formulated in analogy to our experience, a model with which we seek to approach the mystery of the triune God, not in order to comprehend God completely, but rather in order to worship God as the unfathomable and to imitate God in our own, creaturely way" (Volf, *After Our Likeness*, 198; cf. LaCugna and McDonnell, "Far Country," 202–5).

114. Volf, *After Our Likeness*, 198–200. In this sense, for social trinitarians the following methodology to find the trinitarian identity and relation applicable to the church and human society *in* the historical Jesus might be used as an answer to Tanner's critique of the social trinitarianism where "epistemological and ontological abstraction" occurs. See Tanner, *Christ the Key*, 222.

115. Tanner, "Trinity, Christology, and Community," 69. Here Tanner insists that this strategy for "closing the gap" is clear in Moltmann and LaCugna (cf. Zizioulas, *Being as Communion*, 19).

116. Tanner, "Trinity, Christology, and Community," 69. See also Volf, "Trinity Is Our Social Program," 409–411.

117. Moltmann, *Spirit of Life*, 136–37; *Trinity and the Kingdom*, 31–34; Volf, *Exclusion and Embrace*, 25, 29; "Trinity Is Our Social Program," 412–17. Following Moltmann, Volf insists that proposing a social vision based on the doctrine of the Trinity is not so much "projecting" or "representing" the transcendental Trinity, but rather re-narrating the crucified Christ and his cross. The cross shows the *earthly* love of the Trinity that led to the passion of the cross for "those caught in the snares of non-love and seduced by injustice, deceit, and violence," which is what we are called to *imitate*. In this regard, social practices reflect "the Triune God's coming down in self-emptying passion in order to take human beings into their perfect cycle of exchanges in which they give themselves to each other and receive themselves back ever anew

In this way the life and death of Jesus Christ become an interpretative lens by which to see the trinitarian identity and relations that human beings could and should emulate in their finite existence. Hence, the church is called upon not only to embody the fellowship of love and relationship that Jesus had with the one he called Father, but also to participate in Christ's messianic mission, that is, the liberation and restoration of all creation fulfilled through his self-giving love.[118]

All the above briefly expounds the identity and life of the church understood in the social doctrine of the Trinity, which can be summed up as follows: (1) the church is an earthly anticipation of the trinitarian *koinonia* and *perichoresis*, which is embodied in the sacraments where the church is transformed as the image of the Trinity in the trinitarian communion, (2) the church reflects the trinitarian life in its non-hierarchical, circular, inclusive, and participatory structure, order, and relationship, which sheds light on what human life and relations should be, and (3) the fellowship and self-giving love of the Trinity exemplified in Jesus's life and death is the earthly model that the church should imitate, which leads to its social and political involvement.

The ecclesial consideration above might be considered to offer a proper exposition of the nature, life, and mission of the church on a well-balanced theological basis. Further, given that the doctrine of the Trinity is not merely a dogma irrelevant to human life, we could argue that the ecclesiology envisioned by the social trinitarians reveals practical meanings and applications of the divine communion for the church and the world.

However, in the ecclesiology of Torrance, the social trinitarians' views of the church can be critiqued by virtue of its christological and soteriological deficiencies. Firstly, for Torrance, the focus of the social

---

in love" (Volf, "Trinity is Our Social Program," 415–17). According to Bidwell, Volf's central motif for his "theology of embrace" is based on "an anticipation of forgiveness and reconciliation for the oppressed and the oppressors, as exemplified by the crucified Christ" who revealed what the life of the triune God is to the world. Thus, this for Volf forms "a theological paradigm for a nonhierarchical, perichoretic Trinity of self-giving action, a model to be mirrored by the church and the world" (Bidwell, *Church as the Image of the Trinity*, 55).

118. Moltmann, *Church in the Power of the Spirit*, 64–65. The latter point in particular provides a theological motivation for the church's social and political engagement and solidarity with the victims of evil or injustice, poverty, and oppression in the world, which is rooted in the solidarity of Christ on the cross with the victims (Moltmann, *Spirit of Life*, 137; Boff, *Faith on the Edge*, 134–38, 201).

trinitarians on the ways of the church's being and life in practical terms can be regarded as a focus not on "the body *of Christ*," but on "the *body* of Christ" so that the soteriological life and work of Christ for the church are belittled. This focus is clear in the understanding of the sacraments, in which the central point for social trinitarians is not Christ *himself*, but the church *itself* transformed according to the trinitarian communion and its practical relevance to the world.

For instance, it is clear that for Zizioulas the sacraments show how the church can be an image of the Trinity. In the sacrament the Spirit relates us to Christ, the person *par excellence* whose identity is constituted by his relationship with the Father and thus we are constituted as persons through the same trinitarian relationship that exists between the Father and the Son.[119] Hence, the church is *koinonia*, that is, constituted by "the very personal communion between the Father, the Son and the Spirit," and then "the church as a communion reflects God's being as communion."[120] On this basis, Zizioulas develops a relational ontology of personhood applicable to anthropological and ecclesial areas and argues against "individualism" in modern individual and substantialist concepts of human personhood.[121]

Of course, Zizioulas regards the incarnation as significant because in the incarnate Son the human person was united with God and acquired his identity in *theosis*, which is the ground for the human capacity to be the ecclesial *hypostasis* in communion with God.[122] However, when he, unlike Torrance, fails to unfold the fact that Christ did not simply come to live *in* man but *as* man, so as to heal and restore human personhood to proper Sonship in the *imago Dei*, the identity of Christ is read in a philosophical and personalist fashion in order to set up a *fundamental ontology* for his relational anthropology and ecclesiology.[123] It is not surprising, then, that although Zizioulas views the incarnation as the starting point for ecclesial *hypostasis*, he does not pay attention to "atonement" as the *precise point* where "the union between God and humanity in Christ

---

119. Zizioulas, "Human Capacity and Human Incapacity," 442, 438.

120. Zizioulas, "Church as Communion," 105–6.

121. Zizioulas, *Being as Communion*, 16; "Human Capacity and Human Incapacity," 437–47.

122. Zizioulas, "Human Capacity and Human Incapacity," 438–40.

123. Zizioulas, "Human Capacity and Human Incapacity," 438–40; *Being as Communion*, 55–61; cf. Torrance, *Theology in Reconciliation*, 117.

in which the church is rooted could only be consummated through the expiation of sin and the removal of enmity."[124]

This kind of failure is evident in the social trinitarians' consideration of the church, a failure that obscures the soteriological focus on Christ's finished and continuous work for the church, thereby preventing us from properly understanding what the sacraments really point to.[125] Further, this provides a reason why we can easily find a link between the sacraments and the ways of the church's being and life in the social model of the Trinity.

Secondly, when social trinitarians derive the creative source of the ecclesial praxis not from the *participatio Christi*, but from imitation of the trinitarian identity and relations, the church's practices are at risk of merely expressing a series of platitudes on, for instance, "unity in diversity." As expounded, social trinitarians have a twofold source for the ecclesial life: the first is the trinitarian *koinonia* and *perichoresis*, and the second is the earthly image of the trinitarian identity and relationship exemplified by Jesus's fellowship with the Father and self-giving love. Inasmuch as applying the ineffable nature and life of the Trinity directly can be an abstract theological idea, the latter can be seen to offer not only theological validity, but also an effective methodology for ecclesial practices.

However, when the focus is moved from the immanent Trinity to the economic Trinity and it rests on Jesus's relational life and self-donation for the ecclesial imitation, Jesus is simply interpreted as an "exemplar" to show what the church should imitate for human relations and life. This leaves the identity of Jesus isolated from his whole soteriological life, that is, his soteriological identity as the savior who made the church his very body in his vicarious humanity so that the church *in him* had and has the

---

124. Torrance, *Atonement*, 366.

125. According to Hilkert, in LaCugna's thought incorporation into the very life of God that is actualized in baptism and the Eucharist enables and requires "radical transformation of those initiated into the mystery of Christ so that the community of the baptized might respect the full humanity and diverse gifts of all persons and in its common life become a more genuine 'icon of the Trinity'" (Hilkert, "Mystery of Persons in Communion," 242 [italics added]). However, in the ontological connection between the sacraments and the church, LaCugna, like Zizioulas, fails to expound how Christ made the church his very own, his body in his vicarious humanity, and incorporated the church into the trinitarian communion in *soteriological terms*, so her theological vision swiftly moves from the sacraments to the ecclesial applications (LaCugna, *God for Us*, 401–11).

ontological possibility of sharing his fellowship with the Father and the Spirit.

In this sense, it is noteworthy in Tanner's argument that when social trinitarians take the trinitarian relations in the economy as "a model for our imitation," for our human relations without deep theological speculation, they fail to see and follow "what the economy of the Trinity itself is suggesting about human relations."[126] Thus, Jesus's life does not simply show the sort of relations that humans are to have, but it unfolds how the trinitarian persons relate to one another in the incarnate *parousia* in which Christ healed and reconciled us and then shared the trinitarian communion with us.[127] The trinitarian form of human social life, therefore, is only realized not by imitating Jesus's relational life, but by being united with Christ who through the Spirit still draws us into the trinitarian relations.[128]

When Tanner derives the promise of the trinitarian form of human social life from union with Christ, this connotes our ontological transformation and its resultant changes in our social relations from that union. This is a genuine transformation that effects positive relational changes in human social existence.[129] In contrast, social trinitarians relate the trinitarian relations and attributes to ecclesial practices without sufficient christological reasoning and focus on the union with Christ. Here the Trinity cannot work for human ontological transformation and so a superficial reading of the Trinity for human imitation naturally occurs. Thus, the Trinity simply confirms what we already know: "what dialogical relations of loving fellowship are," and therefore "the Trinity offers us nothing more."[130]

In Torrance's language, the ecclesial praxis from "imitation" can be regarded as a supplement to what the state may or may not do or a retreat into religious, social, and political concerns.[131] This explains

---

126. Tanner, "Trinity, Christology, and Community," 71.

127. Tanner, "Trinity, Christology, and Community," 70–73.

128. Tanner, "Trinity, Christology, and Community," 70–73.

129. The way in which Tanner derives social implications from union with Christ is similar to that of Torrance, in which union with Christ, who is the personalizing person, enables human personalization that effects the constant renewal of interpersonal relations within the social structures to which human beings belong. See also Lehmann, *Ethics in a Christian Context*, 177.

130. Tanner, "Trinity, Christology, and Community," 69.

131. Stein, "Editor's Introduction," 14.

why he emphasizes the vicarious and new humanity of Christ and union with him. As elucidated, in union with Christ the church is justified and sanctified, participating in the trinitarian communion. For Torrance, as for Tanner, what the church has to consider with regard to its being and life is not imitation of Christ but "participation in Christ," through which the church is not only united with God, but also transformed as a reconciling community to live out its reconciled life in intercession, witness, reconciliation, and *diakonia* in the world.[132]

Thus, it is evident that for Torrance the *participatio Christi* plays an essential role, not only in facilitating the church's transformation and its transforming impact on human society, but also in making ecclesial practices distinctive and effective. This refers to "the centrality of Christ" in the being and life of the church, on which social trinitarians do not focus attention in terms of the creative source of the church's being, life, and praxis and the transforming power of human society.

Conclusion

This chapter set out to examine Torrance's ecclesiology and its practicality. What we have found through this exploration is that, for Torrance, the church as the body *of* Christ is a christological reality with a teleological and eschatological movement, which is best understood in the incarnation, atonement, and pneumatology. As the *esse* of the church, the *participatio Christi*, which is embodied through the Spirit in the sacraments, enables the church's union with Christ clothed with his gospel and with the misery of humanity and then to live out its reconciled life as

---

132. For Torrance, intercession, witness, and reconciliation are what the church has to pursue above all so as to hold forth Christ, the *diakonos par excellence*, before humankind and to minister the mercy of God to the desperate needs of human beings in their evil and misery. It is only through continuous engagement in *intercession* that the church can "engage in the pure service of divine mercy in utter reliance upon God," so that the church can fulfil its *diaconia* on earth not "through the power of its own action but only through the power of its Lord," its great high priest at the right hand of God almighty. *Witness* is the form that "service takes as it moves from worship and intercession in Christ toward men in their estrangement and separation from God," which enables the church to engage in pure evangelism. *Reconciliation* is the nature and life of the church in which the church that "is committed to the *diakonia* of the divine mercy must live out the reconciled life" in the actualities of human existence where "the bounds of human life break up under the divisive forces of evil." In this sense, for Torrance, living out the reconciled life *per se* becomes *diakonia* (Torrance, *Gospel, Church, and Ministry*, 153–55, 158–61).

a reconciling community and diaconal life in the service of mercy. This focuses on the centrality of Christ's life and work in ecclesiology, in which the ethical life and praxis of the church are understood as resulting from the church's participation in Christ, who creates ethics in his ongoing reconciling and humanizing work.

Although Torrance profoundly articulates the horizontal dimension of the church and its impact on human society constituted by Christ, in this discussion he does not expand on and develop the theological principles applicable to ecclesial life and praxis in a specific social, cultural, and political context. In this respect, the chapter considered Calvin's writing on usury and Barth's on social justice, that is, the financial ethics and the social/political ethics for the church derived from their views of church/culture and church/state relations respectively, in relation to what Torrance could have reflected and developed in his ecclesiology.

Torrance's ecclesiology was further outlined as a corrective to the ecclesiology of social trinitarianism. In the critical dialogue between them, we saw that Torrance has a different approach to the church and its practicality from that of social trinitarians who suggest that the Trinity *per se* or the trinitarian relations and attributes revealed in the economy can be a model for ecclesial life and practices. Through the dialogue, it was unpacked that the insufficient christological reasoning and focus on union with Christ engender overemphasis on the *body* of Christ, the too-swift movement from sacraments to ecclesial and social vision, and the superficial reading of the Trinity for the ecclesial imitation, in which all ecclesial practices are rooted.

In conclusion, it is important to remember that, for Torrance, the life and work of Christ and the *participatio Christi* are linchpins, not only to the church's being, life, and praxis, but also to social transformation. When he argues that living out the church's reconciled life itself in intercession, witness, and reconciliation is its *diakonia* in the world, the church's praxis seems to be confined to the ecclesial area so that the social, cultural, and political implications that the church's praxis should entail in the wider social dimension might be obscured.

However, Torrance insists that although in the early church there was "no programme to commit all members of the Church to political involvement" and "no attempt was made to carry through a programme of social change," the fabric of culture and society was profoundly transformed and thus the church put a strong Christian stamp on the very foundations of western civilization. In this way the church proved to be "the most effective by being faithful to its evangelical mandate," such as meditation, worship, prayer, intercession, witness, and *diakonia*.[133]

This does not mean, however, that the church must exclude social and political engagement with public discourses and issues. Torrance's focus is not simply a matter of choice but, as expounded, a matter of *priority*. He suggests that since the needs of humanity, including hunger and poverty, are bound up with the injustices inherent in social and economic structures, in order to meet human need properly the church has to pay rational attention to its causes and the factors that aggravate it.[134] The problem for him is that a church that does not feel the burden of human misery deeply and take its service of divine mercy seriously cannot but view only the physical aspect of human need. The church is then tempted to make its service effective through social and political methods.[135] In this regard, his ecclesiology can be judged as able to reflect what the church has to pursue as a priority in terms of its praxis.

Nonetheless, when Torrance does not address how the church should participate in public discourses without falling into "the temptation" above, his ecclesiology suffers from the relative absence of practical principles for the church's life in wider realms. Thus, as elucidated, more detailed ecclesial language, expression, and direction for the church's social acts in specific contexts are required for the further development of the church's practicality that his Christocentric ecclesiology unfolds.

---

133. Torrance, *Gospel, Church, and Ministry*, 166–71.
134. Torrance, *Gospel, Church, and Ministry*, 154.
135. Torrance, *Gospel, Church, and Ministry*, 154.

Conclusion

THIS THESIS HAS EXPLORED Torrance's Christocentric anthropology and ethics and the theological validity and effectiveness of this. Through this exploration, we saw that he utilizes wide-ranging theological, philosophical, and scientific knowledge and epistemologies in order to disclose and support his anthropological and ethical thoughts. In particular, Christology plays a central and pivotal role in Torrance's anthropology and ethics. Focusing on the epistemic and ontological significance of Christ's humanity with regard to knowing and participating in the trinitarian personhood and communion, and persons in true relation to God and others, that is, *personalization*, Torrance profoundly and precisely reveals that the vicarious and new humanity of Christ and the *participatio Christi* underlie all important personal and relational thinking and acting in Christian anthropology and ethics. This explains why Torrance's anthropology and ethics should be regarded as *Christocentric*.

Such a Christocentric anthropology and ethics in Torrance not only shows a vertical and doxological dimension, but also horizontal and practical significance. Moreover, Torrance's emphasis on the mediatorial and vicarious life and work of Christ in his humanity in terms of revelation and reconciliation and its resulting new moral life/order and social relations reflects what should be a *primary focus* in our anthropological and ethical thought.

In this regard, the overall argument in this book is that despite the inadequacy of horizontal applications in wider social realms, Torrance does engage in horizontal and practical considerations and implications, and that his understanding of and approach to the trinitarian personhood, communion, and praxis sheds significant light on the *christological deficiency* of the social trinitarians, who draw heavily upon the personal and relational attributes of the Trinity in relative isolation from Christology, and thus it should be considered a *corrective* to social trinitarianism.

Summary of the Chapters

To sum up the four main chapters in which the above argument was addressed, in chapter 1, this thesis explored Torrance's *onto-relational concept of person* in extensive theological, philosophical, and scientific discussions. Rejecting the impersonal and non-relational patterns of thought found in the ancient and modern dualisms that are so pervasive in the fields of anthropology, theology, philosophy, and science, Torrance argues for an onto-relational characteristic to the concept of person. This is supported by his use of theological, philosophical, and scientific epistemology, that is, the concepts of "the relational *imago Dei*," "person in relations," and "personal knowledge." In this process, however, we found insufficient philosophical research to support his interpretation of Aristotle in the context of the history of philosophy as related to the concept of person on the one hand, but, on the other hand, his reflection on Augustine—that by offering a psychological and interiorizing and not a Christocentric approach to God he committed himself to the individual and rational concept of person—was defensible.

In chapter 2, this book set out to examine Torrance's understanding of the *onto-relationality of trinitarian personhood* and *its practical relevance*. For Torrance the concepts of the *homoousion* and *perichoresis* reveal the ontic relations of the divine persons in which the dynamic, personal, and relational being and life of the triune God are clearly unpacked, so that the triune God as a *Being for others, a Being who loves* is known to us. As the creative source of all created personal beings and communities, the personal and relational nature of trinitarian personhood is the *ontological foundation* for the human person and personhood. In this understanding, the particularity and relationality of the divine three persons are neither isolated from nor absorbed into the unity of God, but underlined in their *homoousial* and co-inherent relations. Therefore, Gunton's critique that Torrance's western or Augustinian emphasis on the being (*ousia*) of God at the expense of the particularity and relationality of the persons (*hypostases*) does not offer a trinitarian model for anthropology, was refuted.

Torrance's Christocentric approach to trinitarian personhood, communion, and praxis in comparison with Moltmann, Zizioulas, and other social trinitarians was also explored in order to identify the way in which his approach has practical implications and it can have more appropriate theological validity and effectiveness than the trinitarian-centric approach of social trinitarianism. When social trinitarians draw heavily on the ontology of persons and the personal/relational contents of the trinitarian communion for their social visions, there is an *inadequacy of christological reasoning* in how we are capable of knowing the triune God and participating in the communion. By contrast, Torrance reveals and focuses on the epistemological and ontological role of Christ, not only for the knowledge of and participation in God, but also for true Christian praxis, which can only begin from our reconciliation with God in Christ, the *personalizing person* who heals and restores our dehumanization and creates new moral life, order, and relations. Hence, Torrance's Christocentric approach was suggested as a theological *corrective* to social trinitarianism.

In chapter 3, this thesis articulated Torrance's understanding of *the humanity of Christ* and *its anthropological and ethical significance*. For Torrance the humanity of Christ has an epistemic and ontological significance for revelation and reconciliation. The concepts of the *homoousion* and the hypostatic union in particular expound the actuality of atoning reconciliation as an internal act within Christ's humanity for our new humanity. The fallen, vicarious, and new humanity of Christ articulate the ways in which Christ penetrates our sinful humanity and atones and sanctifies it in order to address "dehumanization" in the ontological depths of our fallen humanity, so that it is *personalized* or *humanized* according to the proper Sonship in the *imago Dei*. As a result, new moral and social life, order, and relations are set up before God and among other persons.

As such, Torrance presents the humanity of Christ as the ontological foundation for the transformation of the human person, that is, it is the *personalization* necessary for and bringing about personal human relations and ethical practice. This proves that Torrance's Christology *does not neglect ethics* in the provision of horizontal and practical implications (contra Webster). Further, Torrance's focus on Christology, particularly Christ's ongoing personalizing work and its ethical effects rejects the *self-justifying ethics* that is evident in "exemplarism" in Christian ethics, pointing out "the acting subject" who grounds and creates ethics in his new humanity.

However, although Torrance offers a foundational basis for Christian anthropology and ethics and addresses some ethical issues in his christological view, he pays little attention to developing *how* Christian moral principles (e.g., love of neighbor and enemy, forgiveness, loving kindness, justice, and mercy for the weak and defenceless) can be applied to human societies to seek inter-personal relationality, community, and morality in religiously plural human communities. Therefore, it was argued that further ethical dialogue and engagement in wider social and political realms are required in order for a theological elaboration of the way in which a Christocentric anthropology and ethics can develop and address wide-ranging practical issues.

In chapter 4, this book explored Torrance's understanding of the *sacramental and diaconal action of the church* and *its practicality*. For Torrance, the body *of* Christ the church is a christological reality with a teleological and eschatological movement, which is best described in the incarnation, atonement, and pneumatology. It is the sacraments where the Spirit facilitates the church's *participatio Christi* clothed in his gospel and the misery of humanity and then the church lives out its reconciled life as a reconciling community and its diaconal life in the service of mercy. This reveals not only the centrality of Christ's life and work for the being, life, and mission of the church, but also the resultant ethical life and praxis of the church from its *participatio Christi*, who creates ethics in his ongoing reconciling and personalizing work. In this regard, Torrance's Christocentric understanding of and approach to the church's identity and life was considered as a corrective to the insufficient christological reasoning and focus on participation in Christ in the ecclesiology of social trinitarianism that engenders over-emphasis on the *body* of Christ, the too-swift movement from sacraments to ecclesial and social vision, and the superficial reading of the Trinity for ecclesial imitation.

However, we saw that although Torrance profoundly articulates the church's horizontal dimension and its distinctive social ethics in its task of reconciliation and *diakonia*, in this discussion he does not develop the concrete theological principles for ecclesial life and praxis in a specific social context. Therefore, this thesis suggested Calvin's writing on usury and Barth's on social justice, that is, financial ethics and social/political ethics for the church derived from their views of church/culture and church/state relations, as examples that Torrance could have reflected on and developed in his ecclesiology.

The Importance and Contributions of This Book

There are several areas of theological importance and contribution that this book achieved. First, this study articulated Torrance's inclusive and holistic understanding of Christian anthropology and ethics. As noted in the introduction, exploring and revealing Torrance's anthropological and ethical thought in an integrated and systematic way has not yet been attempted in relation to research on him. This study not only fully addressed wide-ranging theological, philosophical, and scientific knowledge and epistemologies that he utilized in arguing for the onto-relational concept of the person and the significance of Christ's humanity with regard to personalization and its resultant ethics, but it also presented them in relation to the fields of anthropology, the doctrine of the Trinity, Christology, and ecclesiology. Therefore, the contents and presentation of this study take the first step in this direction, potentially improving our understanding of Torrance in this integrated and systematic manner, in particular the horizontal considerations and practicality of his theology.

Second, there are critical and constructive discussions in each chapter, which means that this study is not merely expository but also critical in nature. This is significant given that through such discussions we can better understand and identify Torrance's system and logic and its validity in terms of his anthropology and ethics. In this respect, this book can provide us with wide-ranging interpretative lenses to help and improve our comprehension of Torrance.

Third, this book examined in depth the anthropological and ethical significance of the humanity of Christ in Torrance's theology and suggested his Christocentric anthropology and ethics as a corrective to social trinitarianism. As expounded in chapters 2 and 4, the theological tendency of social trinitarians that draws heavily upon the relational attributes of the divine persons for their social visions should be corrected by a christological injection. In this regard, as argued, Torrance's Christocentric approach to trinitarian personhood and communion and his focus on the humanity of Christ, the *personalizing person* who still heals and restores our dehumanization and creates new moral life, order, and relations, should be considered as a complement or corrective to this. As a result, the christological deficiencies in the social trinitarian logic can benefit from the Christocentric reasoning in his anthropology and ethics.

The Limitations of This Book and Suggestions for Further Study

Despite the important facets and contributions of this book mentioned above, there are also several limitations in this book. These limitations are by definition closely linked to suggestions for further study. First, while this study engages in various critical and constructive discussions, considering different positions in Torrance, particularly those on the left of social trinitarianism, there are relatively few discussions on other contemporary writers whose positions are close to those of Torrance and therefore it is difficult to *fully* identify how he can be differentiated on the right. Of course, given that the secondary aim of the book is to assess and test the theological validity and effectiveness of his Christocentric anthropology and ethics in critical dialogue with social trinitarians, the focus on critical dialogue with different positions in Torrance has a purpose. Further, despite the limited works in number, the discussions on Pannenberg and Jüngel, and Calvin and Barth in chapters 2 and 4 respectively enable us to identify how Torrance can be distinguished from those close to him. However, it is clear that further comparative discussions that consider those with similar positions to him can enrich his anthropology and ethics and therefore it is necessary to develop and deal with such discussions in greater depth.

Second, this study undertook critical discussions on selective contents and restricted scope. This means that there are subjects in this book that are not dealt with to any profound degree. This is justified with regard to the aims and directions of this book. However, with regard to further understanding and developing Torrance's anthropology and ethics as a whole, it would be important to find and consider more theological, philosophical, and scientific epistemologies related to anthropology and ethics in dialogue with Torrance. This in turn could illustrate how he positively influences other anthropological and ethical thoughts (contributions) on the one hand, and, one the other hand, how his anthropology and ethics is influenced and enriched by them (supplementation).

One viable approach to the above would be to compare Torrance's anthropology and ethics in western thought to Confucianism's in eastern thought. According to Paul Chung, a leading scholar who has dealt directly with comparative research between Christian theology and Confucianism, through inter-connecting western theological terms and concepts with those of Confucianism, we can engage a complementary connection of hermeneutical and historical importance that is significant for discovering their shared anthropological and ethical values and properly contextualizing Christian theologies as the ultimate goal of the Christian mission.[1] In this context, such cross-cultural

1. Chung, "Dietrich Bonhoeffer," 127–46.

research comparing Torrance's anthropology and ethics, particularly his concepts of person and personhood and christological reasoning in terms of personalization and its resultant ethics with the understanding of humanity, self-cultivation for true personhood, and a God for morality in Confucianism, would lead to a constructive discussion with anthropological, ethical, and theological significance, through which we could identify his contributions or works that supplement him.

Conclusion

We have seen that in his anthropology and ethics Torrance sheds significant light on: (1) human existence as *persons in relation* to God and other fellow humans, (2) the *onto-relationality of trinitarian personhood* as the creative source of all personal being and community, and (3) *the humanity of Christ*, the *personalizing person* and its resulting new moral life, order, and relations. By considering the Christocentric anthropology and ethics in the theology of Torrance, we found that Torrance does indeed focus on "where" Christian anthropology and ethics occur and derive their impetus from, that is, "Christ's ongoing humanity" and "its reconciling and personalizing work," thereby revealing the centrality of Christ, not only in soteriology, but also in anthropology and ethics. This rejects any kind of independent Christian ethics, particularly in social trinitarianism, that excludes the ongoing reconciling and personalizing work of Christ as the creative source of all ethical life, order, and relations.

Nevertheless, Torrance's theology needs to address ethical issues in the wider social realm and to develop horizontal applications for the church in specific contexts in order to establish a more holistic Christian ethics. In this regard, a strong moral and social theology can proceed along Torrancian lines even if Torrance himself did not say as much about this subject as we might wish. This theological attempt would enable churches and believers to recognize that as the body *of* Christ they are living in multi-cultural and religiously plural societies. This is the reality they are facing and the reason why so many and such wide-ranging ethical, social, and political issues are now being considered in the field of theology. Thus, I believe that it is incumbent upon theology to fully explore and reveal "how" the Christian understanding of God can have ontological and practical significance and suggest implications for human existence, life, and strife. However, it is particularly in "the humanity of Christ" himself, and the church in Christ, where Christology is lived out, that the contribution of Christian theology and ethics should be most visible. This is what we can and should learn from Torrance's Christocentric anthropology and ethics, in which Christian anthropological and ethical thinking and acting should begin with the understanding of "who Christ is" and "what Christ has done and is continually doing" for our true humanity and morality.

Bibliography

Achtemeier, P. Mark. "Natural Science and Christian Faith in the Thought of T. F. Torrance." In *The Promise of Trinitarian Theology*, edited by Elmer M. Colyer, 269–302. Lanham, MD: Rowman & Littlefield, 2001.

Adams, Robert M. "Faith and Religious Knowledge." In *The Cambridge Companion to Friedrich Schleiermacher*, edited by Jacqueline Mariña, 35–52. Cambridge: Cambridge University Press, 2005.

Allen, Diogenes and Springsted, Eric O. *Philosophy for Understanding Theology*. Louisville: Westminster John Knox Press, 2007.

Anderson, Ray S. "Reading T. F. Torrance as a Practical Theologian." In *The Promise of Trinitarian Theology*, edited by Elmer M. Colyer, 161–84. Lanham, MD: Rowman & Littlefield, 2001.

Aristotle. *De Anima*. Translated by R. D. Hicks. Cambridge: Cambridge University Press, 1907.

Ayres, Lewis. "Augustine on the Trinity." In *The Oxford Handbook of the Trinity*, edited by Gilles Emery and Matthew Levering, 123–37. New York: Oxford University Press, 2011.

———. *Nicaea and Its Legacy: An Approach to Fourth-Century Trinitarian Theology*. New York: Oxford University Press, 2004.

———. "'Remember That You Are Catholic' (Serm. 52.2)': Augustine on the Unity of the Triune God." *Journal of Early Christian Studies* 8 (2000) 39–82.

Barnes, Michel R. "Augustine in Contemporary Trinitarian Theology." *Theological Studies* 56 (1995) 237–50.

———. "Exegesis and Polemic in Augustine's *De Trinitate* I." *Augustinian Studies* 30 (1999) 43–59.

———. "Regarding Augustine's Theology of the Trinity." In *The Trinity: An Interdisciplinary Symposium on the Trinity*, edited by Stephen T. Davis et al., 145–76. Oxford: Oxford University Press, 1999.

Barth, Karl. "The Christian Community and the Civil Community." In *Against the Stream: Shorter Post-War Writings, 1946–1952*, edited by Ronald G. Smith, 15–50. London: SCM, 1954.

———. *Church Dogmatics*. Edited by G. W. Bromiley and T. F. Torrance. Translated by T. F. Torrance et al. 13 vols. Edinburgh: T. & T. Clark, 1956–1975.

———. "The Church—The Living Congregation of the Lord Jesus Christ." In vol. 1 of *Man's Disorder and God's Design*, edited by W. A. Visser't Hooft, 67–76. New York: Harper & Brothers, 1948.

Bauckham, Richard. *The Bible in the Contemporary World: Hermeneutical Ventures*. Grand Rapids: Eerdmans, 2015.
Bevan, Andrew M. "The Person of Christ and the Nature of Human Participation in the Theology of T. F. Torrance." PhD diss., University of London, 2002.
Bidwell, Kevin J. *The Church as the Image of the Trinity: A Critical Evaluation of Miroslav Volf's Ecclesial Model*. Eugene, OR: Wipf & Stock, 2011.
Boethius. *The Theological Tractates*. Translated by H. F. Steward and E. K. Rand. London: William Heinemann, 1926.
Boff, Leonardo. *Faith on the Edge: Religion and Marginalized Existence*. San Francisco: Harper & Row, 1989.
———. *Trinity and Society*. Maryknoll, NY: Orbis, 1988.
Bracken, Joseph. *The Triune Symbol: Persons, Process, and Community*. Lanham, MD: University Press of America, 1985.
Brettmann, Stephanie M. *Theories of Justice: A Dialogue with Karl Wojtyla and Karl Barth*. Cambridge: James Clarke, 2014.
Brink, Gijsbert van den. "Social Trinitarianism: A Discussion of Some Recent Theological Criticisms." *International Journal of Systematic Theology* 16.3 (2014) 331–50.
———. "Trinitarian Ecclesiology and the Search for Unity: A Reformed Reading of Miroslav Volf." In *The Unity of the Church: A Theological State of the Art and Beyond*, edited by E. van der Borght, 313–26. Boston: Brill, 2010.
Brown, Alan. "On the Criticism of Being as Communion in Anglophone Orthodox Theology." In *The Theology of John Zizioulas: Personhood and the Church*, edited by Douglas H. Knight, 35–78. London: Routledge, 2007.
Calvin, John. *Institutes of the Christian Religion*. Edited by John T. McNeill. Peabody, MA: Hendrickson, 2008.
Carr, Anne. *Transforming Grace*. San Francisco: Harper & Row, 1988.
Cavadini, John. "The Structure and Intention of Augustine's De Trinitate." *Augustinian Studies* 23 (1992) 101–23.
Charles, David. *Aristotle's Philosophy of Action*. Ithaca: Cornell University Press, 1984.
Chiavone, Michael L. *The One God: A Critically Developed Evangelical Doctrine of Trinitarian Unity*. Cambridge: James Clarke, 2009.
Chung, Paul S. "Dietrich Bonhoeffer Seen from Asian Minjung Theology and the Fourth Eye of Socially Engaged Buddhism." In *Asian Contextual Theology for the Third Millennium: Theology of Minjung in Fourth-Eye Formation*, edited by Paul S. Chung et al., 127–46. Eugene, OR: Wipf & Stock, 2007.
Chung, Titus. *Thomas Torrance's Mediations and Revelation*. Farnham, UK: Ashgate, 2011.
Coakley, Sarah. "Introduction." In *Re-Thinking Gregory of Nyssa*, edited by Sarah Coakley, 2–11. Oxford: Blackwell, 2003.
———. "Person in the Social Doctrines of the Trinity: A Critique of the Current Analytic Discussion." In *The Trinity: An Interdisciplinary Symposium on the Trinity*, edited by Stephen T. Davis et al., 123–44. New York: Oxford University Press, 1999.
Cobb, John. *God and the World*. Philadelphia: Westminster, 1969.
Cobb, John, and David Griffin. *Process Theology: An Introductory Exposition*. Philadelphia: Westminster, 1976.

Colyer, Elmer M. *How to Read T. F. Torrance: Understanding His Trinitarian and Scientific Theology*. Downers Grover, IL: IVP Academic, 2001.

Copan, Paul. "Review of the Christian Doctrine of God." *Trinity Journal* 18.2 (1997) 245–49.

Cunningham, David. *These Three Are One: The Practice of Trinitarian Theology*. Malden, MA: Blackwell, 1998.

Cvetkovic, Vladimir. "T. F. Torrance as Interpreter of St. Athanasius." In *T. F. Torrance and Eastern Orthodoxy*, edited by Matthew Baker and Todd Speidell, 54–91. Eugene, OR: Wipf & Stock, 2015.

Davidson, Matthew. "The Logical Space of Social Trinitarianism." *Faith and Philosophy* 33.3 (2016) 333–57.

Deddo, Gary W. *Karl Barth's Theology of Relations: Trinitarian, Christological, and Human*. Vol. 1. Eugene, OR: Wipf & Stock, 2015.

Douglass, Jane D. "Calvin's Relation to Social and Economic Change." In *Calvin's Thought on Economic and Social Issues and the Relationship of Church and State*, edited by Richard C. Gamble, 127–33. New York: Garland, 1992.

Ebert, Theodor. "Aristotelian Accidents." In vol. 16 of *Oxford Studies in Ancient Philosophy*, edited by C. C. W. Taylor, 133–60. New York: Oxford University Press, 1998.

Elsee, Charles. *Neoplatonism in Relation to Christianity*. Cambridge: Cambridge University Press, 1908.

Ernest, James D. *The Bible in Athanasius of Alexandria*. Boston: Brill, 2004.

Eugenio, Dick. *Communion with the Triune God: The Trinitarian Soteriology of T. F. Torrance*. Eugene, OR: Wipf & Stock, 2014.

Everson, Stephen. "Psychology." In *The Cambridge Companion to Aristotle*, edited by Jonathan Barnes, 168–94. Cambridge: Cambridge University Press, 1995.

Fergusson, David. "The Ascension of Christ: Its Significance in the Theology of T. F. Torrance." *Participatio: Journal of the Thomas F. Torrance Theological Fellowship* 3.1 (2012) 92–107.

———. "The Contours of Macmurray's Philosophy." In *John Macmurray: Critical Perspectives*, edited by David Fergusson and Nigel Dower, 35–50. New York: Peter Lang, 2002.

———. "The Influence of Macmurray on Scottish Theology." *Journal of Scottish Thought* 1.1 (2007) 141–47.

———. "Karl Barth's Doctrine of Creation: Church-Bells Beyond the Stars." *International Journal of Systematic Theology* 18.4 (2016) 414–31.

———. "Persons in Relation: The Interaction of Philosophy, Theology and Psychotherapy in Twentieth-Century Scotland." *Practical Theology* 5.3 (2012) 287–306.

Folsom, Marty. "John Macmurray's Influence on Thomas F. Torrance." *Scottish Journal of Theology* 71.3 (2018) 339–58.

Ford, David F. *The Modern Theologians*. Oxford: Blackwell, 1997.

Fox, Matthew. *Original Blessing: A Primer in Creation Spirituality*. Santa Fe, NM: Bear and Company, 1983.

Grenz, Stanley J. *Rediscovering the Triune God*. Minneapolis: Fortress, 2004.

———. *The Social God and the Relational Self*. Grand Rapids: Eerdmans, 2001.

———. *Theology for the Community of God*. Grand Rapids: Eerdmans, 1994.

Gunton, Colin E. "Being and Person: T. F. Torrance's Doctrine of God." In *The Promise of Trinitarian Theology*, edited by Elmer M. Colyer, 115–37. Lanham, MD: Rowman & Littlefield, 2001.

———. *Christ and Creation: The Didsbury Lectures 1990*. Carlisle: Paternoster; Grand Rapids: Eerdmans, 1992.

———. *The One, the Three and the Many: God, Creation and the Culture of Modernity*. Cambridge: Cambridge University Press, 1993.

———. "Person and Particularity." In *The Theology of John Zizioulas: Personhood and the Church*, edited by Douglas H. Knight, 97–108. London: Routledge, 2007.

———. *The Promise of Trinitarian Theology*. Edinburgh: T. & T. Clark, 1991.

———. *The Triune Creator: A Historical and Systematic Study*. Grand Rapids: Eerdmans, 1998.

Haas, Guenther. *The Concept of Equity in Calvin's Ethics*. Waterloo, Ontario: Wilfrid Laurier University Press, 1997.

Habets, Myk. "The Doctrine of Election in Evangelical Calvinism: T. F. Torrance as a Case Study." *Irish Theological Quarterly* 73 (2008) 334–54.

———. *Theology in Transposition: A Constructive Appraisal of T. F. Torrance*. Minneapolis: Fortress, 2013.

———. *Theosis in the Theology of Thomas Torrance*. Farnham, UK: Ashgate, 2009.

Hanson, Richard P. *The Search for the Christian Doctrine of God: The Arian Controversy 318-38*. Edinburgh: T. & T. Clark, 1988.

Hardy, Daniel W. "T. F. Torrance." In *The Modern Theologians: An Introduction to Christian Theology since 1918*, edited by David Ford and Rachel Muers, 163–77. Oxford: Blackwell, 2005.

Hart, Trevor A. *Regarding Karl Barth: Essays Toward a Reading of His Theology*. Carlisle: Paternoster, 1999.

Hartman, Edwin. *Substance, Body and Soul: Aristotelian investigations*. Princeton, NJ: Princeton University Press, 1977.

Hasker, William. "Objections to Social Trinitarianism." *Religious Studies* 46 (2010) 421–39.

Heinaman, Robert. "Aristotle and the Mind-Body Problem." *Phronesis* 35 (1990) 83–102.

Hilkert, Mary C. "The Mystery of Persons in Communion: The Trinitarian Theology of Catherine Mowry LaCugna." *Word and World* 18.3 (1998) 237–43.

Ho, Man Kei. *A Critical Study on T. F. Torrance's Theology of Incarnation*. Bern: Peter Lang, 2008.

Holmes, Christopher R. J. *Ethics in the Presence of Christ*. New York: T. & T. Clark, 2012.

Holmes, Stephen R. *The Quest for the Trinity: The Doctrine of God in Scripture, History and Modernity*. Downers Grover, IL: IVP Academic, 2012.

———. "Three Versus One? Some Problems of Social Trinitarianism." *Journal of Reformed Theology* 3 (2009) 77–89.

Horrell, Scott. "Toward a Biblical Model of the Social Trinity: Avoiding Equivocation of Nature and Order." *Journal of the Evangelical Theological Society* 47.3 (2004) 399–421.

Hunsinger, George. *Conversational Theology: Essays on Ecumenical, Postliberal, and Political Themes, with Special Reference to Karl Barth*. London: Bloomsbury, 2015.

———. "The Dimension of Depth: Thomas F. Torrance on the Sacraments." In *The Promise of Trinitarian Theology*, edited by Elmer M. Colyer, 139–60. Lanham, MD: Rowman & Littlefield, 2001.

———. *Evangelical, Catholic, and Reformed: Essays on Barth and Other Themes*. Grand Rapids: Eerdmans, 2015.

Hunt, Anne. "The Trinity and the Church." *Irish Theological Quarterly* 70 (2005) 215–35.

Janson, Robert W. *The Triune Identity: God According to the Gospel*. Philadelphia: Fortress, 1982.

Jing, Wei. "The Theological Anthropology of Thomas F. Torrance: A Critical and Comparative Exploration." PhD diss., University of Edinburgh, 2013.

Jones, David W. *Reforming the Morality of Usury: A Study of Differences that Separated the Protestant Reformers*. Lanham, MD: University Press of America, 2004.

Jüngel, Eberhard. *God's Being Is in Becoming: The Trinitarian Being of God in the Theology of Karl Barth, a Paraphrase*. Translated by John B. Webster. Grand Rapids: Eerdmans, 2001.

———. *Theological Essays II*. Translated by Arnold Neufeldt-Fast and John B. Webster. Edinburgh: T. & T. Clark, 1995.

Kelsey, David. "What Happened to the Doctrine of Sin?" *Theology Today* 50.2 (1993) 169–78.

Kettler, Christian D. *The Vicarious Humanity of Christ and the Reality of Salvation*. Lanham: University Press of America, 1991.

Kilby, Karen. "Perichoresis and Projection: Problems with Social Doctrines of the Trinity." *New Blackfriars* 81 (2000) 432–45.

Kilcrease, Jack D. *The Doctrine of Atonement: From Luther to Forde*. Eugene, OR: Wipf & Stock, 2018.

King, Daniel. "Introduction." In *Three Christological Treatises*, by Cyril of Alexandria, 3–34. Translated by Daniel King. Washington, DC: Catholic University of America Press, 2014.

LaCugna, Catherine Mowry. *God for Us: The Trinity and Christian Life*. New York: Harper San Francisco, 1991.

———. "Philosophers and Theologians on the Trinity." *Modern Theology* 2 (1986) 169–81.

———. "The Practical Trinity." *Christian Century* 109.22 (1992) 678–83.

LaCugna, Catherine Mowry, and Killan McDonnell. "Returning from 'The Far Country': Theses for a Contemporary Trinitarian Theology." *Scottish Journal of Theology* 41 (1998) 191–215.

Lehmann, Paul L. *Ethics in a Christian Context*. New York: Harper & Row, 1963.

Loder, James E., and W. Jim Neidhardt. *The Knight's Move: The Relational Logic of the Spirit in Theology*. Colorado Springs: Helmers & Howard, 1992.

Macmurray, John. *Persons in Relation*. 1961. Reprint, New York: Humanities, 1999.

———. *Reason and Emotion*. 1935. Reprint, New York: Humanities, 1992.

———. *Religion, Art, and Science: A Study of the Reflective Activities in Man*. Liverpool: Liverpool University Press: 1961.

———. *Search for Reality in Religion*. London: Allen & Unwin, 1965.

———. *The Self as Agent*. New York: Harper & Brothers, 1953.

Manson, William. *Jesus and the Christian*. Grand Rapids: Eerdmans, 1967.

McDougall, Joy A. "The Return of Trinitarian Praxis? Moltmann on the Trinity and the Christian Life." *The Journal of Religion* 83.2 (2003) 177–203.

McFague, Sallie. *A New Climate for Theology: God, the World, and Global Warming*. Minneapolis: Fortress, 2008.

McGrath, Alister E. *Thomas F. Torrance: An Intellectual Biography*. Edinburgh: T. & T. Clack, 1999.

Molnar, Paul D. *Divine Freedom and the Doctrine of the Immanent Trinity*. London: T. & T. Clark, 2002.

———. *Faith, Freedom and the Spirit: The Economic Trinity in Barth, Torrance and Contemporary Theology*. Downers Grover, IL: IVP Academic, 2015.

———. "The Function of the Immanent Trinity." *Scottish Journal of Theology* 42.3 (1989) 367–99.

———. *Incarnation and Resurrection: Toward a Contemporary Understanding*. Grand Rapids: Eerdmans, 2007.

———. *Thomas F. Torrance: Theologian of the Trinity*. Farnham, UK: Ashgate, 2009.

Moltmann, Jürgen. *God for a Secular Society: The Public Relevance of Theology*. London: SCM, 1999.

———. *The Church in the Power of the Spirit*. London: SCM, 1977.

———. *The Crucified God: The Cross of Christ as the Foundation and Criticism of Christian Theology*. Translated by R. A. Wilson and John Bowden. Minneapolis: Fortress, 1993.

———. *History and The Triune God*. Translated by John Bowden. New York: Crossroad, 1992.

———. "Some Reflections on the Social Doctrine of the Trinity." In *The Christian Understanding of God Today: Theological Colloquium on the Occasion of the 400th Anniversary of the Foundation of Trinity College, Dublin*, edited by James M. Byrne, 104–11. Dublin: Columba, 1993.

———. *The Spirit of Life: A Universal Affirmation*. Translated by Margaret Kohl. London: SCM, 1992.

———. *The Trinity and the Kingdom*. Minneapolis: Fortress, 1993.

Moore-Keish, Martha L. "Sacraments in General and Baptism in Twentieth-Century and Contemporary Protestant Theology." In *The Oxford Handbook of Sacramental Theology*, edited by Hands Boersma and Matthew Levering, 396–409. Oxford: Oxford University Press, 2015.

Morrison, John D. *Knowledge of the Self-Revealing God in the Thought of Thomas Forsyth Torrance*. New York: Peter Lang, 1997.

Muller, Earl C. "Rhetorical and Theological Issues in the Structuring of Augustine's *De Trinitate*." In vol. 27 of *Studia Patristica*, edited by Elizabeth A. Livingstone, 356–63. Leuven: Peeters, 1993.

Myers, Benjamin. "The Stratification of Knowledge in the Thought of T. F. Torrance." *Scottish Journal of Theology* 61.1 (2008) 1–15.

Nash, Roderick. *The Rights of Nature: A History of Environmental Ethics*. Madison: University of Wisconsin Press, 1989.

Nicholls, David. *Deity and Domination: Images of God and the State in the Nineteenth and Twentieth Centuries*. New York: Routledge, 1989.

Niebuhr, H. Richard. *Christ and Culture*. New York: Harper & Row, 1951.

Noble, Thomas A. "Thomas Forsyth Torrance." In *Dictionary of Scottish Church History and Theology*, edited by Nigel M. de S. Cameron, 823–24. Edinburgh: T. & T. Clark, 1993.

O'Donnell, John. *The Mystery of the Triune God*. New York: Paulist, 1989.

Padgett, Alan G. "Dialectical Realism in Theology and Science." *Perspective on Science and Christian Faith* 54.3 (2002) 184–92.

Pannenberg, Wolfhart. *Systematic Theology*. Vol. 1. Translated by Geoffrey Bromiley. Grand Rapids: Eerdmans, 1988.

Patterson, Sue M. *Realist Christian Theology in a Postmodern Age*. Cambridge: Cambridge University Press, 1999.

Perlman, Helen H. *Persona: Social Role and Personality*. Chicago: University of Chicago Press, 1968.

Peters, Ted. *God as Trinity: Relationality and Temporality in Divine Life*. Louisville, Kentucky: Westminster John Knox, 1993.

Plantinga, Cornelius, Jr. "Social Trinity and Tritheism." In *Trinity, Incarnation, and Atonement: Philosophical and Theological Essays*, edited by Ronald Feensta and Cornelius Plantinga Jr., 21–47. Notre Dame: University of Notre Dame Press, 1989.

Polanyi, Michael. *Personal Knowledge: Towards a Post-Critical Philosophy*. London: Routledge & Kegan Paul, 1958.

———. *Science, Faith, and Society*. New York: Oxford University Press, 1948.

Purves, Andrew. "The Christology of Thomas F. Torrance." In *The Promise of Trinitarian Theology*, edited by Elmer M. Colyer, 51–80. Lanham, MD: Rowman & Littlefield, 2001.

Radcliff, Alexandra S. *The Claim of Humanity in Christ: Salvation and Sanctification in the Theology in T. F. and J. B. Torrance*. Eugene, OR: Wipf & Stock, 2016.

Radcliff, Jason R. *Thomas F. Torrance and the Church Fathers*. Eugene, OR: Wipf & Stock, 2014.

Robinson, Howard. "Aristotelian Dualism." *Oxford Studies in Ancient Philosophy* 1 (1983) 123–44.

Rudman, Stanley. *Concepts of Person and Christian Ethics*. Cambridge: Cambridge University Press, 1997.

Ruether, Rosemary R. *Gaia and God: An Ecofeminist Theology of Earth Healing*. San Francisco: Harper & Row, 1992.

Russell, Edward. "Reconsidering Relational Anthropology: A Critical Assessment of John Zizioulas's Theological Anthropology." *International Journal of Systematic Theology* 5.5 (2003) 168–86.

Sauer, James B. *Faithful Ethics According to John Calvin: The Teachability of the Heart*. New York: Edwin Mellen, 1997.

Schwöbel, Christoph. "The Creature of the Word: Recovering the Ecclesiology of the Reformers." In *On Being the Church*, edited by Colin E. Gunton and Daniel W. Hardy, 110–55. Edinburgh: T. & T. Clark, 1989.

Shields, Christopher. "Soul and Body in Aristotle." *Oxford Studies in Ancient Philosophy* 4 (1988) 103–35.

Sittler, Joseph. "A Theology for Earth." *Christian Scholar* 37 (1954) 367–74.

Speidell, Todd. *Fully Human in Christ: The Incarnation as the End of Christian Ethics*. Eugene, OR: Wipf & Stock, 2016.

Stead, George C. *Divine Substance*. Oxford: Oxford University Press, 1977.

———. *Philosophy in Christian Antiquity*. Cambridge: Cambridge University Press, 1994.

Stein, Jock. "Editor's Introduction." In *Gospel, Church, and Ministry*, by Thomas F. Torrance, 1–24. Eugene, OR: Wipf & Stock, 2012.

Tanner, Kathryn. *Christ the Key*. New York: Cambridge University Press, 2010.

———. "Trinity, Christology, and Community." In *Christology and Ethics*, edited by F. LeRon Shults and Brent Waters, 56–74. Grand Rapids: Eerdmans, 2010.

Thiel, Udo. "Personal Identity." In vol. 2 of *The Cambridge History of Seventeenth-Century Philosophy*, edited by Daniel Garber and Michael Ayers, 868–912. Cambridge: Cambridge University Press, 2003.

Torrance, Alan J. *Persons in Communion: An Essay on Trinitarian Description and Human Participation*. Edinburgh: T. & T. Clark, 1996.

Torrance, James B. "The Place of Jesus Christ in Worship." In *Theological Foundations for Ministry*, edited by Ray S. Anderson, 348–69. Edinburgh: T. & T. Clark, 1979.

Torrance, Thomas F. *Atonement: The Person and Life of Christ*. Edited by Robert T. Walker. Downers Grover, IL: IVP Academic, 2009.

———. *The Being and Nature of the Unborn Child*. Lenior, NC: Glen Lorien, 2000.

———. *Calvin's Doctrine of Man*. Grand Rapids: Eerdmans, 1957.

———. *The Christian Doctrine of God: One Being Three Persons*. Edinburgh: T. & T. Clark, 1996.

———. *The Christian Doctrine of Marriage*. Edinburgh: Handsel, 1992.

———. *The Christian Frame of Mind*. Colorado Springs: Helmers & Howard, 1989.

———. *Christian Theology and Scientific Culture*. Eugene, OR: Wipf & Stock, 1998.

———. "Concerning Amsterdam." *Scottish Journal of Theology* 2 (1949) 241–70.

———. *Conflict and Agreement in the Church I*. London: Lutterworth, 1959.

———. *Conflict and Agreement in the Church II*. London: Lutterworth, 1960.

———. *Divine and Contingent Order*. Oxford: Oxford University Press, 1981.

———. "Divine and Contingent Order." In *The Sciences and Theology in the Twentieth Century*, edited by A. R. Peacocke, 81–92. Notre Dame, IN: University of Notre Dame Press, 1981.

———. *Divine Interpretation*. Edited by Adam Nigh and Todd Speidell. Eugene, OR: Wipf & Stock, 2017.

———. *Divine Meaning: Studies in Patristic Hermeneutics*. Edinburgh: T. & T. Clark, 1995.

———. *The Doctrine of Jesus Christ*. Eugene, OR: Wipf & Stock, 2002.

———. "Eschatology and the Eucharist." In *Intercommunion*, edited by D. M. Baillie and J. Marsh, 303–50. London: SCM, 1952.

———. "The Framework of Belief." In *Belief in Science and in Christian Life: The Relevance of Michael Polanyi's Thought for Christian Faith and Life*, edited by Thomas F. Torrance, 1–27. Edinburgh: Handsel, 1980.

———. *God and Rationality*. London: Oxford University Press, 1971.

———. "The Goodness and Dignity of Man in the Christian Tradition." *Modern Theology* 4 (1988) 309–22.

———. *Gospel, Church, and Ministry*. Edited by Jock Stein. Eugene, OR: Wipf & Stock, 2012.

———. *The Ground and Grammar of Theology*. Charlottesville: University Press of Virginia, 1980.

———. *Incarnation: The Person and Life of Christ*. Edited by Robert T. Walker. Downers Grover, IL: IVP Academic, 2008.
———. "Justification: Its Radical Nature and Place in Reformed Doctrine and Life." *Scottish Journal of Theology* 13 (1960) 225–46.
———. "Karl Barth and the Latin Heresy." *Scottish Journal of Theology* 39.4 (1986) 461–82.
———. *Karl Barth, Biblical and Evangelical Theologian*. Edinburgh: T. & T. Clark, 1990.
———. *The Mediation of Christ*. Colorado Springs: Helmers & Howard, 1992.
———. *The Ministry of Women*. Edinburgh: Handsel, 1992
———. "Notes on Terms and Concepts." In *Belief in Science and in Christian Life: The Relevance of Michael Polanyi's Thought for Christian Faith and Life*, edited by Thomas F. Torrance, 133–47. Edinburgh: Handsel, 1980.
———. "One Aspect of the Biblical Conception of Faith." *The Expository Times* 68.1 (1957) 111–14.
———. "Predestination in Christ." *The Evangelical Quarterly* 13 (1941) 108–41.
———. "The Problem of Natural Theology in the Thought of Karl Barth." *Religious Studies* 6.2 (1970) 121–35.
———. *Reality and Evangelical Theology*. Philadelphia: Westminster, 1982.
———. *Reality and Scientific Theology*. Eugene, OR: Wipf & Stock, 2001.
———. *Royal Priesthood*. Edinburgh: T. & T. Clark, 1993.
———. *The School of Faith: The Catechisms of the Reformed Church*. London: James Clarke, 1959.
———. "A Sermon on the Trinity." *Biblical Theology* 6.2 (1956) 40–44.
———. "The Singularity of Christ and the Finality of the Cross: The Atonement and the Moral Order." In *Universalism and the Doctrine of Hell*, edited by Nigel M. de S. Cameron, 223–54. Grand Rapids: Baker, 1992.
———. "The Soul and Person, in Theological Perspective." In *Religion, Reason and the Self: Essays in Honour of Hywel D. Lweis*, edited by Stewart R. Sutherland and T. A. Roberts, 103–18. Cardiff: University of Wales Press, 1989.
———. *The Soul and Person of the Unborn Child*. Edinburgh: Handsel, 1999.
———. *Space, Time and Incarnation*. London: Oxford University Press, 1969.
———. *Space, Time and Resurrection*. Edinburgh: T. & T. Clark, 1998.
———. *Theological Science*. Oxford: Oxford University Press, 1969.
———. *Theology in Reconciliation*. London: Geoffrey Chapman, 1975.
———. *Theology in Reconstruction*. London: SCM, 1965.
———. "Thomas Torrance Responds." In *The Promise of Trinitarian Theology: Theologians in Dialogue with T. F. Torrance*, edited by Elmer M. Colyer, 303–40. Lanham, MD: Rowman & Littlefield, 2001.
———. *Transformation and Convergence in the Frame of Knowledge*. Eugene, OR: Wipf & Stock, 1998.
———. *The Trinitarian Faith*. Edinburgh: T. & T. Clark, 1991.
———. *Trinitarian Perspectives: Toward Doctrinal Agreement*. Edinburgh: T. & T. Clark, 1994.
———. "Universalism or Election?" *Scottish Journal of Theology* 2 (1949) 310–18.
———. "What Is the Church?" *The Ecumenical Review* 11 (1958) 6–21.
Vogel, C. J. de. "The Concept of Personality in Greek and Christian Thought." In *Studies in Philosophy and the History of Philosophy*, edited by Ryan John Kenneth, 20–60. Catholic University of America Press, 1963.

Volf, Miroslav. *After Our Likeness: The Church as the Image of the Trinity*. Grand Rapids: Eerdmans, 1998.

———. *Exclusion and Embrace: A Theological Exploration of Identity, Otherness, and Reconciliation*. Nashville, TN: Abingdon, 1996.

———. "'The Trinity is Our Social Program': The Doctrine of the Trinity and the Shape of Social Engagement." *Modern Theology* 14.3 (1998) 403–23.

Walker, Robert T. "Editor's Introduction." In *Atonement: The Person and Life of Christ*, by Thomas F. Torrance, xxxv–lxxxiii. Downers Grover, IL: IVP Academic, 2009.

———. "Editor's Introduction." In *Incarnation: The Person and Life of Christ*, by Thomas F. Torrance, xxi–lii. Downers Grover, IL: IVP Academic, 2008.

———. "Glossary." In *Incarnation: The Person and Life of Christ*, by Thomas F. Torrance, 345–67. Downers Grover, IL: IVP Academic, 2008.

———. Review of *Theology in Transposition: A Constructive Appraisal of T. F. Torrance*, by Myk Habets. *Scottish Journal of Theology* 71.1 (2018) 112–14.

Watson, Richard A. "Dualism." In *The Cambridge Dictionary of Philosophy*, edited by Robert Audi, 244. Cambridge: Cambridge University Press, 1999.

Webster, John B. *Barth's Ethics of Reconciliation*. Cambridge: Cambridge University Press, 1995.

———. *Barth's Moral Theology: Human Action in Barth's Thought*. Grand Rapids: Eerdmans, 1998.

———. "The Christian in Revolt: Some Reflections on the Christ Life." In *Reckoning with Barth: Essays in Commemoration of the Centenary of Karl Barth's Birth*, edited by Nigel Biggar, 119–44. London: Mowbary, 1988.

———. "Christology, Imitability and Ethics." *Scottish Journal of Theology* 39.3 (1986) 309–26.

———. *Eberhard Jüngel: An Introduction to His Theology*. Cambridge: Cambridge University Press, 1986.

———. "Editorial: T. F. Torrance 1913–2007." *International Journal of Systematic Theology* 10.4 (2008) 369–71.

———. "The Imitation of Christ." *Tyndale Bulletin* 37 (1986) 95–96.

Weightman, Colin. *Theology in a Polanyian Universe: The Theology of Thomas Torrance*. New York: Peter Lang, 1994.

White, James F. *The Sacraments in Protestant Practice and Faith*. Nashville, TN: Abingdon, 1999.

White, Lynn, Jr. "The Historical Roots of Our Ecological Crisis." *Science* 155 (1967) 1203–7.

Wolterstorff, Nicholas. *Hearing the Call: Liturgy, Justice, Church, and World*. Grand Rapids: Eerdmans, 2011.

Yoder, John Howard. *Body Politics: Five Practices of the Christian Community before the Watching World*. Nashville, TN: Discipleship Resources, 1992.

Ziegler, Geordie W. *Trinitarian Grace and Participation: An Entry into the Theology of T. F. Torrance*. Minneapolis: Fortress, 2017.

Zizioulas, John D. *Being as Communion: Studies in Personhood and the Church*. New York: St Vladimir's Seminary, 2004.

———. "The Church as Communion: A Presentation on the World Conference Theme." In *On the Way to Fuller Koinonia*, edited by Thomas F. Best and Günther Gassmann, 103–11. Geneva: WCC, 1994.

———. *Communion and Otherness: Further Studies in Personhood and the Church.* Edited by Paul McPartlan. London: T. & T. Clark, 2006.

———. "Human Capacity and Human Incapacity: A Theological Exploration of Personhood." *Scottish Journal of Theology* 28.5 (1975) 401–47.

General Index

A

abortion, 87, 123–24, 130–32, 164n83
absolutism, 65, 170n107
adoption, 142, 147, 151, 155n48, 158n59
agent
    human, 37n136, 86, 119
    knowing, 28, 29, 29n107, 30
    personal, 18, 26, 30, 32–33, 43
    rational, 17, 30
anamnesis, 156, 158,
Anderson, Ray, 82, 84n137
anhypostasia, 100n56, 102
anthropocentrism, 135, 136n201, 137, 139
anthropology
    a trinitarian model for, 53n30
    Platonic-Aristotelian, 3, 4n7, 9, 10n33, 25
    Torrance's, 3, 9n30, 25n88, 35
anthropology and ethics
    Christian, 43, 64, 69, 98n48, 116–18, 122–23, 141, 180, 182, 184, 186
    Christocentric, 87, 139, 140, 180, 183–87
Arianism, 48, 62, 89n14, 96n39
Aristotle, 2, 4, 6, 8n28, 17, 35–37, 38–39, 43, 50, 89, 181
Athanasius, 31n113, 42, 45, 48, 49n13, 50, 54n36, 56, 66, 72n105, 96, 148n24, 153n44, 158n59, 158n42

atonement
    actuality of, 96, 98
    incarnational, 98n52, 106
    instrumental and external, 99n52
    internality of, 102
    juridical, 14n49
    reconciliation through, 91n19, 94n35
    substitutionary aspect of, 155
Augustine, 2, 14, 25, 35, 39, 40, 41–43, 57n52, 58n52, 59n60, 73n106
Ayres, Lewis, 2n4, 39, 40, 59n60

B

baptism, 75, 100n56, 113n114, 149n31, 152n39, 153–58, 169, 175n125
Barth, Karl, 16n59, 22n81, 31n113, 35n127, 43, 49n13, 53, 54n36, 64n76, 84n137, 101n58, 119n138, 122n, 126n158, 130n177, 136–37, 140, 146–47, 150n34, 157n59, 164, 166–67, 170n107, 178, 183
Bauckham, Richard, 135n198
being-constituting relation, 19, 21–23, 26, 44
Bevan, Andrew, 7
Bidwell, Kevin, 173n117,
Boethius, 6n17, 13–15, 36, 39, 42
Boff, Leonardo, 47n7, 76, 170n108
Bonhoeffer, Dietrich, 84n137

Bracken Joseph, 77
Brink, Gijsbert van den, 76n112, 77, 79n126
Bultmann, Rudolf, 16n59

C

Calvin, John, 22n81, 31n113, 59n56, 60n62, 102n62, 122n147, 140, 145n11, 153n44, 157n59, 164–65, 178, 183, 185
Cappadocians, 57n52, 61–62, 70
  Basil, 58, 60, 62, 70n94
  Gregory Nazianzen, 45, 55, 60n62, 61, 66
  Gregory of Nyssa, 62, 70n94
Carr, Anne, 76, 77n115
Chalcedon, 96n42
Charles, David, 37n133
Christocentrism, 123
Christopraxis, 82
Chung, Paul, 185
Chung, Titus, 151, 164
church,
  being and life of, 143–150
  body of Christ, 113n114, 126, 141, 145n12, 146–48, 150, 156n54, 159–60, 162n77, 168, 174, 177–78, 183, 186
  diakonia, 151, 161–62, 164, 177–79
  eschatological movement of, 150–51
  horizontal dimension of, 151
  reconciled existence of, 167n96
  sacramental and diaconal action of, 151–167
Coakley, Sarah, 73n106
Cobb, John, 137n204
coinherence, 50n17, 55
Colyer, Elmer, 10n33, 19n64, 51n18, 88n7, 98, 103, 157n56
Confucianism, 185
Constantinople, 48
contingent order, 133, 136, 139n211
conversion, 75n110, 118, 164, 165
creation
  new, 107, 126, 128
  redemption and, 110n99, 124
  human priestly role in, 134–39
critical realism, 17n59, 18, 87, 92–93, 133n191
culture, 17, 28, 66n82, 123n147, 129, 164–65, 178, 183
Cunningham, David, 117n131
Cvetkovic, Vladimir, 96n42
Cyril of Alexandria, 96n42, 100n56

D

dehumanization, 74, 83, 112, 117, 141n1, 160n64, 182, 184
deification, 142, 151
deism, 7n23
Demiurge, 5
Descartes, René, 15, 37n136, 39, 91
  Cartesian idea of self-consciousness, 16n59
  Cartesian approach, 31–32
  Cartesian notion of humanity, 33
determinism, 94n34
divine simplicity, 40
Docetism, 85n1
dualism
  anthropological/body and soul, 4, 6, 9, 36–37
  Platonic-Aristotelian, 8–9
  Neoplatonic, 14n49
  epistemological and cosmological, 17, 27, 89–94

E

Ebionism, 85n1
ecclesiology, 141–43, 144n10, 146n16, 149n31, 150n34, 151, 159, 163–64, 167–70, 173–74, 177–79, 183–84
ecocentrism, 137
ecology, 132, 138–39
egalitarianism, 124–27, 158n59
Einstein, Albert, 16n59, 25n90, 28
election, 135, 136n201, 144, 145n11–12, 166

embryo, 131–32
enhypostasia, 100–102
Epiphanius, 56n47
epistemology
  critical realist, 92–93
  scientific and philosophical, 26, 35, 43
equality, 46, 62, 111n108, 124–27, 158n59, 170n107
eschatology, 150, 152
ethics
  environmental, 132–39
  financial, 164–65
  medical, 130–32
  sexual, 127–30
  social, 111, 151, 163, 166
  suspension of, 115–16, 119
Eucharist, 153–59, 170
Eunomius, 61n63
ex nihilo, 10n33, 20, 133n191
exemplarism, 31, 32n118, 116, 117n131, 163, 168n97, 182
existence
  adamic, 106, 109,
  Christ's reconciling and personalizing, 122
  fallen, 106–7
  God's, 40n144, 100n56
  human, 22, 25, 28, 34, 52, 94, 96, 97, 98n47, 99, 109, 115, 156, 159, 171, 177n132, 186
  human contingent, 21–22
  modes of, 61
  personal, 33, 76n114
  the incommunicable, 12, 13

F

Father, the divine person of
  arche theotetos, 60n62
  monarchy, 62, 63n72
Fergusson, David, 84n137, 112n108, 120–22, 140
filioque, 62n73
forgiveness, 23n84, 156, 173n117
Fox, Matthew, 136

freedom, 66, 68, 70–71, 108, 111n108, 137, 138n208, 150n34, 166

G

God
  and human knowing in Christ, 90–94
  and reconciliation in Christ, 94–99
grace
  inner logic of, 102, 105
Grenz, Stanley, 77
Gunton, Colin, 46, 52–55, 57–60, 66n82, 73n106, 111n108, 137

H

Habets, Myk, 22n81, 98n52, 138, 142, 150n31, 151
Hanson, Richard, 62
Hartman, Edwin, 37n133
Hegel, G. W. F, 16, 64n76
Heinaman, Robert, 37n136, 39
Holmes, Christopher, 116, 117n131, 163n82
Holmes, Stephen, 78–79, 80n127, 97n42
Homoians, 40n144
humanity,
  Greek and Roman view of, 4–8
  Hebrew unitary view of, 2n3, 3, 9–11
  transformation of, 24n88, 67, 86–87, 99, 108–16, 139, 165n84, 182
Hunsinger, George, 64n76, 150n34, 157n59
hylomorphism, 37n136

I

imago Dei, 19–25, 39n143, 67, 80, 156, 174
impassibility, 54n36, 85n1

GENERAL INDEX

individualism, 52n27, 71, 73n106, 74, 75n110, 111, 112n108, 113, 174
Irenaeus, 146n16, 153n44
Israel
    in relation to church, 144–46
    the community of reciprocity between God and, 104

J

Jesus Christ
    ascension, 81, 95n36, 103, 107–9, 120, 145, 148
    cross, 23n84, 54n36, 68n89–90, 98n52, 109, 110, 145n11, 148n24, 155, 161n74, 171n117, 172, 173n118
    crucifixion, 89n14, 98n47, 146n12
    death, 54n36, 68, 81, 94n35, 95n36, 102–3, 108–9, 114, 143n5, 145–46, 148, 153n44, 154–56, 166, 173,
    diakonos par excellence, 161, 177n132
    fallen humanity, 25, 98, 100–102, 105–7, 109, 111–12, 121, 148n24
    homoousios, 40n144, 48, 72n105, 97
    homoousion, 48–52, 55, 59n60, 62, 72n105, 74, 80, 96–97, 99, 181–82
    hypostatic union, 80, 87, 96–99, 101, 103, 105, 111, 182
    incarnation, 90–93, 95, 99, 100n56, 101–3, 105–7, 110, 126, 134, 138, 142n3, 144, 146–48, 153, 155–56, 168, 174, 177, 183
    justification, 87, 100n54, 103–5, 108, 119, 121, 148, 154–56, 159, 161, 166–67
    katabasis and *anabasis*, 157
    new humanity, 106–17, 119, 121–23, 126–28, 140–44, 148–50, 153, 157n59, 160n64, 163, 168, 177, 182
    mediation, 19, 25, 67, 81, 94, 115
    Mediator, 96–97, 113–14, 144n10
    personalizing person, 24, 74, 83, 109, 113, 121, 131
    resurrection, 89n14, 98n47, 102–3, 107–9, 145–46, 148n26, 154, 157
    union with, 24, 68–69, 75n110, 81, 87, 104–5, 114–15, 118, 121–23, 128, 149n31, 150, 152, 157n59, 159, 161, 163, 176–78
    vicarious humanity, 67n85, 84n137, 101, 103–6, 109n94, 119, 140, 146n12, 153–55, 158n59, 161n74, 162–163, 175
    virgin birth, 101, 126n158, 132
Jones, David, 165
judgement, God's, 100, 102, 110, 130n175, 162, 182, 184
Jüngel, Eberhard, 65n76, 67n85

K

Kant, Immanuel, 16n59, 27–28, 9–92
kerygma, 151–52
Kettler, Christian, 106n85
Kilby, Karen, 78–79, 84, 168
Kilcrease, Jack, 67n85
koinonia, 142n4, 169, 173–75

L

LaCugna, Catherine Mowry, 47n7, 66n82, 76, 81, 171n109, 175n125
Lehmann, Paul, 117n131, 163

M

Macmurray, John, 2n3, 18n63, 31–34, 112n108, 137n208

Manson, William, 118
marriage, 21–22, 127–30
Maxwell, Clerk, 16n59
McDougall, Joy, 66n82, 69n91
McFague, Sallie, 137n205
McGrath, Alister, 8, 16n59, 19n64, 43n157, 122n146, 138
modalism, 46–47, 54–55, 58n52, 63, 77n119,
modes of being, 35n127, 61, 64n76
Molnar, Paul, 16n59, 19n64, 57, 62n73, 113, 137n206
Moltmann, Jürgen, 64–69, 76, 142n5, 169,
monotheism, 46n7, 65, 170n107
morality, 69, 105n80, 115–17, 119–20, 122, 129, 183, 186–87

N

nature
    of the Trinity, 11–12, 17–18, 20n65, 44, 51, 67, 69–70, 72–74, 79–80
    of human beings, 5–6, 9, 13–15, 19–21, 23–24, 33, 36, 41, 56
Neoplatonism, 14n49, 39
Nestorianism, 100n56
Newton, Isaac, 15–16, 27–29, 89,
Nicaea, 48, 51, 62, 72n105, 73, 96n39,
Niebuhr, Richard, 165n84
Nicholls, David, 170n107

O

obedience, 29n107, 54n36, 101, 103–8, 150n34, 153n44
oikonomia, 40n143, 47n7, 49, 76n113
onto-relations, 23–24, 42, 62
ontology, 8
    Aristotelian, 59n60, 70
    Cappadocian, 59–60, 63
    realist, 93
    relational, 77, 169
    Torrance's, 8, 71, 74
    trinitarian, 58–59, 136

Zizioulas's, 70–71, 174
organisms, 135–37

P

Padgett, Alan, 92
panentheism, 137
Pannenberg, Wolfhart, 65n76
pantheism, 137
parousia
    divine, 74
    eucharistic, 157
    incarnate, 176
participatio Christi, 141–43, 151–52, 163, 168, 175, 177–78, 183
Pentecost, 146, 149
person(s)
    in relation(s), 3, 12
    the concept of, 11–19, 35–36, 38, 43, 131
personal knowledge, 26–30, 114n116
Plato, 5–7, 8n28, 9, 15, 17, 20, 36–37, 39, 89
pneumatology, 149n31, 168
Polanyi, Michael, 26–31
Purves, Andrew, 138

R

Radcliff, Alexandra, 154n45
Radcliff, Jason, 97n42
Rahner, Karl, 50n16
reconciliation
    atoning, 94n35, 97–100, 108, 146n12, 148, 149n31, 154
    incarnational, 24n88
Régnon, Théodore de, 73n106
revelation, 8, 35, 40, 42, 48–51, 60, 64, 72, 81–82, 86–96, 100, 145–46, 151
Robinson, Howard, 37n136, 39
Rudman, Stanley, 117
Ruether, Rosemary, 139n212
Russell, Edward, 75n110

S

sanctification, 101–2, 111, 155–56, 159, 161
Schleiermacher, Friedrich, 16n59, 91n22
Shields, Christopher, 2n4, 37n136, 39n140
Sittler, Joseph, 135n200
Smail, Thomas, 154n45
social justice, 117n131, 120, 122, 140, 158n59, 163n82, 164, 167, 178
social trinitarianism, 46–47, 52n27, 65n76, 75–84, 142–43, 168, 178, 182–86
Speidell, Todd, 110, 115, 122n146, 125
stewardship, 135, 139
stratification of knowledge, 25
subordinationism, 46–47, 63, 73n106

T

Tanner, Kathryn, 39, 78–80, 84, 117n131, 168n99, 172, 176–77
theosis, 142, 151, 174
Tillich, Paul, 16
Torrance, Alan, 69n92
Trinity
  ad extra/ad intra, 25n90, 48
  economic/immanent, 49–50, 53, 64n76, 74, 76, 81
  mia ousia, treis hypostaseis, 51
  oneness, 47, 54, 57n52, 58–62, 65n76, 72, 77n119, 85n1
  ousia, 11n35, 12, 40, 50–55, 57n52, 59, 60n62, 61–62, 70n94, 72–74, 181
  perichoresis, 15n55, 45–47, 50n17, 55–63, 65–67, 71, 75, 79, 116, 171, 173
  transcendence, 137–138
  threeness, 46, 54, 57n52, 58–59, 72
tritheism, 35n127, 62–63, 77n119

U

universalism, 145n11
usury, 140, 164–66, 178

V

Victor, Richard of St, 12
Vogel, C. J. de, 35–36
Volf, Miroslav, 66n82, 170n108, 171–72, 173n117

W

Walker, Robert, 95n36, 106, 114n116, 142n3, 150n31
Webster, John, 105, 118–21, 122n146
Weightman, Colin, 27n92
White, James, 158n59
White, Lynn, 135n198
Whitehead, Alfred, 137n204
Wolterstorff, Nicholas, 120n144, 167n96
worship, 54n36, 93, 103, 114n116, 142n3, 167n96, 172n113, 177n132, 179

Y

Yoder, John, 158n59
Zizioulas, John, 46n5, 53n30, 58, 63, 69–76, 142n5, 169–70, 174–75

www.ingramcontent.com/pod-product-compliance
Lightning Source LLC
Chambersburg PA
CBHW070254230426
43664CB00014B/2535